T0345930

Trade and Employment
in Developing Countries

2   Factor Supply and Substitution

Trade and Employment in Developing Countries

National Bureau of Economic Research

Trade and Employment in Developing Countries

2 Factor Supply and Substitution

Edited by Anne O. Krueger

The University of Chicago Press

Chicago and London

Anne O. Krueger is director of this study and professor of economics at the University of Minnesota. She was joint director of the NBER study *Foreign Trade Regimes and Economic Development*, author of the NBER volumes *Turkey* and *Liberalization Attempts and Consequences*, and author of *The Benefits and Costs of Import Substitution in India*.

The University of Chicago Press, Chicago 60637
The University of Chicago Press, Ltd., London
© 1982 by The National Bureau of Economic Research
All rights reserved. Published 1982
Printed in the United States of America
89 88 87 86 85 84 83 82   5 4 3 2 1

Library of Congress Cataloging in Publication Data
Main entry under title:
Trade and employment in developing countries.

"[Results] from the research project sponsored by
the National Bureau of Economic Research on alternate
trade strategies and employment."
Includes index.
CONTENTS: v. 1. Individual studies—v. 2. Factor supply
and substitution.
1. Underdeveloped areas—Foreign trade and employment—
Addresses, Essays, Lectures. 2. Underdeveloped areas—Commerce
—Addresses, Essays, Lectures. I. Krueger, Anne O.
II. National Bureau of Economic Research.
HD5852.T7   331.12′09172′4   80-15826
ISBN 0-226-45492-4 (v. 1)   AACR1
    0-226-45493-2 (v. 2)

Relation of the Directors to the
Work and Publications of the
National Bureau of Economic Research

1. The object of the National Bureau of Economic Research is to ascertain and to present to the public important economic facts and their interpretation in a scientific and impartial manner. The Board of Directors is charged with the reponsibility of ensuring that the work of the National Bureau is carried on in strict conformity with this object.

2. The President of the National Bureau shall submit to the Board of Directors, or to its Executive Committee, for their formal adoption all specific proposals for research to be instituted.

3. No research report shall be published by the National Bureau until the President has sent each member of the Board a notice that a manuscript is recommended for publication and that in the President's opinion it is suitable for publication in accordance with the principles of the National Bureau. Such notification will include an abstract or summary of the manuscript's content and a response form for use by those Directors who desire a copy of the manuscript for review. Each manuscript shall contain a summary drawing attention to the nature and treatment of the problem studied, the character of the data and their utilization in the report, and the main conclusions reached.

4. For each manuscript so submitted, a special committee of the Directors (including Directors Emeriti) shall be appointed by majority agreement of the President and Vice Presidents (or by the Executive Committee in case of inability to decide on the part of the President and Vice Presidents), consisting of three Directors selected as nearly as may be one from each general division of the Board. The names of the special manuscript committee shall be stated to each Director when notice of the proposed publication is submitted to him. It shall be the duty of each member of the special manuscript committee to read the manuscript. If each member of the manuscript committee signifies his approval within thirty days of the transmittal of the manuscript, the report may be published. If at the end of that period any member of the manuscript committee withholds his approval, the President shall then notify each member of the Board, requesting approval or disapproval of publication, and thirty days additional shall be granted for this purpose. The manuscript shall then not be published unless at least a majority of the entire Board who shall have voted on the proposal within the time fixed for the receipt of votes shall have approved.

5. No manuscript may be published, though approved by each member of the special manuscript committee, until forty-five days have elapsed from the transmittal of the report in manuscript form. The interval is allowed for the receipt of any memorandum of dissent or reservation, together with a brief statement of his reasons, that any member may wish to express; and such memorandum of dissent or reservation shall be published with the manuscript if he so desires. Publication does not, however, imply that each member of the Board has read the manuscript, or that either members of the Board in general or the special committee have passed on its validity in every detail.

6. Publications of the National Bureau issued for informational purposes concerning the work of the Bureau and its staff, or issued to inform the public of activities of Bureau staff, and volumes issued as a result of various conferences involving the National Bureau shall contain a specific disclaimer noting that such publication has not passed through the normal review procedures required in this resolution. The Executive Committee of the Board is charged with review of all such publications from time to time to ensure that they do not take on the character of formal research reports of the National Bureau, requiring formal Board approval.

7. Unless otherwise determined by the Board or exempted by the terms of paragraph 6, a copy of this resolution shall be printed in each National Bureau publication.
(Resolution adopted October 25, 1926, as revised through September 30, 1974)

Contents

Editor's Preface

This is the second of three volumes emanating from the National Bureau of Economic Research project on alternative trade strategies and employment. It contains a series of papers focusing on important aspects of the analysis of the trade strategies–employment relationship.

The entire project has been devoted to analyzing the extent to which employment and income distribution are affected by the choice of trade strategies and by the interaction of trade policies with domestic policies and market distortions. The trade strategies in question are, of course, import substitution and export promotion as alternative means of encouraging the growth of domestic industry. Although earlier studies, including the NBER project on foreign trade regimes and economic development (see Bhagwati 1978 and Krueger 1978 for details), provided considerable evidence that the economic growth performance of developing countries pursuing export-oriented trade strategies was substantially superior to that of countries under import substitution, little attention was given to the relationship between the choice of trade strategy and conditions in the domestic labor market before this project.

Trade theory, especially the Heckscher-Ohlin-Samuelson model, predicts that poor countries will generally have a comparative advantage in the production of relatively labor-intensive commodities. In light of this, failure to investigate the possible links between different rates of growth of employment and real wages with alternative trade strategies constituted a significant hiatus in our understanding of the trade strategies–growth relationship.

A first task in the research project on alternative trade strategies and employment was to provide an analytical framework within which the links between trade strategies and employment could be identified. This was done in Krueger (1977). A next step was to secure a group of researchers to investigate the empirical dimensions of the relationship. Many of the project participants undertook empirical and analytical studies of individual country experiences. The studies for ten countries were presented in the first volume in this series, Krueger, et al. (1981), which also contains a chapter describing the common concepts and methods employed in all the country studies.

It was clear from the outset that the country studies would provide a great deal of insight into the trade strategies–employment relation, but that there were some interesting questions where comparative analysis, or focus upon a single aspect of the relationship, would yield fruitful results. In addition to the country studies, research on these questions was considered an integral part of the project. This volume presents the results of those endeavors. A final volume will analyze the findings from the entire project, based upon the results reported in both this volume and the individual country studies.

A statement of the theory underlying the links between factor markets, substitution possibilities, and supply responses covered in this volume is not possible here and has been given in Krueger (1977). It suffices to point out that the net result of a change in real exchange rates or other incentives provided through trade regimes is a function of supply response and of underlying conditions within domestic markets. In particular, conditions and regulations covering real wages, social insurance taxes, and the like can affect the sorts of industries that find it profitable to respond to altered incentives. Credit rationing, artificially low costs of capital goods, and other inducements to employ capital-intensive techniques can also affect both the output mix and the factor proportions that will result from any particular set of trade policy instruments. The scope for substitution between factors of production is crucial in determining to what degree factor proportions are affected by domestic factor market distortions. Likewise, the extent to which the industry mix alters in response to changed incentives is a function of the extent of supply responses. Finally, there is an interaction term between prevailing factor market conditions and the mix of outputs that will result from any particular set of incentives conveyed by the trade regime.

Each country author attempted to assess the importance of these phenomena for his country, and the results are highly revealing. The results of the individual country studies point to significant supply responses and to a fairly large scope for altering overall factor proportions within the industrial sector both by altering the mix of output and by altering factor proportions.

There is no substitute for in-depth analysis of individual countries' economies and particular situations. There is, however, scope for complementary analysis. That is what this volume provides. The first study, by James M. Henderson, contains an optimizing model that uses a nonlinear programming framework to investigate what individual countries' optimal export and import vectors might be if they maximized the international value added of a fixed bundle of available domestic resources subject to production functions that permit substitution between labor and capital. Much of the data base for Henderson's study originated with the individual country authors, and there is significant overlap between the countries covered by his study and those covered in the first volume in this series. Henderson's paper makes a twofold contribution: on one hand, his model provides an additional tool that economists can use to estimate the direction of likely changes from a shifting of trade strategies or a removal of factor market distortions, or both; on the other hand, his substantive findings tend to reinforce those of the individual country authors. In particular, his results suggest that countries that have followed export-oriented trade strategies appear to have an output mix fairly close to one the model indicates to be optimal, while some of the countries known to have had fairly severe distortions in the domestic wage/rental ratio and large deviations between domestic and international prices show fairly large scope for gains through resource reallocation and altered factor proportions. Henderson's comparisons with some developed countries further reinforce this finding. By employing capacity constraints he is able to use the shadow prices derived from the optimal program to infer a considerable amount about the direction of likely resource pulls in the event of an alteration in trade strategies, and this should prove a useful tool in future research.

The second chapter by T. Paul Schultz, focuses on the income distribution implications of protecting domestic industry. Using data from Colombia, Schultz estimates earnings functions for workers of various skill categories. He finds a strong and significant relationship between the protection afforded an industry and earnings, even after allowance is made for such factors as schooling and experience. This finding holds for both employers and employees, thus strongly suggesting that protection does protect the incomes of those within the industry. Although it is possible that this might reflect the attraction of more able persons within each schooling and experience category to more highly protected industries, it is more likely that protection has served to shelter the incomes of those in the protected sectors. Particularly in light of the findings in most of the country studies, that import substitution industries tend to employ a relatively larger proportion of skilled workers than do export industries, Schultz's results strongly suggest that the income distribution effects of import substitution regimes, or at least the regime in Colombia, have been to increase the incomes of those already earning more than average. Schultz's effort is the first empirically oriented demonstration of the ways effective protection affects incomes of domestic owners of the factors of production. While the Colombian situation may not be representative, it is a significant first step in documenting the direct effects of effective protection on income distribution.

In chapter 3, José Carvalho and Cláudio Haddad, who also wrote the Brazilian country study in volume 1, provide estimates of the extent to which Brazilian exports responded to changes in incentives. One of the frequently heard arguments against shifting from an inner-oriented import substitution trade strategy to export promotion is that there is little export potential within the domestic economy. "Export pessimism" has, in one form or another, discouraged a shift in strategy. There was considerable pessimism in Brazil before its shift in trade strategy, so the Carvalho-Haddad findings are of particular interest. They conclude that Brazil's exports, especially exports of manufactured products, were very responsive to the altered incentives to export. Their estimates suggest that the overvaluation of the real exchange rate that characterized the Brazilian trade regime during the late 1950s and early 1960s explained a large part of the lagging export performance in those years, and that alteration of those policies after 1964 significantly affected performance. To be sure, other incentives to export appear to have been influential too, though Carvalho and Haddad find that an export subsidy led to a somewhat smaller export response than did an equal increase in incentives by means of the exchange rate. While many unanswered questions remain—such as the role of the increased certainty exporters felt after the adoption of a sliding-peg exchange rate—the Carvalho-Haddad estimates contribute significantly to knowledge about the responsiveness of exports to altered incentives and the empirical orders of magnitude of those responses.

The next two chapters, by Jere R. Behrman and by Vittorio Corbo and Patricio Meller, directly address the question of scope for substitution between labor and capital. Behrman's approach is to use cross-sectional data for seventy countries and as many as twenty-seven two-digit industries for the period 1967 to 1973. This is probably the richest cross-sectional data set to be used in many estimates of substitution possibilities. Using average observed inputs and outputs (to reduce problems associated with year-to-year fluctuations owing to strikes, recessions, and so forth), he estimates that elasticities of substitution are close to the Cobb-Douglas value of unity. His results are robust under alternative specifications of the model, though inclusion of a real per capita income variable yields some puzzling results.

Behrman provides strong evidence in support of the view that policies that affect the payments made for capital services and workers may significantly alter the factor mix in developing countries. They reinforce the notion that some of the capital intensity observed in developing countries may be a function of the distortions in wage/rental ratios

occurring in those countries and thus significant in affecting the employment implications of any trade strategy. His estimates are used as a basis
for inferring some of those costs in the final volume in this series.

Whereas Behrman's estimates are based upon data for many countries,
Corbo and Meller, who also undertook the Chilean country study, base
their estimated production relations upon data for 11,468 establishments
in eighty-five four-digit Chilean industries, though only forty-four industries provide more than ten degrees of freedom and form the basis for
their estimates. Using the general translog model, they test first for
constant returns to scale, then for the validity of the Cobb-Douglas
specification. For thirty-five of the forty-four sectors, Cobb-Douglas
technology could not be rejected, tending to reinforce Behrman's conclusion. Corbo and Meller proceeded to investigate the substitution relationships between unskilled labor, skilled labor, and capital. As they
explain, the nature of this relationship—whether human capital and
unskilled labor are relatively good substitutes while complementary with
physical capital, or whether human capital is more appropriately aggregated with physical capital—is of considerable importance for understanding many aspects of labor market behavior and the determinants of
the pattern of wage differentials in developing countries. They find that,
for Chile at least, there is more econometric support for regarding
unskilled and skilled labor as substitutes and aggregating them than there
is for aggregating human and physical capital. In view of the fact that the
evidence from the country studies (and from Henderson's model) all
suggests that there are strong differences in skill coefficients between
exportable and import competing industries, this finding is important.
For, if import substitution industries are skill-intensive relative to export
industries, a shift in trade strategy would tend to increase the demand for
unskilled labor in exportable industries, while releasing skilled labor (or
failing to absorb the growth in supply of skilled labor) in import substitution industries. If skilled and unskilled labor tend to be substitutes, as
Corbo and Meller's findings suggest, the adjustment process within the
labor market would be relatively straightforward, as skilled workers
could be absorbed in exportable industries.

The final chapter in this volume, by Robert E. Lipsey, Irving B. Kravis,
and Romualdo A. Roldan, focuses upon multinational firms and their
adaptation, or nonadaptation, to altered relative factor prices in developing countries. Using data on the behavior of American firms and Swedish
firms, they investigated factor proportions (by a variety of yardsticks) in
the multinationals' home countries, in other developed countries, and in
developing countries. They found that capital intensity of the multinationals was higher at home than in other developed countries, which in
turn was higher than that in developing countries. In general, a higher

price of labor implied the use of less labor-intensive techniques, thereby providing strong evidence of adaptation by multinationals. In addition, more labor-intensive operations tend to be in lower-wage countries, so that there is adaptation by multinationals both in their choice of technique and in the choice of which activities to locate in which countries. These findings are of interest not only because of the light they shed on the behavior of multinationals, but also because they suggest that the costs of factor market distortions, and especially labor market distortions, in developing labor-abundant countries may be greater than can be inferred by inspection of the behavior of domestic industry. For developing countries that rely upon multinational firms to contribute to the growth of their domestic industry, distortions in the wage structure may either scare off multinationals or induce them to choose more capital-intensive products or techniques than would be optimal given the abundance of labor.

Taken as a whole, the studies included in this volume represent a significant contribution to knowledge about scope for alteration of product mix and factor proportions. In addition, they tend to reinforce the conclusions of the individual country studies and to provide evidence that trade strategy, and its interaction with domestic policies affecting the relative costs of labor and capital services, may significantly affect employment opportunities and their growth.

The authors of the studies included here were all financed in their research by the National Bureau of Economic Research, which in turn received funding for the project from the United States Agency for International Development. Other sources of funding for the individual studies have been noted by the authors. All the authors, as well as the project director, owe Hal B. Lary a considerable debt of gratitude for his careful reading and comments on earlier drafts of the manuscript. Delma Burns capably retyped many of the manuscripts and handled the numerous details of manuscript preparation necessary to ready the studies for press.

References

Bhagwati, Jagdish N. 1978. *Foreign trade regimes and economic development: Anatomy and consequences of exchange control regimes*. Cambridge: Ballinger.

Krueger, Anne O. 1977. *Growth, distortions and patterns of trade among many countries*. Princeton Studies in International Finance, no. 40. Princeton: Princeton University Press.

————. 1978. *Foreign trade regimes and economic development: Liberalization attempts and consequences*. Cambridge: Ballinger.

Krueger, Anne O.; Lary, Hal B.; Monson, Terry; and Akrasanee, Narongchai, eds. 1981. *Trade and employment in developing countries*. Vol. 1. *Individual studies*. Chicago: University of Chicago Press for National Bureau of Economic Research.

1 Optimal Factor Allocations for Thirteen Countries

James M. Henderson

1.1 Introduction

Distortions in commodity and factor markets significantly affect commodity patterns of trade and, perhaps even more important, the factor proportions in individual industries. This is a major conclusion of most of the country studies for the project on alternative trade strategies and employment. This chapter is designed to determine what might happen if trade barriers and factor market distortions were relaxed so resources could be shifted toward sectors with comparative advantage and factor proportions could be adjusted in individual sectors. Many of the individual country studies made estimates of the magnitudes of commodity and factor market distortions, using the assumptions and techniques appropriate for each country. This study is complementary. A broad framework and model are used for the analysis of all countries, complementing the detailed data of the individual studies. The model is applied to determine some of the short- to medium-run effects of distortion relaxation for nine developing countries and, for comparison, four developed countries.

The basic model is constructed within a nonlinear programming format. Each country is assumed to face fixed international prices, and the model is implemented for one country at a time. The maximand is the international value added (IVA) of domestic production. Optimality thus is guided by international, rather than domestic, prices. Each country is assumed to have a fixed endowment of labor and capital. Intermediate

James M. Henderson is associated with the University of Minnesota.

I gratefully acknowledge the many constructive comments of Anne O. Krueger and Larry E. Westphal. I also thank the country authors for the NBER project on alternative trade strategies and employment for making their data available to me.

good inputs are used in fixed proportions relative to the output of each industry. Input-output coefficients provide the requisite data. Labor and capital inputs are governed by Cobb-Douglas production functions, and thereby continuous substitution between these factors is allowed for each industry.

Upper and lower limits relative to historical levels are imposed for the outputs of traded goods. The limits prevent solutions with extreme specialization and allow consideration to the short- to medium-run directions of movements toward comparative advantage allocations from observed allocations. The limits reflect some relaxation rather than total elimination of distortions. Solutions of the model describe freer trade but do not go all the way to free trade. In addition, the limits reflect both the fixity of capital and unobserved constraints that in the real world would result in upward-sloping supply curves. The optimal solutions of the model thus provide indications of the directions of change. The shadow prices corresponding to the output constraints indicate the gains from such changes and also may suggest the severity of underlying distortions.

It must be recognized from the outset that the freer trade described by the model has not been observed, and that neither exact nor stochastic measures of its consequences are possible. However, it is possible to confront the solutions of the model with the individual country studies described in Krueger et al. (1981). That volume and this chapter have six countries in common—Chile, Indonesia, the Ivory Coast, South Korea, Tunisia, and Uruguay. These studies rely heavily upon census data rather than on the comprehensive input-output data used here. Comparisons of the two types of studies show general comparability and compatibility. The present study provides information that supplements and extends the country studies with regard to the implications of alternative trade strategies.

Section 1.2 contains a discussion of the structure of the model, that is, its underlying assumptions and definitions. The properties of optimal solutions are the subject of section 1.3. Kuhn-Tucker conditions are applied to determine equilibrium conditions, and optimal shadow prices are derived. A three-factor extension of the model is obtained by separating labor into unskilled and skilled components. The empirical implementation of the model is covered in section 1.4.

Optimal solutions are analyzed in section 1.5 in terms of (1) implied employment changes, (2) implied IVA and DVA (domestic value added) changes, (3) a measure of comparative advantage, (4) implications for trade, and (5) implied capital/labor ratio changes. A three-factor application for Chile is also described. Section 1.6 contains conclusions and suggestions for further research.

There are four appendixes. Appendix A contains a description of some of the model's mathematical properties. Data sources and rectification procedures are described in Appendix B. Appendix C contains some detailed sectoral data to supplement the more aggregative data presented in the text. Computational procedures to obtain optimum solutions are described in Appendix D.

1.2   Structure of the Model

1.2.1   Classification of Goods

Each of $(n + 1)$ sectors is assumed to have a single homogeneous good. The terms "good" and "sector" are used interchangeably, as are the terms international good and traded good. The outputs of the sectors numbered 1 through m are international goods that can be exported to and imported from other countries. A subset, the outputs of the sectors numbered 1 through $r < m$, are natural resource based (NRB). These require the existence of natural resources such as cropland, forests, or bodies of ore before production can take place. The remaining $(m–r)$ international goods do not directly require the existence of such natural resources. These are designated "HOS" (Heckscher-Ohlin-Samuelson) sectors in conformity with the nomenclature of the individual country studies (see Krueger et al. 1981). Sectors $(m + 1)$ through n cover home goods that are consumed in the country in which they are produced. The output of sector $(n + 1)$ is a noncompetitive import that is consumed but not produced within a given country. Consequently, there are $(m + 1)$ traded goods. The composition of noncompetitive imports, of course, differs from country to country.

1.2.2   The International Trade System

The country under consideration is free to import and export at the fixed international prices $(p_1, p_2, \ldots, p_m)$ and p_{n+1} measured in domestic currency units. These prices are unaffected by its trade levels.

Following input-output practice, physical units are defined so that the base-year domestic price for each good equals one. Each country is assumed to have a fixed exchange rate, and international prices are measured in terms of domestic currency units. Since the model treats real rather than monetary phenomena, nothing is lost by this assumption. International prices could be measured equivalently in terms of United States dollars or any other foreign currency unit for which there is a fixed exchange rate. Factor prices are also measured in domestic currency units. They reflect international prices in that they are used in the production of international goods as well as home goods. Home goods prices also reflect international values as transmitted through the price system in that inputs used in home goods production have opportunity costs in terms of international goods production.

1.2.3   Domestic Production

Produced intermediate inputs are assumed to be required in fixed proportions for the production of each good. The input-output coefficient a_{ij} gives the quantity of the ith good required to produce one unit of the jth. Accordingly, $a_{ij}X_j$ units of good i are required to produce X_j units of good j. The nonproduced factors, labor and capital, are also required for each good as specified by the Cobb-Douglas production functions:

$$(1) \qquad X_j = A_j L_j^{\alpha_j} K_j^{(1-\alpha_j)}, \; (j = 1, \ldots, n)$$

where $A_j > 0$ and $0 \leq \alpha_j \leq 1$ are given parameters. The respective inputs of labor and capital for the production of good j are denoted by L_j and K_j. In section 1.3 it is shown that the labor and capital shares of DVA are α_j and $(1 - \alpha_j)$ respectively under competitive assumptions. The marginal products of labor and capital, that is, the partial derivatives of (1) are denoted by

$$MPL_j = \frac{\partial X_j}{\partial L_j} = \alpha_j A_j L_j^{(\alpha_j - 1)} K_j^{(1-\alpha_j)}$$

$$(j = 1, \ldots, n)$$

$$MPK_j = \frac{\partial X_j}{\partial K_j} = (1 - \alpha_j) A_j L_j^{\alpha_j} K_j^{-\alpha_j}$$

respectively.

The Cobb-Douglas functions become

$$(2) \qquad X_j = A_j U_j^{\alpha_j} S_j^{\beta_j} K_j^{(1-\alpha_j-\beta_j)} \qquad (j = 1, \ldots, n)$$

when labor is separated into skilled and unskilled components with the respective input levels U_j and S_j.[1] The coefficients again sum to one with $0 \leq \alpha_j, \beta_j \leq 1$. The exponent for each factor input again gives its competitive share of DVA.

The country under investigation has the fixed endowments L^0 units of labor and K^0 units of capital available for use in production. It may leave some of its endowments unused, but it cannot use more than its endowments. Specifically,

$$(3) \qquad \sum_{j=1}^{n} L_j \leq L^0$$

$$(4) \qquad \sum_{j=1}^{n} K_j \leq K^0.$$

Factors are completely immobile among countries but are mobile between sectors within a given country subject to the output limits described below.

For three factors the labor endowment consists of U^0 units of unskilled and S^0 units of skilled labor, and (3) becomes:

(5)
$$\sum_{j=1}^{n} (U_j + S_j) \leqq U^0 + S^0$$

(6)
$$\sum_{j=1}^{n} S_j \leqq S^0.$$

These constraints allow skilled laborers to work at unskilled tasks but do not allow unskilled laborers to work at skilled tasks. The sum of the U_j can exceed U^0 if the sum of the S_j falls short of S^0 by at least the amount of this difference.

It is assumed that the output level for each international good cannot be increased or decreased from its base value (X_j^0) by more than 100δ percent ($0 < \delta < 1$):

(7)
$$(1 - \delta)X_j^0 \leqq X_j \leqq (1 + \delta)X_j^0. \qquad (J = 1, \ldots, m)$$

Individual sectoral values for δ and differential values for increases and decreases are easily introduced when circumstances warrant. Alternatively, limits could be placed upon factor service changes rather than output changes. The output constraints provide indirect short- to medium-run limits on labor and capital mobility. They serve as proxies for other institutional and real constraints to output flexibility that cannot be explicitly introduced into the model. They allow for a relaxation, rather than an elimination, of distortions. They permit consideration of movements within a neighborhood of an observed base-year solution and indicate the directions in which changes might take place. These limited changes are more useful for a consideration of alternative trade strategies than unconstrained long-run changes, because the latter would result in very high levels of specialization and fail to reflect the conditions that give rise to upward-sloping supply curves. Policy determination is often in terms of small and gradual changes with slow relaxation of institutional constraints. "Shadow prices" corresponding to (7) are derived in section 1.3.

1.2.4   Domestic Consumption and Home Goods Outputs

Home goods final consumption levels for a base year, denoted by C_i^0 ($i = m + 1, \ldots, n$), include all uses observed during the base year other than intermediate input uses. These cover net trade,[2] final purchases by consumers and governments, investment, and inventory change. Home goods final consumption levels are treated as constants. The optimization problem is to maximize IVA given these final consumption levels. Relaxation of the constant level assumption would substantially complicate the model with little alteration of major results.

The output level for each home good is determined by its fixed final consumption level and its use as an intermediate input:

$$X_i = C_i^0 + \sum_{j=1}^{n} a_{ij}X_j. \qquad (i = m + 1, \ldots, n)$$

Solving these $(n - m)$ linear equations for the $(n - m)$ home goods output levels,

$$(8) \qquad X_i \geq k_i + \sum_{j=1}^{m} \sigma_{ij} X_j, \qquad (i = m + 1, \ldots, n)$$

where $\qquad k_i = \sum_{j=m+1}^{n} \mu_{ij} C_j^0$ and $\sigma_{ij} = \sum_{h=m+1}^{n} \mu_{ih} a_{hj}.$

The coefficient μ_{ij} is the quantity of the ith home good required directly and indirectly to produce one unit of the jth home good. Here, k_i is a constant giving the gross output of the ith home good necessary to meet the direct and indirect requirements for the fixed home goods final demands.[3] The coefficient σ_{ij} is the quantity of the ith home good necessary directly and indirectly to support one unit of output of international good j. The μ and σ coefficients are derived from the input-output coefficients in Appendix A. The inequality in (8) facilitates the derivations of section 1.3. It specifies that the output of each home good be *at least as great* as final consumption and production requirements. It is shown that the exact equality holds in equilibrium.

The assumptions of the model allow a two-stage procedure for the optimization of a country's welfare or utility under free trade. First, let the country maximize IVA for its production of traded goods. Second, let it spend the maximum IVA to buy an optimal consumption bundle. This procedure corresponds very closely to the tradition in international trade theory of treating production choices as separate from consumption choices because of the availability of international markets. It has considerable value for empirical application. It means that optimal production specialization patterns can be determined without having to either model or forecast international goods final consumption patterns. Opportunities for errors thus are normally lessened. Of course it is necessary to forecast final consumption for international goods before optimal trading patterns can be determined.

1.3   Equilibrium Properties of the Model

1.3.1   The Objective Function

The IVA for a representative country's production is

$$(9) \qquad V = \sum_{j=1}^{m} p_j X_j - \sum_{j=1}^{n} \sum_{i=1}^{m} p_i a_{ij} X_j - \sum_{j=1}^{n} p_{n+1} a_{n+1,j} X_j,$$

which is simply the international value of its traded outputs less the international value of its traded inputs. Let γ_j be the fixed value of the traded inputs necessary to produce one unit of good j:

$$\gamma_j = \sum_{i=1}^{m} p_i a_{ij} + p_{n+1} a_{n+1,j}, \qquad (j=1, \ldots, n)$$

and rewrite (9) as

(10) $$V = \sum_{j=1}^{m} p_j X_j - \sum_{j=1}^{n} \gamma_j X_j.$$

Now let

(11) $$\hat{z}_j = p_j - \gamma_j - b_j \qquad (j=1, \ldots, m)$$

for international goods where $\hat{z}_j$ is direct and indirect IVA per unit of j and b_j (see Appendix A) is the international value of the international goods used as inputs directly and indirectly to produce the home goods used as inputs in the production of j. Direct IVA per unit of j is simply $z_j = p_j - \gamma_j$. The IVA coefficients are constants because the underlying international prices and input-output coefficients are constants. A coefficient will be negative if the international value of its direct and indirect inputs exceed its international price. Equation (10) may be rewritten as

(12) $$V = \sum_{j=1}^{m} \hat{z}_j X_j - K,$$

where K (see Appendix A) is a constant giving the international value of the traded goods necessary to directly and indirectly support the fixed home goods final demands.

The constant K has no effect upon the determination of an optimum solution and may be omitted from (12) so that each country is assumed to maximize the direct and indirect IVA from its production of traded goods. Note that indirect IVA in this context is traded goods used to produce home goods used to produce traded goods. There are no indirect international good requirements, since inputs may be directly purchased in the international markets without transaction costs.

1.3.2 An Illustration

A simple system is pictured in figure 1.1 within a standard international trade format. There are two traded goods and no home goods. The output transformation curve for the fixed labor and capital endowments is given by DBACE. Point A represents base-year output levels. The maximum and minimum limits as defined by the broken lines allow outputs to increase or decrease by 40 percent. The feasible point set, that is, the output levels that satisfy all the constraints, is FBC. Both labor and capital are fully utilized for points on the transformation curve arc BC. One or both the primary factors are underutilized at all interior points in the feasible set. Good 1 is at its minimum limit at B, and good 2 is at its minimum limit at C. In this particular example the maximum limits lie

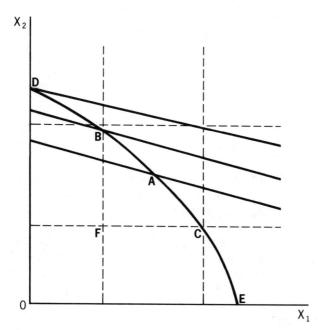

Fig. 1.1

above the transformation curve and therefore are not binding for any set of international prices.

An optimal point maximizes IVA within the feasible set. Let an iso-value line be the locus of all output combinations that yield a particular IVA for specified international prices. Its slope equals the negative of the IVA ratio: $-\hat{z}_2/\hat{z}_1$. The lines containing points A, B, and D give increasing IVAs for a particular IVA ratio. The base point A gives the lowest value of the three, and the tangent point D gives the highest.[4] However, D is not feasible because it violates the lower output limit for good 1. If this constraint did not exist, D would be optimal, and there would be almost complete specialization in good 2. Point B is optimal. It gives the highest IVA of any point in the feasible set. For B, both factors are fully utilized. Good 1's output is at its minimum limit, good 2's output is between its minimum and maximum limits.

Another example is pictured in figure 1.2. The transformation curve is the same as in figure 1.1, but the base output point and IVA ratio are different. The feasible point set is FBCE. The transformation curve segment BC is bounded by the upper and lower limits for good 1. The tangent point D is optimal for the unit IVA ratio corresponding to the line on which it lies. In this case none of the output limits is effective.

The positively sloped line containing B in figure 1.2 is an isovalue line for which IVA per unit of good 1 is negative. Total IVA increases as the

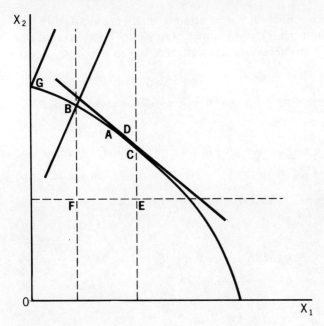

Fig. 1.2

line moves to the left with X_2 increasing relative to X_1. The complete specialization point G would be optimal if there were no lower limit for good 1. The optimal point in this case is B with the smallest possible output for good 1.

1.3.3 The Kuhn-Tucker Conditions

A representative country desires to select nonnegative values for its output and primary input levels that maximize its IVA subject to the constraints given by (1), (3), (4), (7), and (8). For the Lagrange function

$$(13) \qquad Z = \sum_{i=1}^{m} p_j X_i - \sum_{i=1}^{n} \gamma_i X_i + w(L^0 - \sum_{i=1}^{n} L_i) + c(K^0 - \sum_{i=1}^{n} K_i)$$

$$+ \sum_{i=1}^{n} q_i (A_i L_i^{\alpha_i} K_i^{1-\alpha_i} - X_i) + \sum_{i=1}^{m} u_i [(1+\delta)X_i^0 - X_i]$$

$$+ \sum_{i=1}^{m} v_i [X_i - (1-\delta)X_i^0] + \sum_{i=m+1}^{n} \pi_i (X_i - k_i - \sum_{j=1}^{m} \sigma_{ij} X_j),$$

where the parenthesized constraints have been rewritten so that each is in the form $\geqq 0$. It is more convenient to use (10) than (12) at this juncture. A Lagrange multiplier is introduced for each of the $(2n + m + 2)$ constraints. These increase the total number of variables to $(5n + m + 2)$.

Since the objective function and constraints of (13) are all concave and the Slater constraint qualification is met,[5] the Kuhn-Tucker conditions (see Hadley 1962) are necessary and sufficient for an optimum. Specifically,

(14.1)
$$\frac{\partial Z}{\partial X_j} = p_j - \gamma_j - q_j - u_j + v_j - h_j \leq 0, \frac{\partial Z}{\partial X_j} X_j = 0, X_j \geq 0$$
$$(j = 1, \ldots, m)$$

(14.2)
$$\frac{\partial Z}{\partial X_j} = \pi_j - \gamma_j - q_j - h_j \leq 0, \frac{\partial Z}{\partial X_j} X_j = 0, X_j \geq 0$$
$$(j = m+1, \ldots, n)$$

(14.3)
$$\frac{\partial Z}{\partial L_j} = q_j(MPL_j) - w \leq 0, \frac{\partial Z}{\partial L_j} L_j = 0, L_j \geq 0$$
$$(j = 1, \ldots, n)$$

(14.4)
$$\frac{\partial Z}{\partial K_j} = q_j(MPK_j) - c \leq 0, \frac{\partial Z}{\partial K_j} K_j = 0, K_j \geq 0$$
$$(j = 1, \ldots, n)$$

(14.5)
$$\frac{\partial Z}{\partial w} = L^0 - \sum_{i=1}^{n} L_i \geq 0, \frac{\partial Z}{\partial w} w = 0, w \geq 0$$

(14.6)
$$\frac{\partial Z}{\partial c} = K^0 - \sum_{i=1}^{n} K_i \geq 0, \frac{\partial Z}{\partial c} c = 0, c \geq 0$$

(14.7)
$$\frac{\partial Z}{\partial q_i} = A_i L_i^{\alpha_i} K_i^{(1-\alpha_i)} - X_i \geq 0, \frac{\partial Z}{\partial q_i} q_i = 0, q_i \geq 0$$
$$(i = 1, \ldots, n)$$

(14.8)
$$\frac{\partial Z}{\partial u_i} = (1+\delta)X_i^0 - X_i \geq 0, \frac{\partial Z}{\partial u_i} u_i = 0, u_i \geq 0$$
$$(1 = 1, \ldots, m)$$

(14.9)
$$\frac{\partial Z}{\partial v_i} = X_i - (1+\delta)X_i^0 \geq 0, \frac{\partial Z}{\partial v_i} v_i = 0, v_i \geq 0$$
$$(1 = 1, \ldots, m)$$

(14.10)
$$\frac{\partial Z}{\partial \pi_i} = X_i - k_i - \sum_{j=1}^{n} \sigma_{ij} X_j \geq 0, \frac{\partial Z}{\partial \pi_i} \pi_i = 0, \pi_i \geq 0,$$
$$(i = m+1, \ldots, n)$$

where $h_j = \sum_{i=m+1}^{n} \pi_i a_{ij}$ is the direct unit cost in terms of the prices π_i $(i = m+1, \ldots, n)$ of the home goods inputs used for the production of a unit of good j.

Conditions (14) are necessary and sufficient for optimal solutions, but they do not guarantee that such solutions exist. Fortunately, existence is no problem for the present model. The parameters of the model are defined (see section 1.4) so that base-year outputs provide feasible solutions, and that points in neighborhoods—perhaps large neighborhoods—about these outputs are also feasible.

1.3.4 Shadow Prices and Equilibrium Conditions

In general, a Lagrange multiplier is a shadow price—sometimes called an efficiency price—that gives the rate at which the maximum value of the objective function would increase per unit increase in the quantity being constrained. For example, w is the increment of optimal IVA per marginal unit of labor, that is, the value of the marginal product of labor. It is interpreted as the optimal wage rate. Table 1.1 contains economic interpretations of the shadow prices corresponding to each group of constraints.

Enough is known about the specifics of the present model to allow considerable specification of conditions (14). Since each international good is subject to a positive lower limit, and each home good has a positive final demand, is used in the production of other goods, or both, *all optimal output levels are positive*. Since $X_j > 0$, $\partial Z/\partial X_j = 0$ follows from the condition $(\partial Z/\partial X_j)X_j = 0$, and the first two sets of conditions in (14) are strict equalities in equilibrium. Rearranging terms,

$$(15) \qquad p_j = \gamma_j + h_j + q_j + r_j \qquad (j = 1, \ldots, m)$$

$$(16) \qquad \pi_j = \gamma_j + h_j + q_j, \qquad (j = m+1, \ldots, n)$$

where $r_j = (u_j - v_j)$. Following the interpretations given in table 1.1, the price of an international good equals the sum of the unit costs of its international inputs (γ_j), its home goods inputs (h_j), and its factor inputs (q_j) plus the net unit rent (r_j) arising from its output limits. A positive (negative) r_j is the unit profit (loss) arising from difference between unit international price and unit shadow costs for a good at its maximum (minimum) limit. Zero profits would prevail if the government imposed unit taxes equal to positive r_js and paid unit subsidies equal to the absolute value of negative r_js. The rents would all be zero if there were no

Table 1.1		Shadow Prices
Con-straint	Shadow Price	Definition
1	q_j	Optimal DVA per unit of output
3	w	Wage per unit of labor
4	c	Price per unit of capital service
7	u_i	Rent for one more unit of capital output i
7	v_i	Rent for one less unit of output i
8	π_i	Price per unit of a home good

output limits. They are a consequence of relaxing rather than eliminating the causes of distortion.

The imputed price for a home good (π_j) equals the unit cost of its inputs given by (16). Home goods are not traded, but their prices reflect international prices because home and international goods are used in each other's production, and because labor and capital are used for the production of both.

The eighth set of conditions in (14) states that u_i can be positive only if X_i is at its upper limit, and the ninth set states that v_i can be positive only if X_i is at its lower limit. Consequently, u_i and v_i cannot both be positive for the same good, though both can be zero. In fact, normally there is at least one marginal good that is at neither its upper nor its lower limit with $r_i = 0$.[6] Such goods provide reference points for the calculation of unit rents. A positive rent corresponds to a good at its maximum limit. A positive IVA increment could be achieved if its output could be increased by drawing the requisite factor quantities from the marginal goods. IVA exceeds factor cost for such goods, and IVA equals factor costs for the marginal goods.

Similarly, a negative rent corresponds to a good at its minimum limit. A positive IVA increment could be achieved if its output could be decreased with the released factor quantities used for the production of the marginal good. IVA is less than factor costs for such goods.[7]

Since all primary factor production functions are Cobb-Douglas and all outputs are positive, positive amounts of labor and capital are used in the production of each good.[8] This means that the second and third sets of (14) are also satisfied as strict equalities with

(17) $\qquad q_j(MPL_j) = w \qquad (j=1, \ldots, n)$

(18) $\qquad q_j(MPL_j) = c. \qquad (j=1, \ldots, n)$

These state the well-known conditions for profit maximization that the value of the marginal product for each factor equals the factor's price.

The marginal products of each factor are always positive for Cobb-Douglas production functions. Consequently, an incremental quantity of either factor can be used to increment the output of the marginal good and thereby increment total IVA.[9] It follows that both factors are fully utilized for optimal solutions. This means that optimal solutions will be on the transformation surface. The shadow price w is the rate of increase of optimal IVA per unit increase of labor endowment. It is positive and is interpreted as the wage rate. Similarly, c is interpreted as the price of capital services. The partial derivatives of (14.5) and (14.6) equal zero in equilibrium. Since marginal products are positive for the Cobb-Douglas functions, it follows that the q_j are positive for positive w and c.

The strict equalities in (14.7) and (14.10) are satisfied in equilibrium, since a strict inequality would entail producing an output and throwing it away.

Utilizing (17) and (18), total factor payments for the production of good j are

$$wL_j + cK_j = q_j(\alpha_j \frac{X_j}{L_j}) L_j$$

$$+ q_j [(1-\alpha_j) \frac{X_j}{K_j}] K_j = q_j X_j,$$

which equals optimal DVA. Thus (15) and (16) state that the whole of optimal DVA is absorbed by factor payments.

An equilibrium solution may be interpreted as the outcome of competitive behavior in which people optimize subject to the domestic prices $(p_j - r_j)$. The output limits prevent the equalization of the domestic and international prices and prevent the equalization of IVA and optimal DVA. Let the government impose a system of taxes and subsidies as given by the optimal r_js. Assume that the net tax revenue, $\sum_{j=1}^{n} r_j X_j$, which may be positive, negative, or zero, is redistributed.

1.3.5   Measures of IVA and DVA

IVA and DVA are each used in two different senses in this paper, and it is necessary to keep track of which concepts are being used in particular instances. In general, value added per unit for a good is simply the difference between unit price and unit costs on some set of inputs for that good. Different concepts result from the use of different price or cost concepts.

Direct and indirect unit IVA as defined by (11):

$$\hat{z}_j = p_j - \gamma_j - b_j$$

is international price less the unit costs of international inputs used directly and the international inputs used to produce direct and indirect home goods inputs. Since international prices and input-output coefficients are constant, this concept of IVA can be defined without reference to an optimal solution.

Direct unit IVA (z_j) is international price minus the cost of all international inputs:

(19) $z_j = p_j - \gamma_j.$ $(j=1, \ldots, m)$

Since b_j (see Appendix A) is assumed to be positive, it follows that $\hat{z}_j < z_j$.

Optimal direct unit DVA for an international good differs from unit IVA by the amount of its unit rent and home goods inputs:

(20) $q_j = z_j - r_j - h_j,$ $(j=1, \ldots, m)$

which follows from (15). The q_j are always positive even though a corresponding z_j may be negative. This concept of DVA is relevant only with reference to an optimal solution.

Base-year unit DVAs for international goods are

$$(21) \qquad q_j^0 = 1 - \sum_{i=1}^{n} a_{ij}, \qquad (j=1, \ldots, m)$$

since unit prices prevailed. These may deviate substantially from the other DVA and IVA measures. Negative q_j^0s arc possible. However, it is more common to have a positive q_j^0 corresponding to a negative z_j.[10] Production of such outputs is made viable through domestic policies, such as high rates of protection, that make base-year DVAs positive.

1.3.6   The Cost of Distortions

Commodity and factor market distortions prevent a country from obtaining the maximum IVA that would be realized in the absence of such distortions. The difference between actual and maximum IVA is the cost of the distortions. This concept represents a generalization of the concept of the cost of protection.[11] The difference between observed IVA and the optimal IVA given by the present model provides an overall measure of the cost of distortions. Looked at from a more positive viewpoint, it provides a measure of the gains from relaxing distortions. Empirical measures of these costs (gains) are given in section 1.5.

Analysis of the relative magnitudes of distortion costs on a sectoral basis is useful in considering alternative trade strategies. The following measure of sectoral distortion costs is used in section 1.5:

$$(22) \qquad g_j = \frac{\hat{z}_j}{w\hat{\ell}_j^* + c\hat{k}_j^*} - 1, \qquad (j=1, \ldots, m)$$

where $\hat{\ell}_j^*$ and $\hat{k}_j^*$ respectively are the optimal direct and indirect labor and capital requirements per unit output.[12] This measure gives the number of currency units of IVA obtained per unit expenditure for domestic factors in the production of international good j *relative to the marginal good*.[13] The coefficient is zero for the marginal good, positive for a good with a positive rent and negative for a good with a negative rent. Sector distortion costs are indicated by the absolute values of the g_j coefficients.

The g_j coefficients are constructed to represent changes in factor allocations constrained by the upper and lower output limits. The total costs of distortions may be substantially understated if larger output variations are allowed.

1.3.7   A Three-Factor Extension

A three-factor version of the model has been constructed with two classes of labor—unskilled and skilled, allowing one-way mobility between labor classes. A skilled worker may take an unskilled job, but an unskilled worker may not take a skilled job. The three-factor programming format is very similar to the two-factor format: select nonnegative values for outputs, unskilled labor inputs, skilled labor inputs, and capital inputs that maximize IVA as represented by (11) subject to the production functions (2); the factor endowments (5), (6), and (3); the output limits (7); and the home goods requirements (8). The appropriate Lagrange function is

$$
\begin{aligned}
Z = & \sum_{i=1}^{m} p_i X_i - \sum_{i=1}^{n} \gamma_i X_i + w(U^0 + S^0 - \sum_{i=1}^{n} U_i \\
& - \sum_{i=1}^{n} S_i) + s(S^0 - \sum_{i=1}^{n} S_i) \\
& + c(K^0 - \sum_{i=1}^{n} K_i) + \sum_{i=1}^{n} q_i (A_i U_i^{\alpha_i} S_i^{\beta_i} K_i^{(1-\alpha_i-\beta_i)} - X_i) \\
& + \sum_{i=1}^{m} U_i[(1+\delta)X_i^0 - X_i] + \sum_{i=1}^{m} v_i[X_i - (1-\delta)X_i^0] \\
& + \sum_{i=m+1}^{n} \pi_i(X_i - k_i - \sum_{j=1}^{m} \sigma_{ij} X_j).
\end{aligned}
$$

(23)

Kuhn-Tucker conditions again are applicable. Conditions (14.1), (14.2), (14.4), (14.6), (14.8), (14.9), and (14.10) are applicable for three factors as well as two. The remaining conditions for the three-factor extension are

(24.3a) $\dfrac{\partial Z}{\partial U_j} = q_j(MPU_j) - w \leq 0, \dfrac{\partial Z}{\partial U_j} U_j = 0, U_j \geq 0$

$$(j = 1, \ldots, m)$$

(24.3b) $\dfrac{\partial Z}{\partial S_j} = q_j(MPS_j) - (w + s) \leq 0, \dfrac{\partial Z}{\partial S_j} S_j = 0, S_j \geq 0$

$$(j = 1, \ldots, n)$$

(24.5a) $\dfrac{\partial Z}{\partial w} = U^0 + S^0 - \sum_{i=1}^{n} U_i \geq 0, \dfrac{\partial Z}{\partial w} w = 0, w \geq 0$

(24.5b) $\dfrac{\partial Z}{\partial s} = S^0 - \sum_{i=1}^{n} S_i \geq 0, \dfrac{\partial Z}{\partial s} s = 0, s \geq 0$

(24.7) $\dfrac{\partial Z}{\partial q_i} = A_i U_i^{\alpha_i} S_i^{\beta_i} K_i^{(1-\alpha_i-\beta_i)} - X_i \geq 0, \dfrac{\partial Z}{\partial q_i} q_i = 0, q_i \geq 0.$

$$(i = m+1, \ldots, n)$$

For the reasons explained earlier, the equilibrium values for all the variables—other than the u_i, v_i, and s—are always positive, and the corresponding derivatives equal zero.

Equations (14), (15), and (16) hold for both two and three factors, but (17) is replaced by

(25a) $q_j(MPU_j) = w$

(25b) $q_j(MPS_j) = w + s.$

The wage rates for unskilled and skilled workers are w and $(w + s)$ respectively. The equilibrium skill premium, s, will be zero if skilled labor is not scarce; that is, the strict equality in (6) does not hold for an optimal solution. If some skilled workers are employed in unskilled jobs, all skilled workers will receive the unskilled wage, w.

It is easily verified that $wU_j + (w + s)S_j + cK_j = q_jX_j (j=1, \ldots, n)$ so that zero profits would prevail throughout the system with the appropriate unit taxes and subsidies.

1.4 Empirical Implementation

The model has been applied for nine developing countries: Chile, Indonesia, Ivory Coast, Kenya, South Korea, Taiwan, Tunisia, Turkey, and Uruguay; and for four developed countries: Belgium, France, Germany, and Italy. To a large degree the data are drawn from input-output studies. For the developing countries other than Kenya, Taiwan, and Turkey, the input-output studies are the same as used for NBER individual country studies. Some price and skill data were also drawn from these six country studies. Summaries for six of the studies are contained in Krueger et al. (1981). The country studies rely more heavily upon the census data than input-output data whereas the current study requires the comprehensive input-output data. Consequently, the data in this study and the country studies are not always strictly comparable. Nonetheless they are complementary, with a great deal of common ground.

This section begins with a general discussion of empirical implementation, followed by a discussion of the determination of the requisite data and parameters. The following are required: (1) input-output coefficients, the a_{ij}; (2) international prices, the p_j; (3) labor and capital data to provide the L^0 (or U^0 and S^0) and K^0; (4) Cobb-Douglas parameters, the A_j and α_j (also for the three-factor version β_j); and (5) base-year outputs and home goods final demands, the X_i^0 and C_i^0. The coefficient δ was arbitrarily set equal to 0.25 to restrict output changes to plus or minus 25 percent. Experimentation suggests that "reasonable" variation of δ will not trigger major changes in the solution results.

The use of base-year data to implement the model ensures that the base-year outputs provide a feasible solution. Consequently, optimal solutions in terms of IVA may be viewed as movements from the base-year observations. In interpreting the optimal solutions, it is assumed that the base-year observations describe optimal solutions giving maximum DVA subject to the constraints in force during the base year. Thus, base-year distortions are built in. Optimal solutions in terms of DVA differ from base solutions in two major regards. First, the optimal solutions are subject to fewer constraints. Second, they entail maximization of IVA rather than DVA. Base-year observations provide feasible, but not optimal, solutions for the IVA programs.

1.4.1 Base Years, Sector Classifications, and Adjustments

Some particulars for the applications are contained in table 1.2. More specific detail for the individual applications is given in Appendix B. There are sixteen applications in total for thirteen countries. There are separate applications for 1966, 1970, and 1973 for South Korea in order to investigate changes in comparative advantage over time. In addition, a three-factor extension of the model is applied for Chile.

The base years as listed in table 1.2 span the thirteen years from 1961 through 1973. The input-output tables differ markedly in procedures and span a wide range of reliability. The data for South Korea are perhaps the best. The sector classifications differ in a number of important regards. Value added for labor is used to represent physical labor inputs, and nonlabor value added is used to represent physical capital inputs. The definitions of nonlabor value added differ somewhat between countries. Consequently, comparison of capital labor ratios for pairs of countries must be made with great care.

The second column of table 1.2 indicates whether the input-output agricultural value added was adjusted. The adjustments consist of shifts to the labor component of value added from the nonlabor component. The labor component is understated in most cases because income to owner-operators is treated as profit rather than labor income. A common adjustment was to assume that two-thirds of value added for agriculture as a whole is labor income. Particulars are given in Appendix B.

The solutions as presented in section 1.5 normally have sectoral data aggregated into the following six major divisions: (1) agriculture, including forestry and fisheries; (2) other natural resource based (NRB) industries; (3) food production; (4) textiles including clothing, furs, and leather; (5) other manufacturing industries; and (6) home goods industries.

Table 1.2   **Particulars for Applications of the Optimal Trade Model**

Country	Base Year	Agricultural Adjustment
Chile	1962[a]	Yes
Indonesia	1971	Yes
Ivory Coast	1972	Yes
Kenya	1967	Yes
South Korea	1966–70–73	Yes
Taiwan	1971	No
Tunisia	1972	No
Turkey	1973[b]	No
Uruguay	1961	Yes
Europe	1963	No

[a]International prices for 1961 are used.
[b]International prices for 1968 are used.

Divisions 1 and 2 contain the NRB sectors, and 3, 4, and 5 contain the HOS sectors. The number of sectors contained in each major division for each country is listed in table 1.3.

The total number of sectors ranges from a low of 20 for Uruguay to a high of 168 for Indonesia. The number of HOS sectors is less than 20 for three of the nine developing countries. The classification of sectors into the traded and home goods categories differs somewhat from country to country. In some cases a good is classified as a home good because it does not appear desirable to consider an expansion of trade for that good. For example, the sector "undistributed" may have had a substantial volume of foreign trade, but it is difficult to imagine a country specializing in the production of its output. Tobacco products are treated as an international good for Turkey, which is a major exporter, and as home goods for the other twelve countries. Alcoholic beverages are treated as home goods for all thirteen countries. It is very difficult to determine international prices for these heavily taxed and highly protected sectors. Furthermore, few if any countries are likely to consider relaxing their controls for these sectors. Consequently, current consumption and trade levels were frozen.

In some cases nontradable services required for the production of a particular international good are included within the sector for that good. In other cases, separate service sectors are defined. Textile dyeing and finishing in Korea is an example. Such sectors are treated as home goods even though they are part of a sequence leading to a traded good. In some cases nonexportable agricultural produce is placed in an individual sector. Paddy rice and sugarcane in Taiwan are examples. These are inputs for the international goods rice and sugar and are treated as home goods. Diverse treatments mean that one country may have a higher proportion of its labor force in home goods sectors than another solely as a result of

Table 1.3   Numbers of Sectors in Each Major Division

Country	Agri-culture	Other NRB	Food	Tex-tiles	Other Manu-facturing	Home Goods	Total
Chile	2	6	2	3	14	27	54
Indonesia	29	12	23	11	48	45	168
Ivory Coast	6	1	9	3	17	11	47
Kenya	1	1	2	4	8	10	26
South Korea	8	3	9	16	52	30	118
Taiwan	8	4	9	6	29	20	76
Tunisia	7	4	6	6	25	20	68
Turkey	4	6	8	5	24	16	63
Uruguay	2	1	2	3	9	3	20
Europe	2	5	9	7	31	8	62

classification differences. This problem is somewhat ameliorated by focusing upon direct plus indirect factor use.

The breakdown of traded goods into the NRB and HOS categories is particularly troublesome for Korea, Taiwan, and to some degree Tunisia for which the input-output data combine extraction and processing of nonmetallic minerals. The combined sectors are classed as HOS, which causes some noncomparability for major division results. Different levels of aggregation present major comparability problems. A typical optimal solution has every sector but one[14] at either its maximum or its minimum output limit. The Ivory Coast, Kenya, and Uruguay have only one sector in the other NRB division, and as a result they will normally realize output changes of plus or minus 25 percent for this division, while countries with more sectors in the division may have smaller absolute changes. Similarly, a country with an aggregative sector such as "machinery" normally realizes a 25 percent output change, whereas a country with fifteen machinery sectors normally has some at their output maxima and others at their minima. Consequently, the absolute value of the aggregate change in machinery output may be smaller in the second country even though the underlying conditions are the same for both. As more information is gained, it may prove desirable to let δ vary with the level of aggregation. These and other problems are considered in section 1.5.

1.4.2 Input-Output Coefficients

The a_{ij} were taken from base-year input-output tables and follow the input-output definition whereby the domestic price for each sector equals one (or sometimes, one million), with the corresponding physical output units being the quantities that could have been purchased for one (or one million) domestic currency unit(s) during a base year. The typical input-output coefficient gives the number of physical units of the output of sector i defined in this manner necessary to produce one physical unit of the output sector j defined in this manner. This definition is retained throughout.

1.4.3 International Prices

The domestic currency price of a traded good is denoted by ρ_j, and its international dollar price is denoted by p_j. The two are related as follows:

$$(26) \qquad \rho_j = (1/R)p_j(1 + t_j), \qquad (j = 1, \ldots, m)$$

where t_i is an implicit tariff rate with a negative value indicating an implicit subsidy and R is an exchange rate giving the number of units of domestic currency per dollar. Nothing essential is lost by letting $R = 1$ and thereby measuring international prices in domestic currency units. It is customary to define units so that $p_j = 1$ and $\rho_j = (1 + t_j)$. Here, however, the input-output convention $\rho_j = 1$ is retained so that

$$(27) \qquad p_j = 1/(1 + t_j). \qquad (j = 1, \ldots, m)$$

The essential results of the analysis are independent of the units in which goods are defined. The individual sectoral prices used for the model applications are listed in Appendix C.

The implicit tariff rate t_j provides a measure of the divergence between domestic and international prices. It reflects quantitative restrictions and a variety of other influences as well as tariffs. The ideal way to measure the rate is to compute it directly from measures of domestic and international prices. This procedure was used for Chile, the Ivory Coast, and Uruguay. Appropriate nominal tariff rates were used for some of the other countries, and the ratios of duty collections to imports were used for others. The use of such rates introduces an error insofar as they fail to reflect domestic/international price differences accurately. For countries such as South Korea and Taiwan, where nontariff barriers are relatively unimportant, the error is probably small. For some of the other countries it may be large for some sectors. International prices are the most difficult data to obtain.

1.4.4   Labor and Capital Data

The input-output tables also are the principal source of labor and capital information. Wage payments and employer contributions to Social Security are used to measure labor input, and all other value added except taxes and subsidies is used to measure capital input. Thus it is assumed that the productivities of individual laborers are directly proportional to their wage rates. The capital data were adjusted in cases where abnormally low profits were earned. There are occasional cases where a capital input as defined above is negative. This is a particular problem for sectors that are run as State Economic Enterprises in Turkey. Comparable data for other sectors are used to make the capital adjustments. Particulars are given in Appendix B. The L^0 and K^0 estimates were obtained by summing the individual sector quantities for the base year.

The Chile study in Krueger et al. (1981) provided supplementary information that allowed a breakdown of input-output labor data into skilled and unskilled categories. For Chile it is a white-collar/blue-collar distinction. There are no data for the agricultural sectors. It is assumed somewhat arbitrarily that 5 percent of agricultural labor is skilled. Values for U^0 and S^0 were obtained by summing individual sector data. By this criterion 18 percent of the Chilean labor force is skilled. The Tunisia study also has a skill breakdown, with unskilled workers, apprentices, and seasonal employees constituting the unskilled group. These data were used to provide a skill breakdown for the input-output labor coefficients. Again, 5 percent of agricultural labor is assumed to be skilled. The aggregates indicate that 43 percent of the Tunisian labor force is skilled by this criterion. The Tunisian and Chilean data are not comparable, since many Tunisian blue-collar workers are classed as skilled.

Labor and capital inputs can be measured in terms of either stocks or flows. The choice often depends upon data availability. The individual country studies sometimes use stock measures and sometimes use flow measures. Flows are used here with factor payments as proxies for the flow of factor services. The use of stocks and flows are equivalent if stock/flow ratios are constant over an economy as a whole, as is assumed here. Errors may be introduced if stock/fllow ratios differ between sectors within a given economy, or if a uniform overall ratio varies in response to factor price changes. The costs of distortion will be understated if factors, particularly unskilled labor, were underutilized in the base year. Corrections are straightforward wherever such variations in stock/flow ratios can be identified and measured.

The definition of uniform labor units always presents problems whether the unit is man-hours or wage payments. It is by no means clear which metric is preferable. The wage metric can introduce errors if intersectoral wage differentials reflect distortions rather than productivity differences. Again, corrections can be made wherever the requisite information is available.

1.4.5   Cobb-Douglas Coefficients

Let ℓ_j and k_j denote the respective base-year adjusted labor and capital inputs per unit of output. These provide the basis for the Cobb-Douglas coefficients on the assumption that α_j is labor's share of base-year of DVA in sector j:[15]

$$(28) \qquad \alpha_j = \ell_j/(\ell_j + k_j). \qquad (j = 1, \ldots, n)$$

The sectoral alphas used for the applications are listed in Appendix C. The A_j are determined by dividing the production function (1) by X_j and solving for

$$(29) \qquad A_j = 1/(\ell_j^{\alpha_j} k_j^{(1-\alpha_j)}). \qquad (j = 1, \ldots, n)$$

A similar procedure is used for the three-factor extension.

1.4.6   Base-Year Outputs and Home Goods Final Demands

The X_j^0 are simply the base-year gross output levels provided by the input-output tables. Base-year import and export data also were secured directly from the input-output tables for most of the countries. These are not necessary for implementing the model, but they are useful for interpreting its solutions as described in section 1.5.

The fixed home goods final demand levels were computed from the input-output data as follows:

(30) $$C_i^0 = X_i^0 - \sum_{j=i}^{n} a_{ij} X_j^0. \qquad (i = m+1, \ldots, n)$$

These equal total final demands less imports as given by the input-output data.

1.5 The Optimal Solutions

1.5.1 Implied Labor Service Shifts

Table 1.4 shows labor changes, on a major-division basis implied by shifts from base-year observations to optimal solutions. Columns 1 and 3 contain percentage distributions by division of direct labor services, and column 2 contains the differences between the two distributions that sum to zero, since labor service totals are the same for corresponding base years and optimal solutions.

Labor services are measured in terms of factor payments. Consequently, for a relative low-wage sector such as agriculture the percentage of labor shown in table 1.4 is smaller than the percentage of the labor force working in agriculture. The converse normally is true for manufacturing. There are some differences in the definitions of the home goods sectors between countries. Some services that are included in the agricultural sectors for one country are included in separate home goods sectors for another. In Taiwan, for example, the home goods sector "paddy" supplies the international goods sector "rice." The two activities are combined in a single sector in other countries. The agriculture and home goods percentages for the Ivory Coast and Kenya are an example of different classification procedures that do not represent massive structural differences. Intercountry comparisons of labor distributions must be made with care.

For the base year, the three manufacturing divisions constitute from 10 to 12 percent of total labor services for Indonesia, the Ivory Coast, Kenya, and Tunisia and about 20 percent for South Korea, Taiwan, and Turkey. The figure is almost 27 percent for Uruguay, where meat-packing is a major activity. Also, some of Uruguay's NRB activities are included in other manufacturing as a result of a very aggregative sectoral classification. Manufacturing constitutes more than 40 percent of total labor services for Germany and about 30 percent for the other European countries.

The optimal solutions indicate agricultural expansions for all of the developing countries except South Korea 1973 and Tunisia. Table 1.4 shows a decline of 0.66 percent of the total labor services for agriculture

Table 1.4   **Base-Year and Optimal Solution Labor/Service Distributions by Major Division (Percentages of Total Labor Services)**

Country	Base Year (1)	Solution Shift (2)	Optimal Direct (3)	Optimal Indirect (4)	Optimal Direct and Indirect (5)
Chile					
Agriculture	20.59	3.16	23.75	3.73	27.48
Other NRB	8.99	1.75	10.74	2.16	12.90
Food	3.90	−1.15	2.75	2.22	4.97
Textiles	4.55	−1.36	3.19	1.33	4.52
Other manufacturing	14.51	−3.94	10.57	5.13	15.70
Home goods	47.46	1.54	49.00	−14.57	34.43
Total	100.00	0.00	100.00	0.00	100.00
Indonesia					
Agriculture	42.75	2.11	44.86	0.43	45.29
Other NRB	1.56	−0.32	1.24	0.23	1.47
Food	6.10	0.02	6.12	0.64	6.76
Textiles	1.84	−0.40	1.44	0.19	1.63
Other manufacturing	4.71	−0.71	4.00	0.58	4.58
Home goods	43.04	−0.70	42.34	−2.07	40.27
Total	100.00	0.00	100.00	0.00	100.00
Ivory Coast					
Agriculture	48.01	−0.66	47.37	10.01	57.38
Other NRB	0.32	−0.08	0.24	0.06	0.30
Food	3.46	−0.06	3.40	1.38	4.78
Textiles	2.93	−0.70	2.23	0.50	2.73
Other manufacturing	4.21	0.21	4.40	3.94	8.34
Home goods	41.07	1.29	42.36	−15.89	26.47
Total	100.00	0.00	100.00	0.00	100.00
Kenya					
Agriculture	21.04	3.55	24.59	1.44	26.03
Other NRB	0.60	−0.15	0.45	0.10	0.55
Food	2.13	−0.54	1.59	0.87	2.46
Textiles	1.19	−0.01	1.18	0.27	1.45
Other manufacturing	8.24	−1.81	6.43	1.57	8.00
Home goods	66.80	−1.04	65.76	−4.25	61.51
Total	100.00	0.00	100.00	0.00	100.00
South Korea, 1966					
Agriculture	51.21	−0.50	50.71	0.55	51.26
Other NRB	2.29	−0.51	1.78	0.14	1.92
Food	2.41	0.46	2.87	0.66	3.53
Textiles	4.10	0.59	4.70	0.93	5.63
Other manufacturing	7.84	−0.39	7.45	2.82	10.27
Home goods	32.15	0.34	32.49	−5.10	27.39
Total	100.00	0.00	100.00	0.00	100.00

Table 1.4 (continued)

Country	Base Year (1)	Solu-tion Shift (2)	Optimal Direct (3)	In-direct (4)	Direct and Indirect (5)
South Korea, 1970					
Agriculture	36.98	1.29	38.27	1.02	39.29
Other NRB	1.90	−0.33	1.57	0.27	1.84
Food	2.58	0.28	2.86	0.90	3.76
Textiles	4.76	0.01	4.77	1.33	6.10
Other manufacturing	9.43	−0.49	8.94	3.57	12.51
Home goods	44.35	−0.76	43.59	−7.09	36.50
Total	100.00	0.00	100.00	0.00	100.00
South Korea, 1973					
Agriculture	35.79	−1.54	34.25	0.89	35.14
Other NRB	1.77	−0.35	1.42	0.65	2.07
Food	2.62	−0.14	2.48	0.84	3.32
Textiles	5.42	1.31	6.73	1.86	8.59
Other manufacturing	11.86	0.14	12.00	3.15	15.15
Home goods	42.54	0.58	43.12	−7.39	35.73
Total	100.00	0.00	100.00	0.00	100.00
Taiwan					
Agriculture	11.08	0.04	11.12	7.74	18.86
Other NRB	1.21	0.33	1.54	0.12	1.66
Food	1.49	0.40	1.89	1.98	3.87
Textiles	3.13	1.05	4.18	1.26	5.44
Other manufacturing	18.36	−4.52	13.84	4.55	18.39
Home goods	64.73	2.70	67.43	−15.65	51.78
Total	100.00	0.00	100.00	0.00	100.00
Tunisia					
Agriculture	47.50	−2.04	45.46	1.54	45.49
Other NRB	3.27	−0.67	2.60	0.70	3.30
Food	2.24	−0.31	1.93	0.78	4.22
Textiles	2.14	0.46	2.60	0.53	3.13
Other manufacturing	6.02	1.30	7.32	1.99	9.31
Home goods	38.83	1.26	40.09	−5.54	34.55
Total	100.00	0.00	100.00	0.00	100.00
Turkey					
Agriculture	50.49	3.87	54.36	1.51	55.87
Other NRB	3.17	−0.74	2.43	0.37	2.80
Food	3.68	0.36	4.04	0.90	4.94
Textiles	4.69	0.43	5.12	0.87	5.99
Other manufacturing	12.14	−2.74	9.40	2.05	11.45
Home goods	25.83	−1.18	24.65	−5.70	18.95
Total	100.00	0.00	100.00	0.00	100.00

Table 1.4 (continued)

Country	Base Year (1)	Solution Shift (2)	Optimal Direct (3)	Optimal In-direct (4)	Optimal Direct and Indirect (5)
Uruguay					
Agriculture	23.49	4.14	27.63	4.60	32.23
Other NRB	1.75	−0.45	1.30	0.13	1.43
Food	7.53	1.14	8.67	5.94	14.61
Textiles	4.55	−0.67	3.88	0.63	4.51
Other manufacturing	14.60	−3.76	10.84	3.19	14.03
Home goods	48.08	−0.40	47.68	−14.49	33.19
Total	100.00	0.00	100.00	0.00	100.00
Belgium					
Agriculture	6.71	−1.62	5.09	0.37	5.46
Other NRB	4.98	−0.54	4.44	0.60	5.04
Food	2.42	0.09	2.51	0.87	3.38
Textiles	5.45	−0.24	5.21	0.75	5.96
Other manufacturing	22.21	2.00	24.21	4.81	29.02
Home goods	58.23	0.31	58.54	−7.40	51.14
Total	100.00	0.00	100.00	0.00	100.00
France					
Agriculture	9.17	2.35	11.52	1.22	12.74
Other NRB	2.38	−0.01	2.37	0.47	2.84
Food	2.48	−0.08	2.40	0.75	3.15
Textiles	3.74	0.04	3.78	0.64	4.42
Other manufacturing	24.35	−2.24	22.11	4.79	26.90
Home goods	57.88	−0.06	57.82	−7.87	49.95
Total	100.00	0.00	100.00	0.00	100.00
Germany					
Agriculture	5.79	−1.43	4.36	0.43	4.79
Other NRB	2.75	0.69	3.44	0.80	4.24
Food	2.62	0.26	2.88	0.76	3.64
Textiles	4.64	0.11	4.75	0.49	5.24
Other manufacturing	36.97	−0.02	36.95	6.12	43.07
Home goods	47.23	0.39	47.62	−8.60	39.02
Total	100.00	0.00	100.00	0.00	100.00
Italy					
Agriculture	14.16	−3.47	10.69	0.40	11.09
Other NRB	1.42	0.35	1.77	0.34	2.11
Food	2.53	0.29	2.82	0.74	3.56
Textiles	4.49	−0.32	4.17	0.65	4.82
Other manufacturing	19.99	2.86	22.85	4.43	27.28
Home goods	57.41	0.29	57.70	−6.56	51.14
Total	100.00	0.00	100.00	0.00	100.00

in the Ivory Coast. However, this is more than offset by an expansion of home goods labor services that involve the processing of agricultural produce. Similarly, the slight increase of 0.04 percent for Taiwan is much larger when paddy is included. The South Korea 1973 solution suggests a move from agriculture to textiles. A similar shift is indicated for South Korea 1966, but 1970 indicates a shift to agriculture. A shift away from agriculture is suggested for each of the European countries except France.

The labor service shifts from manufacturing to agriculture suggested by the optimal solutions must be interpreted with care. Such shifts are not likely to be realized. The significant thing is that agriculture has comparative advantage over manufacturing and should be expanded relative to manufacturing. The shifts are large for Chile, Kenya, and Turkey, countries with trade strategies heavily oriented toward import substitution. The shifts to agriculture may reflect the lack of comparative advantage for import substitution manufacturing endeavors more than strong comparative advantage for agriculture. It is possible that other manufacturing industries with some competitive advantage that are currently small or nonexistent could absorb labor released from import substitution sectors.

A substantial increase for other NRB sectors is indicated for Chile with its rich mines, and there is a small increase for Taiwan. Declines are indicated for other developing countries. Labor service declines for all the manufacturing divisions are in order for Chile and Kenya. Indonesia has a small increase for food and shows declines for the other two. The Ivory Coast has declines for food and textiles and a modest increase for other manufacturing. Taiwan shows a sizable reduction for other manufacturing. Turkey has expansion for food and textiles and contraction for other manufacturing. Uruguay has expansion for food and contraction for the other two sectors. South Korea 1973 shows a large expansion for textiles and a modest expansion of other manufacturing. South Korea 1966 also shows a sizable textile expansion. It is significant that textiles did expand substantially in the late 1960s when Korean producers were confronted with international prices.

Belgium, Germany, and Italy all show reductions in agriculture. Belgium and Italy show corresponding increases for other manufacturing. The major thing that comes through for Germany is that its comparative advantage does not lie in agriculture. This has been confirmed by the decline of German agriculture since 1963 and the need for EEC protection of agriculture. The solutions suggest that France is the exception. An increase for agriculture and a decline for other manufacturing is indicated.

Two major uses have been indicated for home goods: the direct and indirect support of home goods final demands, and inputs for the production of international goods. For example, column 3 of table 1.4 shows that

49.00 percent of Chile's labor is used in the home goods division. Some 34.43 percent is attributable to home goods final demands, and 14.57 percent to inputs for the production of international goods. These indirect uses are allocated to the appropriate international goods sectors in column 4. Some 3.73 percent constitutes the home goods labor services that support agricultural output, and so on. Column 4 sums to zero, since total labor services are being reallocated but not changed in total. Column 5 is the sum of columns 3 and 4. For the five international goods divisions it gives total direct plus home goods indirect labor services. For home goods it gives the total home goods labor services that support home goods final demands.

Home goods indirect labor services for traded goods differ a great deal from country to country, indicating differing input-output accounting schemes. It is about 15 percent of total employment for Chile, the Ivory Coast, Taiwan, and Uruguay but is less than 6 percent for the other developing countries except South Korea. It is only 2 percent for Indonesia. The direct plus home goods indirect distributions are somewhat more comparable among countries than the direct, since differences attributable to classification differences are reduced.

Direct plus home goods indirect measures are used for the remaining evaluations of the optimal solutions, since these more closely represent the total impact of output and trade changes.

1.5.2 Implied IVA and DVA Changes

Since the model is designed to maximize IVA and since base-year solutions are feasible, it is not surprising that optimal IVAs are greater than base-year IVAs. It is of interest to ask, How much greater? Can substantial income increments be achieved by moving to a regime of freer trade? IVA increases by major divisions as percentages of base-year values are listed for each of the solutions in the top half of table 1.5. These are calculated by multiplying the base and optimal outputs by the corresponding direct and home goods indirect IVA coefficients, that is, the $\hat{z}_j$s as given by (11). A coefficient is negative if the international value of its traded inputs exceeds its international price. For the present applications there are ten negative $\hat{z}_j$s for the 847 individual sectors in the fifteen applications. Indonesia has six, Taiwan has three, and Turkey has one. The particular sectors can be found by finding g_j values smaller than -1 in Appendix C.

The maximum possible change for total IVA is substantially less than 25 percent. The output constraints limit the IVA increment for each individual sector to 25 percent, but the labor and capital constraints limit the number of sectors that can achieve their maxima. These restrictions suggest that the model may provide underestimates of the gains from free trade. Under these conditions IVA increments of 5 percent or more are

Table 1.5   **Optimum Solution Changes of IVA and DVA**
(Percentages of Base-Year Values)

Country	Agri-culture	Other NRB	Food	Tex-tiles	Other Manu-facturing	All Traded
			IVA			
Chile	25.0	25.0	−25.0	−25.0	−3.1	3.6
Indonesia	8.2	−0.4	6.2	−6.3	−16.2	3.3
Ivory Coast	8.3	−25.0	1.8	−25.0	10.2	6.7
Kenya	17.7	−25.0	−25.0	−14.0	−11.7	10.8
South Korea, 1966	1.9	−25.0	18.7	18.0	2.2	3.9
South Korea, 1970	7.2	−8.5	13.5	7.7	−1.0	4.2
South Korea, 1973	−5.1	0.5	−6.8	23.5	5.7	2.8
Taiwan	15.2	25.0	10.7	−0.6	3.6	8.4
Tunisia	−4.2	12.6	−2.2	19.8	17.7	2.8
Turkey	10.7	−23.5	15.9	8.3	−14.2	5.3
Uruguay	19.3	−25.0	22.1	−25.0	−25.0	8.9
Belgium	−24.1	−13.3	8.6	2.7	10.2	3.0
France	25.0	3.5	1.4	4.8	−6.2	2.7
Germany	−17.7	24.1	10.6	3.5	5.8	6.8
Italy	−24.0	25.0	17.4	−6.1	15.8	2.8
			DVA			
Chile	25.0	25.0	−25.0	−25.0	−7.9	−4.9
Indonesia	3.2	−0.3	−1.6	−20.8	−4.2	0.1
Ivory Coast	1.2	−25.0	−2.9	−25.0	7.7	−1.0
Kenya	17.7	−25.0	−25.0	−16.2	−10.5	−8.1
South Korea, 1966	−1.1	−25.0	17.9	15.3	0.5	0.7
South Korea, 1970	2.6	−9.8	13.6	1.9	−5.3	1.0
South Korea, 1973	−5.8	−12.8	−7.6	23.0	3.6	0.4
Taiwan	15.0	25.0	−21.0	−14.9	−0.8	1.6
Tunisia	−4.1	13.9	−20.0	18.0	18.8	−1.4
Turkey	10.2	−24.2	11.1	5.1	−13.4	1.8
Uruguay	18.5	−25.0	19.8	−25.0	−25.0	−4.8
Belgium	−24.3	−12.8	6.6	−0.7	10.0	1.7
France	25.0	5.0	−3.2	1.9	−7.2	0.7
Germany	−24.4	24.3	13.9	2.6	7.6	5.2
Italy	−24.0	−25.0	13.1	−8.8	14.8	0.4

substantial. Five of the nine developing countries show increments of 5 percent or more. The gains for Kenya and Turkey are the result of the lessening importance of import substitution sectors. The large gain for Taiwan is to a large degree the consequence of reductions in the outputs of food sectors with negative IVAs, and it should be interpreted with care.

The sizable IVA gain for Germany is largely the result of the reduction of its inefficient agricultural sector. The European countries and South Korea 1973 show gains of about 3 percent. South Korea is much closer to a free-trade regime than the other eight developing countries, and as a result it has less to gain from a move toward freer trade. South Korea 1966 and 1970 show greater opportunities for gain during the earlier years of rapid growth. Perhaps some of that rapid growth can be interpreted in terms of movement away from an earlier heavily distorted situation.

The relatively small gains for Chile, Indonesia, and Tunisia, which are a long way from free trade, must be explained in other terms. A possible explanation is that the few sectors in which these countries compete effectively in international trade are already operating at prices very close to international prices and consequently offer small unit gains.

The breakdown of IVA changes again confirms the strong agricultural advantage for most of the developing countries. Only South Korea 1973 and Taiwan show declines of agricultural IVA. Turkey and Uruguay show substantial food IVA gains for processing their agricultural produce. The Ivory Coast and Tunisia are the only countries that show substantial gains for other manufacturing.

The DVA figures in the bottom half of table 1.5 are obtained by multiplying the base and optimal outputs by the base DVA coefficients as defined by (21). Here the optimal solution changes are evaulated in terms of prevailing domestic prices. The relevant question is, Are there incentives to shift to the optimal outputs, given prevailing, distorted prices? Generally the answer is no. The overall DVA increments are much smaller than overall IVA increments. In fact, the overall DVA increments are negative for five of the nine developing countries. The largest increment is 1.8 percent for Turkey. The explanation is straightforward. The developing countries have domestic relative prices that are far removed from international relative prices. The domestic prices serve to protect existing industrial structures and give little or no incentive for further movement toward comparative advantage as defined by international prices.

The differences between IVA and DVA rates of change are smaller for the European countries than for the developing countries. This reflects the smaller gap between domestic and international prices for the European countries.

1.5.3 The Costs of Distortions

The g_j coefficients as defined by (22) provide an opportunity cost measure of the costs of commodity and factor market distortions upon the jth sector. It gives the profit rate in terms of net IVA of allocating a dollar's (or other currency units) worth of factors to sector j where factor prices and proportions are defined in terms of the optimal solutions. Absolute as well as algebraic values are of significance in interpreting the g_j. A positive (negative) g_j gives the increase of IVA that would be achieved if one more (less) dollar's worth of factor was allocated to its production.

From another viewpoint the g_js rank sectors in terms of comparative advantage, or lack thereof, relative to the base-year observations. The magnitudes of the coefficients also provide indicators of the magnitudes of potential gains for alternative trade strategies. In general, countries with domestic prices close to international prices and few factor market distortions will have relatively small g_j coefficients. However, some problems of comparability between countries exist because of difference in levels of aggregation and differences in the accuracy with which international prices can be measured. Coefficients for individual sectors are given in Appendix C.

The major division coefficients given in table 1.6 were calculated by dividing the aggregate optimal direct and home goods indirect IVA for each division by its aggregate value of the factors used directly and indirectly. The coefficients in the last column for all traded sectors are the quotients of the aggregate of IVA and factor values over the five major divisions. The agricultural coefficient is at or close to zero for each of developing countries except South Korea and Tunisia, reflecting comparative advantage in agriculture. The South Korean coefficient is low, with a substantial advantage elsewhere, particularly in textiles. The Tunisian case is more complicated. One possible explanation is that comparative advantage lies in manufacturing because of relative inefficiency of Tunisian agriculture. France is the only one of the European countries with an advantage in agriculture. German agriculture is particularly inefficient.

Table 1.6   **Distortion-Cost Coefficients by Major Division**

Country	Agri-culture	Other NRB	Food	Tex-tiles	Other Manu-facturing	All Traded
Chile	0.320	0.657	−0.291	−0.557	0.042	0.089
Indonesia	0.024	−0.009	−0.092	−0.626	0.083	−0.038
Ivory Coast	0.169	−0.115	−0.055	−0.340	0.285	0.142
Kenya						
South Korea, 1966	−0.080	−0.073	0.854	0.114	−0.017	−0.033
South Korea, 1970	−0.104	−0.001	0.851	0.042	−0.044	−0.049
South Korea, 1973	−0.022	−0.406	−0.070	0.078	−0.041	0.007
Taiwan	0.072	0.132	−0.299	−0.307	−0.016	−0.033
Tunisia	−0.071	−0.060	−0.036	0.150	0.169	−0.016
Turkey	−0.004	−0.404	0.086	−0.020	−0.725	−0.299
Uruguay	0.033	−0.627	0.177	−0.517	−0.496	−0.451
Belgium	−0.107	−0.176	0.151	0.035	0.046	0.023
France	0.068	0.051	0.199	0.026	0.059	0.069
Germany	−0.165	0.195	0.122	0.018	0.050	0.059
Italy	−0.035	0.140	0.241	0.051	0.207	0.134

Chile shows a strong comparative advantage in other resources—copper, nitrate, and iron-ore mining.

Each European country shows comparative advantage for each of the three manufacturing divisions, with all twelve manufacturing coefficients positive. Manufacturing advantage for the developing countries is much spottier. Turkey and Uruguay show advantage for food sectors. Turkey has clear advantages for canned fruits and vegetables, other food products, and tobacco, as indicated in Appendix C. The Uruguayan advantage is in processing its own beef. South Korea has an advantage in a wide range of textile sectors.

The developing countries show a variety of expansion advantages for other manufacturing. The aggregate other manufactures coefficient is positive for five of the ten developing country applications. The top-ranked individual sectors for Chile are petroleum and coal products; wood products; pulp, paper, and products; and fabricated metal products. On the whole these sectors are close to natural resources. Only wood and paper have realized sizable exports thus far. The Indonesian coefficient is dominated by petroleum refining. Its exclusion would reduce the other manufacturing coefficient to -0.138. The Ivory Coast coefficient is dominated by petroleum products, which includes both production and refining. Its exclusion would reduce the other manufacturing coefficient to -0.088.

South Korea has a number of other manufacturing sectors with advantage and has far and away the broadest manufacturing export base of the developing countries. Taiwan, despite an overall coefficient of -0.016, also has a broad range of manufacturing sectors with advantage. Tunisia also shows many manufacturing sectors with advantage.

Turkey and Uruguay show little if any advantage for other manufacturing. Much of the poor showing for Turkey may result from the poor performance of State Economic Enterprises and an extensive import substitution policy. The poor showing for Uruguay is partially comparative disadvantage because agriculture, livestock, and food have such strong advantage.

The aggregate coefficients for all traded goods have the same signs as the aggregate rents, that is, the $\sum_{j=1}^{m} r_j X_j$. These weighted averages provide some information of interest but must be interpreted with care. The European coefficients are all positive. These countries do not subsidize inefficient industries to the same degree as the developing countries, for which seven of ten coefficients are negative. South Korea 1973 has a small but positive coefficient, indicating broad expansion potentials. The Chilean coefficient reflects its efficient mining sectors, and the Ivory Coast coefficient reflects advantages in coffee, cocoa, and timber. Turkey's inefficient State Economic Enterprises and its import substitution are reflected in its strongly negative coefficient.

1.5.4   Implications for Trade

Optimal net trade levels might be determined by subtracting optimal consumption levels from optimal output levels where consumption levels are determined on the basis of country preference functions subject to balance-of-payments constraints, but the determination of optimal consumption levels is beyond the scope of this chapter. Consequently, trade implications of the optimal solutions must be investigated by more indirect procedures.

Table 1.7 contains major division IVA growth rates with export and import weights. The export figures are calculated using the formula

$$\gamma_J = \frac{\sum\limits_{j \varepsilon J} \rho_j \hat{z}_j E_j^0}{\sum\limits_{j \varepsilon J} \hat{z}_j E_j^0}, \qquad (J = 1, \ldots, 5)$$

where j refers to individual sectors, J refers to major divisions, and the ρ_j are the individual sector growth rates, usually plus or minus 25 percent. The last column of table 1.7 contains the growth rates for total IVA as taken from table 1.5.

An overall export expansion advantage would be reflected in an export rate higher than the corresponding import rate, and an overall import substitution advantage would be reflected in an import rate higher than the corresponding export rate. By these criteria, overall export expansion advantages are indicated for seven of the eleven applications for the developing countries. The overall import substitution advantages for South Korea 1966 and 1970 apparently were realized through its rapid industrialization and had been converted to an overall export expansion by 1973 as growth took place and exports expanded. The overall import substitution advantage for Taiwan may indicate that export expansion had been pushed too far by 1971 and that some retrenchment was desirable. Nonetheless, export expansion appears desirable for some of Taiwan's individual sectors. Again, the Tunisian result suggests contraction of agriculture and expansion of manufacturing. The low export and import growth rates suggest near optimality for the highly industrialized European countries.

Comparing the Chilean and Indonesian figures shows that much richer results may be achieved for more disaggregate sectoral classifications. Little of interest is found by examining the major division growth rates for the highly aggregate Chilean classification. Four of the five major division rates are at extremes. The rates for all traded goods are meaningful, however, because of the differential distributions of exports and imports among divisions. The major division rates for the much more disaggregate Indonesia data are of interest. The export growth rate exceeds the import growth rate for every major division except agriculture.

Table 1.7   **Implied IVA Growth Rates with Export and Import Weights (Percentages of Base-Year Values)**

Country	Agri-culture	Other NRB	Food	Tex-tiles	Other Manu-facturing	All Traded	Total IVA
Chile							
Exports	25.0	25.0	−25.0	−25.0	−6.7	23.7	3.6
Imports	25.0	25.0	−25.0	−25.0	−9.9	−4.4	
Indonesia							
Exports	−9.6	2.4	14.1	−17.3	23.2	2.8	3.3
Imports	−4.5	−8.8	8.7	−24.6	−22.4	−18.9	
Ivory Coast							
Exports	19.7	−25.0	10.4	−25.0	9.6	16.5	6.7
Imports	−24.8	—[a]	5.4	−25.0	−11.3	−13.9	
Kenya							
Exports	17.7	−25.0	−25.0	−9.9	−0.1	4.9	10.8
Imports	17.7	−25.0	−25.0	−18.1	−18.2	−16.0	
South Korea, 1966							
Exports	7.6	−25.0	−20.8	15.6	−6.8	−3.7	3.9
Imports	7.2	−25.0	24.7	23.8	13.7	13.3	
South Korea, 1970							
Exports	−24.5	19.1	11.2	2.7	1.8	0.5	4.2
Imports	17.4	6.1	3.5	19.3	7.8	11.5	
South Korea, 1973							
Exports	−19.2	23.7	2.5	22.8	4.8	8.0	2.8
Imports	−5.7	11.4	−15.9	24.4	−0.7	−1.0	
Taiwan							
Exports	−4.2	25.0	−17.2	−21.1	−3.3	−7.5	8.4
Imports	22.7	25.0	−13.7	7.0	−7.1	8.7	
Tunisia							
Exports	−19.4	15.7	−22.0	24.1	13.6	9.4	2.8
Imports	7.4	24.9	24.1	4.3	20.1	17.8	
Turkey							
Exports	11.6	−25.0	15.8	−6.1	−8.1	5.3	5.3
Imports	10.3	−22.8	15.0	4.6	−23.8	−20.8	
Uruguay							
Exports	16.6	−25.0	24.8	−25.0	−25.0	11.3	8.9
Imports	25.0	−25.0	24.2	−25.0	−25.0	−15.5	
Belgium							
Exports	−22.7	−8.9	−8.5	−14.4	11.5	3.7	3.0
Imports	−14.7	−12.1	2.6	−13.1	−1.7	3.0	
France							
Exports	25.0	16.0	4.9	−5.2	−13.8	−7.1	2.7
Imports	25.0	14.0	16.4	−10.7	−14.5	−0.8	
Germany							
Exports	−18.9	23.2	11.9	7.6	−2.5	−1.6	6.8
Imports	−23.3	25.0	13.1	−10.4	16.8	−1.7	
Italy							
Exports	−24.8	25.0	−8.6	−13.0	11.0	1.8	2.8
Imports	−23.3	25.0	13.1	−10.4	16.8	3.5	

[a]Less than 0.05 in absolute value.

At first glance Indonesia might appear to have a general export expansion advantage for other manufacturing, since this division has a 23.2 percent export growth rate. This is not the case, however. Indonesia's other manufacturing exports are dominated by petroleum refining and reprocessed rubber, for which it has major export advantages. The optimal solutions suggest increased imports, with few minor exceptions, for the remainder of other manufacturing.

In summary, the optimal solutions suggest that within the relevant range export expansion is superior to import substitution for most developing countries. To be sure, large policy shifts might lead to opposite results, but for countries and policies covered by the model applications, moves away from import substitution are clearly indicated.

1.5.5 Maximum and Minimum Output Distributions

The optimal solution for each country, except South Korea 1973, has only one sector with an output that is at neither its maximum or its minimum limit. South Korea 1973 has two. The numbers of sectors at each limit for each country is given by major division in table 1.8. A marginal sector is included with the maxima if its output increases and with the minima if it decreases. The reader may determine the status of individual sectors by consulting the g_j values in Appendix C. The value $g_j = 0$ designates a marginal sector, $g_j > 0$ designates a maximum, and $g_j < 0$ designates a minimum.

The relative numbers of other manufacturing sectors in the two categories indicate the status of the various countries in terms of world trade potential. Those with a relatively high number of maxima have broadly based comparative advantage. This is the case for the European countries, South Korea, Taiwan, and Tunisia. Chile has some maxima, but its minima reflect its import substitution policies. Indonesia, Kenya, Turkey, and Uruguay are at the opposite extreme with little general advantage in manufacturing. South Korea 1966 and 1970 and Turkey show advantages for a majority of their food-processing sectors. South Korea for all three years and Tunisia show substantial advantages for textiles.

1.5.6 Implied Capital/Labor Service Ratio Changes

The value-added measures of labor and capital services, and the resultant capital/labor ratios, are not strictly comparable between countries. Differences result from different rates of remuneration for labor and capital, and from differences in accounting procedures. Column 1 of table 1.9 contains overall capital/labor ratios. These are K^0/L^0 in the notation of the model. The ratios range from a low of 0.63 for capital-poor Kenya to a high of 1.68 for Chile, which has high mining investments. The European ratios are lower than those for most of the developing countries. It appears that, when labor services are measured by payments, the

Table 1.8   Number of Traded-Good Sectors at Maximum and Minimum Limits by Major Division

Country	Agriculture		Other NRB		Food		Textiles		Other Manufacturing		All Traded	
	Max.	Min.	Max.	Min.	Max.	Min.	Max.	Min.	Max.	Min.	Max.	Min.
Chile	2	0	6	0	0	2	0	3	5	9	13	14
Indonesia	14	15	2	10	6	17	2	9	5	43	29	94
Ivory Coast	3	3	0	1	3	6	0	3	5	12	11	25
Kenya	1	0	0	1	0	2	1	3	1	7	3	13
South Korea, 1966	3	5	0	3	8	1	13	3	25	27	49	39
South Korea, 1970	2	6	1	2	6	3	12	4	20	32	41	47
South Korea, 1973	2	6	1	2	4	5	13	3	22	30	42	46
Taiwan	6	2	4	0	2	7	1	5	14	15	27	29
Tunisia	3	4	1	3	3	3	5	1	20	5	32	16
Turkey	3	1	1	5	5	3	1	4	3	21	13	34
Uruguay	2	0	0	1	1	1	0	3	0	9	3	14
Belgium	1	1	1	1	6	3	2	5	20	11	30	21
France	2	0	1	4	6	3	3	4	16	15	28	26
Germany	1	1	3	2	5	4	4	3	25	6	38	16
Italy	1	1	5	0	5	4	3	4	23	8	37	17

Table 1.9 Average and Marginal Capital/Labor Service Ratios

| | All | Capital/Labor Service Ratios | | | | Rates of Substitution | | Percentage Shifts to Traded | |
| | Goods | Base | | Optimal | | Optimal | Average | | |
Country	(1)	Traded (2)	Home (3)	Traded (4)	Home (5)	MRS (6)	Shift (7)	Labor (8)	Capital (9)
Chile	1.68	1.73	1.59	1.69	1.67	1.076	0.974	1.0	−0.6
Indonesia	1.53	1.37	1.75	1.32	1.84	1.071	1.034	1.3	−0.9
Ivory Coast	0.78	0.68	1.08	0.68	1.06	0.973	0.864	−0.3	0.3
Kenya	0.63	0.67	0.61	0.66	0.62	1.014	1.015	0.2	−0.4
South Korea, 1966	1.01	0.79	1.58	0.81	1.54	0.997	49.584	−a	1.2
South Korea, 1970	1.07	0.91	1.35	0.90	1.38	1.076	0.916	0.4	−0.4
South Korea, 1973	1.29	1.11	1.61	1.12	1.59	0.982	0.403	−0.4	0.1
Taiwan	0.67	0.83	0.52	0.84	0.52	0.985	0.994	−0.2	0.3
Tunisia	1.43	0.95	2.41	0.98	2.28	0.938	0.965	−1.3	0.9
Turkey	1.66	1.19	2.85	0.94	4.77	1.058	0.902	9.7	−5.3
Uruguay	1.25	1.09	1.56	1.08	1.60	1.023	1.001	0.5	−0.4
Belgium	0.83	0.60	1.05	0.60	1.05	1.001	0.103	−a	−a
France	0.73	0.58	0.87	0.59	0.86	0.988	1.076	−0.3	0.4
Germany	0.66	0.64	0.70	0.64	0.69	0.996	0.696	−0.1	0.1
Italy	0.84	0.68	0.99	0.68	0.99	0.996	0.519	−0.1	0.1

aLess than 0.005 in absolute value.

developed countries have more labor per unit of capital than the developing, and when labor is measured in man-years they have less.

Base-year capital/labor service ratios are computed separately for traded and home goods in columns 2 and 3 of table 1.9. The variance for home goods is much greater than that for traded goods. This reflects some major differences in the treatment of home goods among the countries. For six of the developing countries home goods are more capital-intensive than traded goods, for Kenya intensities are about the same, and for two countries traded goods are more intensive than home goods. The high capital-intensity of traded goods for Chile follows from specialization in mining. The very high home goods capital/labor service ratios for Tunisia and Turkey are the result of accounting rather than real differentials vis-à-vis the other developing countries.

The model is defined so that the marginal rate of substitution (MRS) between capital and labor, $-dL_j/dK_j = MPK_j/MPL_j$, for a base year equals one for each sector. The optimal rates given in column 6 of table 1.9 differ from one but are the same for all sectors for any given country solution. An optimal rate greater than one means that the wage rate increases more than the price of capital services, which suggests that existing factor market distortions favor use of capital relative to labor. This is the result for five of the nine developing countries and for South Korea for 1970. The optimal solutions sometimes dictate movements away from highly protected capital-intensive import substitution sectors to less capital-intensive resource and resource-processing sectors. The Ivory Coast, South Korea 1966 and 1973, Taiwan, and Tunisia have optimal MRSs less than one, suggesting that distortions favor labor more than capital.

By assumption, the total quantities of labor and capital services are unaffected by movements from base to optimal solutions. Consequently, the overall capital/labor service ratio is unaltered. However, the ratios for the traded and home goods sectors do change as shown in columns 4 and 5 of table 1.9. The decreases of the capital/labor service ratios for traded goods coincident with increases for home goods for Chile, Indonesia, Kenya, Turkey, and Uruguay provide additional labor for the production of goods for export. In these cases labor services are shifted from home to traded goods and capital services are shifted from traded to home. The rates of substitution for the shifts are given in column 7 of table 1.9. These rates are less than one for Chile and Turkey, indicating that these shifts yield substantially more labor services per unit of capital services than do shifts on the margin. The very large rate for Korea 1966 corresponds to a very small quantity of labor services. The magnitudes of these factor shifts are expressed as percentages of the base-year labor and capital service quantities devoted to traded goods in the last two columns of table 1.9. The shift for Turkey is particularly large as a consequence of a shift away from capital-intensive import substitutes. The most dramatic aspect of table 1.9 is the fall of Turkey's traded goods capital/labor service ratio from 1.19 to 0.94. The Ivory Coast, South Korea, Taiwan, and Tunisia shift capital from the home to the traded goods sectors. The relative shifts for the European countries are quite small.

1.5.7   A Three-Factor Extension

The three-factor version of the model described in sections 1.2 and 1.3 was applied for Chile, with blue-collar and white-collar workers representing unskilled and skilled labor as described in Appendix B. Skill breakdowns also were made for Tunisia and Turkey, but three-factor applications were not made.

Base-year and optimal-solution labor service summaries for Chile are given in table 1.10. Almost 18 percent of the base-year labor services are classified as skilled. The HOS divisions are considerably more skill-intensive than the NRB divisions and home goods. The optimal solution shows a surfeit of skilled labor services, with 1.64 percent of total labor services—9.2 percent of the skilled labor services—shifted from skilled to unskilled employment. This shift follows the shift from skill-intensive import substituting HOS sectors to NRB export sectors. Chile simply has

Table 1.10   **Base-Year and Optimal Solution Chilean Unskilled and Skilled Labor Service Distributions by Major Division (Percentages of Total Labor Services)**

Sector	Base Year	Solution Shift	Optimal Direct	Optimal Indirect	Direct and Indirect
Unskilled labor services					
Agriculture	19.56	3.00	22.56	3.33	25.89
Other NRB	8.08	1.59	9.67	1.94	11.61
Food	1.98	−0.59	1.39	2.00	3.39
Textiles	2.52	−0.72	1.80	1.41	3.21
Other manufacturing	8.14	−2.37	5.77	4.49	10.26
Home goods	41.94	0.73	42.67	−13.17	29.50
Unskilled services	82.22	1.64	83.86	0.00	83.86
Skilled labor services					
Agriculture	1.03	0.16	1.19	0.37	1.56
Other NRB	0.91	0.16	1.07	0.74	1.81
Food	1.91	−0.55	1.36	0.22	1.58
Textiles	2.03	−0.64	1.39	0.15	1.54
Other manufacturing	6.37	−1.57	4.80	0.43	5.23
Home goods	5.53	0.80	6.33	−1.91	4.42
Skilled services	17.78	−1.64	16.14	0.00	16.14
Total	100.00	0.00	100.00	0.00	100.00

more skilled labor than is required if it seeks its comparative advantage. This result is very strong. However, one must not conclude that skilled labor would actually move from the factories to the farms and the mines. A more likely result would be increased skill intensity in all sectors including agriculture and mining. There might also be some narrowing of the unskilled/skilled wage differential.

The three-factor optimal solution for Chile is very similar to the two-factor optimal solution. Output levels, g-coefficients, home goods prices, and most other variables have the same values for both. The optimal MRS between skilled and unskilled labor is one. The optimal skilled and unskilled wage rates are the same, with an optimal skill premium of zero. The sum of the unskilled and skilled optimal direct employment distributions in table 1.10 is the same as the aggregate optimal direct distribution in table 1.5. The direct and indirect distributions sum to the table 1.5 distribution in the aggregate, but not for each individual division. In general, two-factor and three-factor solutions are not much different unless skilled labor is scarce.

A simple test to determine whether skilled labor is scarce can be performed if a two-factor optimal solution and unskilled and skilled base coefficients are available. Assume that skilled labor is not scarce, that equilibrium conditions are

$$\frac{MPU_j}{MPK_j} = \frac{\alpha_j}{(1 - \alpha_j - \beta_j)} \frac{X_j^*/U_j^*}{X_j^*/K_j^*} = \frac{w^*}{c^*} \qquad (j = 1, \ldots, n)$$

$$\frac{MPS_j}{MPK_j} = \frac{\beta_j}{(1 - \alpha_j - \beta_j)} \frac{X_j^*/S_j^*}{X_j^*/K_j^*} = \frac{w^*}{c^*},$$

where * denotes equilibrium values with c^*, w^*, K_j^*, and X_j^* given by the two-factor solution. Now solve for U_j^* and S_j^*:

$$U_j^* = \frac{\alpha_j}{(1 - \alpha_j - \beta_j)} \frac{c^*}{w^*} K_j^* \qquad (j = 1, \ldots, n)$$

$$S_j^* = \frac{\beta_j}{(1 - \alpha_j - \beta_j)} \frac{c^*}{w^*} K_j^*.$$

Finally, sum the S_j^* for all sectors. If this sum is greater than the skill endowment, skilled labor is scarce.

This test was performed for some preliminary skill data for Turkey and Tunisia. The Turkish results are similar to the Chilean. Turkey would have a surfeit of skilled labor if a movement were made toward its comparative advantage in agriculture and food-processing. The test for Tunisia suggests that skilled labor is scarce. This is not surprising, since the optimal solution indicates movement from NRB to HOS sectors with higher skill intensity.

A simple generalization appears to be in order: Skilled labor is not scarce for countries moving from HOS import substitutes to NRB and HOS exportable sectors, but it would be scarce for countries moving in the opposite direction. This result parallels the findings of the individual country studies in which import substituting industries are shown to be skill-intensive.

1.6   Conclusions

The research described here was designed to ask what might happen if the causes of trade and factor market distortions were relaxed *and* economic activities were guided by prices closer to international prices in some nine developing countries. For comparison, the same questions were asked for four developed European countries. On the whole, the results are encouraging and are consistent with detailed individual country studies.

The empirical results show export expansion to be superior to import substitution for the developing countries except Taiwan and Tunisia. The South Korea solutions for 1966 and 1970 suggest import substitution, but many of the former import substitutes had become exports by 1973. The solution for that year suggests manufacturing export promotion. For most of the developing countries, advantage appears to lie in NRB sectors and HOS sectors that process NRB outputs *given existing production patterns*. Since movement of labor back to agriculture is unlikely, and probably undesirable, the developing countries might well look for currently small or nonexistent sectors with export advantage. The Korean successes might be duplicated to some degree in other countries.

Some of the developing countries with advantage in the NRB sectors have developed labor force skills in connection with import substitution. The optimal solutions suggest a surplus of skilled labor for those countries should trade policies alter. This suggests that some reported "shortages" of skilled workers may have been a consequence, at least in part, of choice of trade strategy.

The empirical applications proved a number of results beyond the primary question of where advantage lies. The use of home goods as indirect inputs was measured, and vast differences in treatment of home goods among countries were noted. The short-run opportunity costs of not relaxing current distortions were measured. The average for the developing countries is a bit over 5 percent, which, given the structure of the model, is sizable. Estimated gains are bounded by existing production structures and factor quantities.

The empirical applications indicate that there is little if any incentive for producers in the developing countries to move toward the optimal solutions. Their citizens appear to be optimizing given current domestic prices, which are often far removed from corresponding international prices. South Korea is an exception in that its domestic prices are close to their international counterparts. Factor distortions appear to favor capital more than labor in five of nine cases and to favor labor more than capital in the remaining four.

Fortunately, the results for most of the countries are very robust. In most cases, international price estimates could be subject to substantial error without altering the principal findings about where comparative advantage lies. Some parametric analysis was done by asking how optimal solutions might change if some key prices were to change by 10 to 20 percent. There were some individual changes, but on the whole not much change of significance. A solution for Chile was calculated with 1967 prices substituted for the 1961 prices. The same broad NRB advantage again emerged.

A conclusion of all empirical studies is that better data would be a great help. That is true here. International prices, in particular, are both very important and very difficult to estimate. Ideally, they should be derived from implicit tariff rate studies, as was done for Chile, the Ivory Coast, and Uruguay. Implicit tariff rates measure proportionate difference between domestic and international prices. Average tariff collections rates may be far removed from the desired implicit rates, and nominal tariff rates may be even further removed. But each had to be used for some countries in the absence of implicit rates.

This is the first study for which the current model has been applied. Use of the model for the study of countries other than those covered here provides an obvious line for future research. There are also many possibilities for further study of the properties of the model's optimal solutions and for extensions of the model. Three of them are mentioned here: (1) an investigation to determine the relation of the g_j coefficients to domestic resource cost and effective protection rates; (2) applications in which several distinct labor skill classes are incorporated; and (3) extensions in which alternative trade strategies are more explicitly introduced into the model.

Appendix A: Some Mathematical Properties of the Model

Some of the coefficients of the model are explicitly derived here in terms of the underlying input-output matrixes. The input-output balance equation is

(A1) $X = AX + C,$

where X and C are n-component row vectors of output and final consumption levels respectively, and A is an $(n \times n)$ matrix of input-output coefficients with typical element a_{ij} that gives the quantity of good i necessary to produce a unit of good j. Partitioning (A1) into international and home good blocks,

$$(A2) \qquad \begin{pmatrix} X_T \\ X_H \end{pmatrix} = \begin{bmatrix} A_{TT} & A_{TH} \\ A_{HT} & A_{HH} \end{bmatrix} \begin{pmatrix} X_T \\ X_H \end{pmatrix} + \begin{pmatrix} C_T \\ C_H \end{pmatrix},$$

where the subscript T designates the m international goods and the subscript H designates the $(n - m)$ home goods. For example, the sub-matrix $A_{HT}[(n - m) \times m]$ gives the home goods input requirements for the production of international goods. By block multiplication of (A2),

$$(A3) \qquad X_T = A_{TT}X_T + A_{TH}X_H + C_T$$
$$X_H = A_{HT}X_T + A_{HH}X_H + C_H.$$

Solving (A3) for home goods outputs,

$$(A4) \qquad X_H = (I - A_{HH})^{-1}A_{HT}X_T + (I - A_{HH})^{-1}C_H,$$

which is the same as equation (8) in the text. The coefficient k_i is the ith element of the matrix product $(I - A_{HH})^{-1}C_H$, and σ_{ij} is an element of the $[(m - n) \times m]$ matrix product $(I - A_{HH})^{-1}A_{HT}$. The coefficient μ_{ij} is an element of the home goods inverse matrix $(I - A_{HH})^{-1}$.

Rewriting (10) in matrix terms,

$$(A5) \qquad V = P_T X_T - \Gamma_T X_T - \Gamma_H X_H,$$

where P_T is an m-component row vector of international prices, and Γ_T and Γ_H are row vectors containing the γ_j coefficients for international and home goods respectively. Substituting for X_H from (A4),

$$(A6) \qquad V = [P_T - \Gamma_T - \Gamma_H(I - A_{HH})^{-1}A_{HT}]X_T$$
$$- \Gamma_H(I - A_{HH})^{-1}C_H,$$

which is the same as (12). The square bracketed term on the right is an m-component vector of the $\hat{z}_j$ coefficients, and K equals the second term on the right. The b_j of (11) are given by the vector $\Gamma_H(I - A_{HH})^{-1}A_{HT}$.

Let L_T^* and L_H^* be vectors of labor services per unit output coefficients that correspond to an optimal solution. Let W denote total labor service use so that

$$W = L_T^*X_T + L_H^*X_H.$$

Substituting from (A4),

$$(A7) \qquad W = [L_T^* + L_H^*(I - A_{HH})^{-1}A_{HT}]X_T$$
$$+ L_H^*(I - A_{HH})^{-1}C_H.$$

The square bracketed term on the right is a vector of the $\hat{\ell}^{*}_j$ used in (22). The second term on the right is the quantity of labor services used to support the home goods final demands. A similar derivation is applicable for capital service coefficients.

Appendix B: Data Sources and Rectification Procedures

Data sources and data adjustments for each country are described here under four headings: (1) Input-output data: sources for the base-year data are given. (2) Value-added adjustments: adjustments to make the input-output value-added data more adequately represent labor and capital service inputs are described. (3) International prices: sources are described. (4) Skill breakdown: the procedures for separating the input-output value-added labor input data into skilled and nonskilled service components are described for Chile, Tunisia, and Turkey.

For some countries the labor value added for agriculture covers only hired employees. Family labor income is treated as profit and thus included in nonlabor value added. Adjustment is necessary to make the labor components reflect labor service inputs. Lacking specific information, it was assumed that labor services constitute two-thirds of agriculture value added and capital services constitute one-third. The adjustment for a country with one agricultural sector is very easy.

For a country with N agricultural sectors it is assumed that the two-thirds rule holds for the aggregate:

(B1) $$\sum_{j=1}^{N} L_j = \frac{2}{3} \sum_{j=1}^{N} (\bar{L}_j + \bar{K}_j),$$

where $\bar{L}_j$ and $\bar{K}_j$ denote respective labor and capital value added before adjustment and L_j and K_j denote them after adjustment. Aggregate value added is assumed to remain unchanged in each sector:

(B2) $$L_j + K_j = \bar{L}_j + \bar{K}_j, \qquad (j = 1, \ldots, N)$$

and the adjusted capital/labor service ratios are assumed to be proportional to the unadjusted:

(B3) $$\frac{L_j}{K_j} = \gamma \frac{\bar{L}_j}{\bar{K}_j}. \qquad (j = 1, \ldots, N)$$

The system (B1), (B2), and (B3) has $(2N + 1)$ equations that can be solved for the $(2N + 1)$ variables, γ, L_j, K_j $(j = 1, \ldots, N)$.

For a few sectors the nonlabor value-added coefficients are negative or very small and do not reasonably represent capital service inputs. Capital service data for similar sectors were used to construct capital service coefficients for such sectors. After adjustment these sectors normally show a loss at base-year prices. Such losses are often partially offset by government subsidy.

International prices often are constructed from tariff collection and import data according to the formula

$$p_j = \frac{1}{(1 + T_j/M_j)},$$

where T_j and M_j are tariff collections and import levels c.i.f. for sector j.

Chile

Input-output data. Source was the Chilean input-output table for 1962 prepared by the Oficina de Planificación Nacional, Departamento de Cuentas Sociales.

Value-added adjustments. The two-thirds adjustment was made for one agricultural sector. The banking and other financial services sectors have negative nonlabor value-added coefficients. Capital service coefficients were constructed from the value-added data for other Chilean service sectors.

International prices. Prices were constructed from implicit tariff rates, which reflect international/domestic price ratios, given by Jere R. Behrman, *Foreign Trade Regimes and Economic Development: Chile* (New York: Columbia University Press, 1976), tables 5.3 and A.3.

Skill breakdown. The census data used for the Chile study gave a white-collar/blue-collar labor breakdown for four-digit ISIC manufacturing industries. These data were used to disaggregate the value-added labor service coefficients into skilled and unskilled components. Agriculture, forestry, and fisheries were assumed to have 5 percent skilled labor. Individual service sectors were assumed to have either 5, 10, 15, or 20 percent skilled labor depending upon their characteristics.

Indonesia

Input-output data. Source was the Indonesia study with data derived from government sources.

Value-added adjustments. The two-thirds adjustment was made for twenty-four agricultural sectors. Output and value-added adjustments were made for a number of sectors as a part of the Indonesia study.

International prices. Prices were constructed from nominal tariff rates used for the Indonesia study.

Ivory Coast

Input-output data. Source was the Ivory Coast country study with data derived from governmental sources.

Value-added adjustments. None. The Ivory Coast study provided appropriate data.

International prices. Prices were constructed as a part of the country study to reflect the ratio of domestic to world prices.

Kenya

Input-output data. Source was *Input-Output Table for Kenya 1967* (Central Bureau of Statistics, Ministry of Finance and Planning, December 1972).

Value-added adjustments. The two-thirds adjustment was made for one agricultural sector.

International prices. Prices were constructed from tariff and import data given in the input-output table.

South Korea

Input-output data. Sources were data tapes prepared by the Korean Development Institute (KDI) for all three years.

Value-added adjustments. The two-thirds adjustment was made for six agricultural sectors.

International prices. Prices for 1970 and 1973 were constructed from tariff and import data on the KDI data tapes. Prices for 1966 were constructed from tariff and import data given in Wontack Hong, *Statistical Data on Trade and Subsidy Policy in Korea* (KDI, August 1976), tables B.35 and B.36.

Taiwan

Input-output data. Source was the official publication *Taiwan Input-Output Tables, Republic of China, 1971*, compiled by Overall Planning Department, Economic Planning Council (Executive Yuan, June 1974).

Value-added adjustments. Two sectors, edible vegetable oils and tea, have negative nonlabor value added. The input-output study gives physical capital data for the sectors. Value-added capital service coefficients were constructed by assuming that the ratio of value added to physical capital is the same for these sectors as the aggregate for the other food sectors.

International prices. Prices were constructed from tariff and import data given in the input-output study.

Tunisia

Input-output data. Source was the Tunisia study with data from governmental sources.

Value-added adjustments. The two-thirds adjustment was made for four agricultural sectors. Four sectors had negative nonlabor value added: other livestock, sugar, lumber, and pulp and paper. Capital service coefficients were constructed by assuming that these sectors have the same capital/labor service ratios as similar Tunisian sectors.

International prices. Prices were constructed from nominal tariff rates for the 150-sector classification used in the Tunisia study. Some adjustments were made on the basis of that study.

Skill breakdown. The census data used for the Tunisian study contain a labor breakdown by seven skill classes. Four are considered skilled: management and engineers, white-collar employees, supervisory personnel, and skilled and semiskilled workers. Three are considered unskilled: unskilled workers, apprentices, and seasonal workers. The value-added labor service coefficients were distributed in proportion to the distributions for corresponding census sectors. It was assumed that 5 percent of agricultural labor is skilled.

Turkey

Input-output data. Source was the 1973 input-output table constructed by the State Institute of Statistics.

Value-added adjustments. Six sectors—coal mining, nonferrous ore mining, nonmetallic mineral mining, nonferrous metal basic industries, railroad equipment, and railway transport—have negative nonlabor value added. These sectors are mainly State Economic Enterprises that are run at losses. Capital service coefficients were constructed using data for similar Turkish sectors.

International prices. Prices were constructed from nominal tariff rates for 1968 given by Tercan Baysan, *Economic Implications of Turkey's Entry into the Common Market*, (Ph.D. diss., University of Minnesota, 1974), table 3.

Skill breakdown. Skilled data for 1968 developed in Baysan, *Economic Implications*, were used.

Uruguay

Input-output data. Source is 1961 tables prepared and published by government agencies.

Value-added adjustments. The two-thirds adjustment was made individually for two agricultural sectors.

International prices. Prices were constructed from the implicit tariff rates, reflecting international/domestic price ratios, used for the Uruguay study.

European Countries

Input-output data. Source is the European Economic Community tables for 1965 published in 1970.

Value-added adjustments. It is assumed that three-fifths of value added for the single agricultural sector for each country is attributable to labor services.

International prices. Prices were constructed from the tariff collection and import data given in the input-output tables.

Appendix C: Sectoral Data

Table 1.A.1 contains selected data for the NRB and HOS sectors for each of the fifteen two-factor applications of the model. A descriptive name is given for each sector. Commas are used in place of the word *and*. For example, "other beans, nuts" means other beans and nuts. Sector type codes are: A (agriculture, forestry, and fisheries), R (other natural resource based sectors), F (food), T (textiles, textile products, leather, leather products, and furs), and M (other manufacturing sectors). The p_j are international prices that are defined relative to unit base-year prices. The α_j are the labor-share exponents for the Cobb-Douglas production functions; these are derived from the base-year input-output tables with adjustments as described in Appendix B. The X_j^* are outputs drawn from the optimal solutions and are measured in appropriate value units.

The g_j coefficients are defined by equation (22). A positive coefficient for a sector means that the sector is at its maximum output limit in the optimum solution with a positive u_j and zero v_j. A negative coefficient means that the sector is at its minimum limit with a positive v_j and zero u_j. A zero value indicates a marginal sector for which both u_j and v_j are zero. The $\hat{\ell}_j^*$ and $\hat{k}_j^*$ are the respective optimal direct plus indirect labor and capital service coefficients per unit of output. Indirect means the labor and capital services required to produce the home goods outputs that are required for the production of a unit of an international good.

Table 1.A.1   Selected Sectoral Data

Sector	Type	p_j	α_j	X_j^*	g_j	ℓ_j^*	k_j^*
Chile							
Agriculture, forestry	A	0.70	0.67	1,133	0.20	0.43	0.34
Fisheries	A	0.83	0.12	55	0.59	0.13	0.64
Coal mining	R	0.73	0.78	57	0.20	0.54	0.25
Iron mining	R	0.98	0.30	90	0.74	0.25	0.52
Copper mining	R	1.00	0.30	510	0.82	0.23	0.55
Nitrate mining	R	0.99	0.58	62	0.94	0.36	0.26
Stone, clay, glass	R	0.60	0.36	47	0.05	0.25	0.57
Other nonmetallic mining	R	0.68	0.45	72	0.12	0.40	0.49
Food	F	0.55	0.35	722	-0.31	0.09	0.20
Beverages	F	0.45	0.21	255	-0.26	0.11	0.38
Textiles	T	0.35	0.31	232	-0.59	0.14	0.34
Apparel, shoes	T	0.28	0.21	433	-0.54	0.11	0.43
Leather, products	T	0.38	0.25	42	-0.54	0.10	0.31
Wood	M	0.74	0.46	171	0.25	0.22	0.27
Furniture, accessories	M	0.43	0.33	116	-0.32	0.16	0.39
Pulp, paper, products	M	0.65	0.28	99	0.21	0.14	0.35
Printing, publishing	M	0.58	0.42	50	-0.05	0.25	0.42
Rubber products	M	0.50	0.17	32	-0.15	0.09	0.42
Chemicals	M	0.52	0.30	169	-0.04	0.15	0.37
Petroleum, coal products	M	0.67	0.09	240	0.55	0.10	0.40
Nonmetallic mineral products	M	0.42	0.27	111	-0.42	0.17	0.44
Basic metals	M	0.60	0.44	125	-0.11	0.21	0.29
Fabricated metal products	M	0.63	0.39	187	0.21	0.19	0.37
Machinery	M	0.54	0.38	136	0.00	0.18	0.36
Electrical machinery	M	0.49	0.23	84	-0.10	0.14	0.46
Transport equipment	M	0.54	0.33	128	-0.02	0.18	0.39
Miscellaneous manufactures	M	0.44	0.15	68	-0.25	0.11	0.50

Table 1.A.1 (continued)

Sector	Type	p_j	α_j	X_j^*	g_j	ℓ_j^*	k_j^*
Indonesia							
Paddy	A	1.15	0.69	580.0	0.02	0.62	0.31
Maize	A	1.18	0.77	46.5	0.05	0.70	0.23
Cassava	A	1.11	0.77	46.8	-0.01	0.71	0.23
Other root crops	A	1.11	0.68	11.9	-0.01	0.61	0.31
Vegetables	A	1.11	0.65	53.2	-0.01	0.57	0.33
Fruits	A	1.00	0.65	70.1	-0.11	0.49	0.29
Peanuts	A	1.11	0.53	11.8	-0.01	0.44	0.42
Soybeans	A	1.11	0.41	28.4	0.01	0.35	0.53
Other beans, nuts	A	1.00	0.41	2.5	-0.09	0.35	0.53
Rubber	A	1.15	0.77	66.8	0.05	0.65	0.23
Sugarcane	A	0.80	0.85	16.1	-0.32	0.63	0.17
Coconut	A	1.33	0.68	74.8	0.19	0.64	0.32
Palm	A	1.11	0.64	25.4	0.04	0.47	0.30
Other crops	A	1.54	0.73	5.5	0.41	0.65	0.27
Tobacco	A	0.95	0.77	12.5	-0.15	0.64	0.23
Coffee	A	1.18	0.74	25.4	0.06	0.66	0.26
Tea	A	1.11	0.83	11.3	0.03	0.61	0.16
Cloves	A	0.86	0.47	12.1	-0.23	0.43	0.52
Nutmeg	A	1.11	0.67	3.2	0.01	0.55	0.29
Spices	A	1.14	0.77	14.6	0.02	0.70	0.23
Other agricultural products	A	1.06	0.78	2.4	-0.06	0.68	0.20
Cattle	A	1.11	0.64	26.3	0.02	0.57	0.34
Milk-cow raising	A	1.00	0.54	1.0	-0.14	0.21	0.20
Other livestock	A	1.11	0.80	1.0	0.01	0.72	0.19
Poultry	A	1.00	0.06	34.4	-0.05	0.05	0.80

Forest products	A	1.00	0.21	71.4	−0.06	0.18	0.67
Bamboo	A	1.00	0.17	14.7	−0.09	0.16	0.82
Other forest products	A	1.05	0.22	2.8	0.01	0.18	0.64
Marine fishing	A	1.00	0.09	71.0	−0.06	0.08	0.83
Inland fishing	A	1.00	0.14	36.6	−0.07	0.13	0.81
Coal mining	R	1.00	0.15	0.5	−0.11	0.14	0.41
Crude petroleum, natural gas	R	1.00	0.03	291.0	0.00	0.03	0.85
Iron ore	R	1.00	0.26	0.4	−0.07	0.23	0.68
Tin ore	R	1.00	0.33	15.5	−0.08	0.23	0.49
Nickel ore	R	1.00	0.03	3.4	−0.06	0.04	0.85
Bauxite	R	1.00	0.23	2.0	−0.09	0.19	0.65
Other nonferrous ore	R	1.00	0.72	0.6	0.10	0.41	0.22
Stone, clay	R	1.00	0.52	18.6	−0.06	0.41	0.42
Chemicals for fertilizer	R	0.97	0.48	0.1	−0.01	0.39	0.45
Salt	R	1.00	0.51	4.4	−0.10	0.45	0.47
Asphalt mining	R	1.00	0.17	0.3	−0.08	0.15	0.78
Other nonmetal mining	R	0.87	0.54	*	−0.19	0.45	0.41
Poultry products	F	1.00	0.01	12.5	−0.05	0.01	0.94
Meat products	F	0.95	0.07	48.4	−0.36	0.02	0.32
Dairy products	F	0.58	0.19	3.9	−0.71	0.04	0.17
Canned fruit	F	0.56	0.39	0.3	−0.88	0.18	0.31
Canned fish	F	1.00	0.19	62.2	−0.08	0.05	0.19
Coconut oil	F	1.11	0.18	58.8	−0.41	0.05	0.23
Other vegetable, animal oil	F	1.11	0.13	47.9	0.06	0.04	0.26
Rice milling, cleaning	F	1.15	0.44	741.0	0.07	0.08	0.11
Grain milling	F	1.22	0.29	6.6	0.51	0.06	0.15
Tapioca flour	F	1.11	0.39	36.8	0.12	0.08	0.13
Bakery products	F	0.53	0.73	6.1	−1.92	0.16	0.09
Noodles, macaroni	F	1.00	0.25	3.3	−0.31	0.10	0.32
Sugar refining	F	0.79	0.23	62.0	−0.31	0.12	0.40
Cocoa, chocolate	F	0.77	0.36	1.8	−0.52	0.12	0.23

Table 1.A.1 (continued)

Sector	Type	p_j	α_j	X_j^*	g_j	ℓ_j^*	k_j^*
Coffee	F	1.18	0.24	61.2	0.14	0.10	0.31
Tea	F	1.00	0.67	21.2	-0.21	0.28	0.16
Soybean products	F	1.00	0.31	24.7	-0.25	0.08	0.19
Other food products	F	0.90	0.37	10.7	-0.28	0.13	0.23
Alcoholic beverages	F	0.72	0.28	3.6	-0.33	0.13	0.32
Nonalcoholic beverages	F	0.60	0.45	10.6	-0.76	0.13	0.19
Tobacco processing	F	1.11	0.54	59.5	0.22	0.16	0.16
Cigarettes	T	0.55	0.25	64.0	-1.12	0.06	0.16
Spinning	T	1.08	0.37	19.5	-0.49	0.13	0.23
Weaving	T	0.69	0.37	65.8	-1.06	0.11	0.20
Textile bleaching, printing	T	0.91	0.26	4.5	-0.23	0.17	0.45
Batik	T	1.00	0.45	30.8	0.38	0.13	0.18
Knitting	T	0.57	0.37	2.5	-1.30	0.13	0.22
Textiles	T	0.56	0.26	9.1	-1.34	0.07	0.20
Clothing	T	0.64	0.46	57.9	-0.67	0.15	0.19
Carpets, ropes	T	0.74	0.74	1.7	-1.18	0.28	0.14
Tanneries	T	1.00	0.27	3.2	-0.03	0.13	0.36
Leather products	T	1.00	0.33	0.9	0.01	0.14	0.30
Leather shoes	T	0.61	0.26	12.5	-0.63	0.13	0.40
Sawmills	M	1.00	0.18	45.6	-0.04	0.09	0.37
Wood, cork products	M	1.00	0.25	10.0	-0.04	0.08	0.22
Furniture, fixtures	M	0.76	0.51	10.9	-0.73	0.17	0.18
Pulp, paper	M	0.77	0.25	3.9	-0.40	0.12	0.35
Paper products	M	0.69	0.22	2.3	-0.39	0.12	0.43
Printing, publishing	M	0.80	0.39	24.0	-0.26	0.22	0.36
Basic industrial chemicals	M	0.93	0.32	1.5	-0.19	0.16	0.35
Fertilizer, pesticides	M	1.00	0.52	2.4	-0.04	0.18	0.21
Paints, lacquers	M	0.61	0.43	5.0	-0.70	0.20	0.29

Drugs, medicines	M	0.73	0.37	6.1	−0.45	0.16	0.30
Soap, cleaners	M	0.71	0.24	21.8	−0.88	0.09	0.29
Cosmetics	M	1.72	0.28	11.7	1.86	0.10	0.27
Matches	M	0.57	0.31	0.9	−0.85	0.14	0.32
Other chemical products	M	0.78	0.64	1.5	−0.90	0.11	0.09
Petroleum refining	M	1.14	0.11	238.5	0.25	0.06	0.46
Other petroleum products	M	1.06	0.23	1.5	−0.21	0.05	0.18
Tires, tubes	M	0.64	0.40	7.6	−0.87	0.10	0.17
Reprocessed rubber	M	1.12	0.52	112.9	0.05	0.10	0.11
Other rubber products	M	0.76	0.30	1.5	−0.64	0.12	0.30
Plastic products	M	0.75	0.34	3.6	−0.53	0.13	0.27
Ceramics, earthenware	M	0.61	0.20	0.5	−0.64	0.12	0.49
Glass products	M	0.71	0.25	1.7	−0.51	0.14	0.43
Structural clay products	M	0.68	0.28	17.2	−0.49	0.17	0.45
Cement	M	0.82	0.32	12.6	−0.37	0.12	0.26
Other nonmetallic products	M	0.83	0.46	4.8	−0.48	0.19	0.25
Iron steel	M	0.96	0.45	3.9	−0.03	0.13	0.18
Nonferrous metals	M	1.00	0.07	22.2	0.02	0.03	0.32
Cutlery, general hardware	M	0.78	0.46	4.9	−0.45	0.19	0.25
Metal furniture, fixtures	M	0.83	0.43	9.4	−0.35	0.12	0.18
Structural metal products	M	0.89	0.39	10.5	−0.26	0.14	0.23
Other fabricated metal products	M	0.84	0.32	16.7	−0.33	0.12	0.26
Machinery	M	0.96	0.80	1.0	−0.07	0.21	0.24
Electrical machinery	M	0.89	0.70	13.9	−0.20	0.33	0.17
Radio, television equipment	M	0.68	0.31	1.3	−0.43	0.13	0.28
Household electrical appliances	M	0.69	0.40	0.6	−0.42	0.12	0.19
Batteries	M	0.68	0.26	3.0	−0.61	0.13	0.36
Other electrical equipment	M	0.89	0.36	1.1	−0.14	0.16	0.29
Shipbuilding	M	0.96	0.25	7.6	−0.10	0.13	0.40
Railroad equipment	M	1.00	0.33	3.0	−0.06	0.16	0.33
Motor vehicles	M	0.48	0.26	46.1	−0.67	0.13	0.36

Table 1.A.1 (continued)

Sector	Type	p_j	α_j	X_j^*	g_j	$\hat{\ell}_j^*$	$\hat{k}_j^*$
Motorcycles	M	0.64	0.19	10.7	−0.57	0.06	0.29
Aircraft	M	0.91	0.46	2.4	−0.09	0.15	0.18
Instruments	M	0.92	0.42	0.1	−0.15	0.18	0.28
Photographic equipment	M	0.88	0.38	*	−0.21	0.18	0.31
Jewelry	M	0.82	0.48	4.5	−0.69	0.17	0.20
Musical instruments	M	0.71	0.34	*	−0.78	0.18	0.37
Sporting goods	M	0.67	0.41	0.2	−0.58	0.17	0.27
Other manufactures	M	1.00	0.41	10.5	0.08	0.17	0.26
Ivory Coast							
Traditional agriculture	A	0.99	0.76	44,771	−0.17	0.65	0.22
Coffee	A	1.47	0.70	60,808	0.35	0.54	0.29
Cocoa	A	1.59	0.50	31,245	0.27	0.49	0.47
Other export agriculture	A	1.10	0.74	13,907	−0.06	0.53	0.23
Timber	A	1.20	0.55	48,281	0.33	0.33	0.27
Fisheries	A	0.78	0.65	3,563	−0.33	0.45	0.28
Minerals	R	0.87	0.51	1,867	−0.11	0.28	0.27
Flour	F	0.78	0.21	2,504	−0.71	0.08	0.19
Other milled products	F	0.99	0.49	4,105	−0.13	0.22	0.22
Bakery products	F	0.98	0.46	8,393	0.00	0.20	0.23
Canned fruit	F	1.00	0.47	3,793	−0.11	0.15	0.16
Processed coffee	F	0.78	0.20	1,529	−0.68	0.12	0.33
Processed cocoa	F	1.16	0.10	4,361	−0.21	0.04	0.26
Other processed foods	F	0.96	0.83	19,560	0.06	0.14	0.07
Edible oils	F	0.85	0.41	7,040	−0.43	0.20	0.26
Miscellaneous foods, tobacco	F	0.82	0.25	8,320	0.82	0.09	0.16
Textiles	T	0.79	0.40	16,531	−0.29	0.19	0.24
Clothing	T	0.66	0.63	3,406	−0.47	0.29	0.21

Shoes	T	0.65	0.82	2,131	−0.47	0.32	0.14
Lumber mills	M	1.04	0.67	7,100	−0.08	0.27	0.15
Wood products	M	0.78	0.77	1,470	−0.42	0.34	0.12
Petroleum products	M	0.89	0.25	35,819	1.39	0.09	0.12
Fertilizers	M	0.94	0.41	2,015	−0.19	0.13	0.17
Paint	M	0.69	0.42	1,156	−0.68	0.16	0.19
Soap, detergents	M	0.71	0.23	3,371	−0.38	0.14	0.27
Basic chemicals	M	0.92	0.50	372	−0.32	0.17	0.17
Plastics	M	0.76	0.52	2,075	−0.34	0.21	0.20
Other chemicals	M	0.74	0.39	897	−0.39	0.28	0.38
Rubber	M	0.94	0.42	1,207	−0.27	0.11	0.14
Cement, building products	M	0.98	0.39	8,223	0.15	0.15	0.19
Auto manufacture	M	0.87	0.35	3,748	−0.13	0.10	0.15
Other vehicles	M	1.00	0.62	2,450	0.06	0.24	0.18
Metalwork	M	0.98	0.57	11,768	0.03	0.21	0.17
Machinery	M	0.85	0.66	2,234	−0.26	0.26	0.17
Paper	M	0.77	0.45	1,586	−0.33	0.12	0.14
Printing, other manufacturing	M	1.05	0.59	5,259	0.01	0.38	0.28
Kenya							
Agriculture, fishing, forestry	A	0.98	0.67	85,658	0.00	0.57	0.30
Mining, quarrying	R	0.66	0.52	3,113	−0.40	0.34	0.31
Other food	F	0.84	0.59	37,001	−0.45	0.11	0.10
Bakery, cocoa, chocolate	F	0.82	0.58	2,749	−0.19	0.18	0.16
Textile, raw materials	T	0.97	0.63	3,239	0.01	0.23	0.16
Finishing textiles	T	0.71	0.66	2,393	−0.42	0.24	0.16
Knitting garments	T	0.75	0.57	4,876	−0.22	0.21	0.18
Shoes, leather	T	0.85	0.47	2,402	−0.16	0.16	0.19
Sawmills	M	0.89	0.60	2,204	−0.14	0.30	0.25
Wood, printing, publishing	M	0.93	0.59	9,171	−0.03	0.29	0.22
Rubber products	M	0.80	0.42	728	−0.30	0.19	0.26

Table 1.A.1 (continued)

Sector	Type	p_j	α_j	X_j^*	g_j	ℓ_j^*	k_j^*
Paint, varnish, soap	M	0.85	0.49	3,769	-0.01	0.19	0.20
Petroleum, chemicals	M	0.93	0.27	34,101	0.98	0.06	0.14
Nonmetallic products	M	0.89	0.33	4,489	-0.06	0.28	0.41
Metal products, machinery, miscellaneous	M	0.94	0.57	11,390	-0.02	0.27	0.22
Transport equipment	M	0.86	0.69	11,302	-0.11	0.40	0.20
South Korea, 1966							
Rice, barley, wheat	A	0.96	0.66	279.0	0.00	0.55	0.29
Pulses, cereals	A	0.97	0.81	17.4	0.01	0.68	0.17
Vegetables	A	0.57	0.76	63.8	-0.48	0.58	0.19
Fruits	A	0.66	0.49	7.1	-0.41	0.34	0.38
Industrial crops	A	0.75	0.82	14.7	-0.27	0.63	0.15
Livestock, poultry	A	0.87	0.46	42.3	-0.13	0.25	0.32
Forest products	A	0.95	0.42	20.6	-0.01	0.35	0.50
Fishing	A	1.00	0.39	30.6	0.07	0.28	0.47
Coal mining	R	0.90	0.76	11.6	-0.05	0.54	0.22
Metal ores	R	0.83	0.37	5.5	-0.13	0.29	0.51
Raw salt	R	0.93	0.72	0.6	-0.02	0.52	0.28
Meat, dairy foods	F	0.93	0.43	26.6	0.29	0.08	0.14
Processed fruits, vegetables	F	0.93	0.33	0.6	0.29	0.14	0.29
Processed seafoods	F	0.93	0.35	10.3	-0.09	0.14	0.27
Grain milling	F	0.93	0.47	25.1	0.01	0.23	0.30
Bakery, confectionery	F	0.93	0.58	9.0	0.02	0.14	0.14
Refined sugar	F	0.93	0.18	7.9	1.00	0.06	0.23
Seasonings, oils	F	0.93	0.45	21.0	0.22	0.15	0.22
Other foods	F	0.93	0.42	16.6	0.07	0.13	0.20
Soft drinks	F	0.96	0.55	2.3	0.32	0.17	0.24
Cotton yarn	T	0.96	0.50	26.6	0.37	0.10	0.12

	Type						
Silk yarn	T	0.96	0.40	5.4	0.32	0.12	0.18
Worsted, woolen yarns	T	0.70	0.52	6.8	-0.71	0.15	0.17
Hemp, flax yarns	T	0.96	0.67	0.8	0.52	0.21	0.13
Other yarns	T	0.96	0.42	6.7	0.70	0.11	0.19
Cotton fabrics	T	0.96	0.47	20.9	0.09	0.10	0.12
Silk fabrics	T	0.97	0.41	1.9	0.06	0.17	0.26
Worsted, woolen fabrics	T	0.97	0.40	12.1	0.49	0.14	0.23
Hemp fabrics	T	0.97	0.43	1.3	0.04	0.23	0.32
Other fabrics	T	0.97	0.55	14.2	0.11	0.18	0.20
Knit products	T	0.86	0.48	9.4	-0.02	0.17	0.22
Rope, fishnets	T	0.86	0.53	3.5	0.09	0.15	0.16
Apparel, accessories	T	0.86	0.49	47.9	0.04	0.17	0.23
Miscellaneous textile products	T	0.86	0.51	10.0	0.02	0.23	0.26
Leather, fur	T	0.96	0.38	3.0	0.14	0.13	0.23
Leather products	T	0.84	0.61	4.6	-0.14	0.23	0.20
Lumber, plywood	M	0.83	0.42	17.0	-0.13	0.12	0.23
Wood products	M	0.97	0.55	3.7	0.14	0.22	0.26
Furniture	M	0.97	0.52	4.8	0.18	0.19	0.24
Pulp	M	0.96	0.79	*	0.06	0.42	0.22
Paper, paperboard	M	0.90	0.39	9.1	-0.04	0.15	0.30
Other paper products	M	0.74	0.48	5.0	-0.41	0.19	0.26
Printing, publishing	M	0.99	0.72	19.1	0.01	0.29	0.17
Rubber products	M	0.87	0.51	18.4	0.01	0.17	0.23
Basic inorganic chemicals	M	0.73	0.08	2.0	-0.17	0.23	0.33
Basic organic chemicals	M	0.73	0.39	3.3	-0.42	0.13	0.23
Explosives	M	0.77	0.35	1.0	-0.24	0.13	0.27
Paint, printing ink	M	0.74	0.30	2.0	-0.36	0.12	0.29
Drugs	M	0.77	0.33	6.8	-0.19	0.16	0.32
Soap surfactants	M	0.67	0.39	2.7	-0.76	0.11	0.19
Cosmetics	M	0.95	0.35	2.1	0.23	0.18	0.32
Pesticides	M	0.79	0.32	1.2	-0.15	0.21	0.45

Table 1.A.1 (continued)

Sector	Type	p_j	α_j	X_j^*	g_j	ℓ_j^*	$\hat{k}_j^*$
Miscellaneous chemical products	M	0.89	0.34	6.0	0.19	0.14	0.29
Fertilizers	M	0.99	0.39	6.1	0.17	0.21	0.37
Petroleum products	M	0.95	0.12	23.1	0.59	0.04	0.21
Coal products	M	1.00	0.42	13.4	-0.06	0.15	0.20
Cement	M	0.96	0.22	11.1	0.15	0.18	0.46
Clay, concrete products	M	0.83	0.57	7.1	0.03	0.32	0.30
Glass products	M	0.76	0.52	2.5	-0.06	0.25	0.33
Pottery	M	0.83	0.69	2.0	0.03	0.37	0.26
Other nonmetallic products	M	0.68	0.63	2.3	-0.23	0.35	0.32
Pig iron	M	0.92	0.68	0.5	0.08	0.19	0.19
Steel ingots	M	0.92	0.48	5.5	-0.01	0.09	0.39
Steel sheet, bars	M	0.91	0.47	6.3	-0.02	0.10	0.16
Pipes, galvanized, plated steel	M	0.91	0.41	3.5	-0.07	0.11	0.19
Cast, forged steel	M	0.91	0.45	2.1	-0.02	0.18	0.43
Nonferrous metals	M	0.93	0.45	4.2	0.08	0.13	0.38
Nonferrous primary products	M	0.85	0.60	1.6	-0.15	0.18	0.43
Structural metal products	M	0.93	0.57	6.7	0.01	0.18	0.21
Miscellaneous metal products	M	0.93	0.63	8.4	0.01	0.21	0.22
Prime movers, boilers	M	0.96	0.58	3.2	0.08	0.25	0.27
Machine tools	M	0.96	0.59	1.0	0.08	0.24	0.28
Special industrial machinery	M	0.96	0.57	5.4	0.08	0.24	0.27
General industrial machinery	M	0.96	0.56	1.1	0.07	0.25	0.30
Office service machinery	M	0.76	0.60	0.3	-0.33	0.26	0.23
Sewing machines	M	0.96	0.44	1.1	0.11	0.20	0.32
Machinery components	M	0.88	0.47	1.0	-0.11	0.22	0.30
Electrical equipment	M	0.95	0.48	4.6	0.06	0.20	0.29
Electronics	M	0.92	0.42	6.7	0.04	0.17	0.28
Electrical products	M	0.85	0.50	1.8	-0.05	0.21	0.26

Miscellaneous electrical equipment	M	0.84	0.36	2.8	−0.20	0.11	0.27
Shipbuilding	M	0.98	0.61	5.5	0.12	0.25	0.20
Railroad equipment	M	1.00	0.89	6.5	0.43	0.12	0.09
Motor vehicles	M	0.69	0.56	9.6	−0.37	0.22	0.24
Bicycles, carts	M	0.83	0.55	1.9	−0.22	0.20	0.23
Instruments	M	0.73	0.62	2.6	−0.37	0.24	0.23
Synthetic resin products	M	0.91	0.93	4.2	−0.08	0.16	0.26
Miscellaneous manufactures	M	0.90	0.93	8.8	−0.59	0.21	0.31
South Korea, 1970							
Rice, barley, wheat	A	1.00	0.67	546.5	0.01	0.54	0.29
Pulses, cereals	A	0.91	0.82	31.5	0.00	0.69	0.19
Vegetables	A	0.59	0.76	111.4	−0.49	0.58	0.20
Fruits	A	0.68	0.32	17.2	−0.36	0.25	0.54
Industrial crops	A	0.77	0.81	28.2	−0.26	0.59	0.17
Livestock, poultry	A	0.89	0.46	95.4	−0.18	0.18	0.23
Forest products	A	0.92	0.27	49.1	−0.06	0.24	0.65
Fishing	A	0.59	0.59	49.3	−0.52	0.39	0.30
Coal mining	R	0.92	0.76	18.8	−0.05	0.58	0.23
Metallic ores	R	0.99	0.38	16.4	0.06	0.31	0.51
Raw salt	R	0.97	0.52	2.9	−0.01	0.44	0.42
Meat, dairy products	F	0.89	0.43	57.7	−0.05	0.09	0.17
Processed fruits, vegetables	F	0.74	0.32	3.1	−0.27	0.19	0.25
Processed seafoods	F	0.83	0.51	27.0	0.07	0.19	0.27
Grain milling	F	1.00	0.08	71.9	0.07	0.18	0.23
Bakery, confectionery	F	0.87	0.47	15.0	−0.16	0.15	0.20
Refined sugar	F	0.89	0.24	27.9	1.07	0.06	0.18
Seasonings, oils	F	0.92	0.40	43.6	0.22	0.14	0.24
Other foods	F	0.97	0.39	69.6	0.13	0.12	0.21
Soft drinks	F	0.96	0.40	8.7	0.59	0.13	0.25
Cotton yarn	F	1.00	0.69	40.3	0.37	0.14	0.13

Table 1.A.1 (continued)

Sector	Type	p_j	α_j	X_j^*	g_j	$\hat{\ell}_j^*$	$\hat{k}_j^*$
Silk yarn	T	1.00	0.47	21.1	0.22	0.15	0.19
Worsted, woolen yarns	T	0.70	0.55	8.6	-0.60	0.15	0.17
Hemp, flax yarns	T	1.00	0.65	1.3	0.46	0.17	0.15
Other yarns	T	0.99	0.49	32.2	0.54	0.13	0.18
Cotton fabrics	T	0.99	0.64	29.6	0.04	0.14	0.10
Silk fabrics	T	1.00	0.18	5.4	0.09	0.25	0.17
Worsted, woolen fabrics	T	0.99	0.38	23.9	0.58	0.17	0.17
Hemp fabrics	T	0.98	0.56	2.6	0.04	0.24	0.23
Other fabrics	T	0.99	0.56	40.3	0.14	0.19	0.21
Knit products	T	0.96	0.55	69.1	0.02	0.20	0.19
Rope, fishnets	T	0.96	0.49	8.4	0.04	0.15	0.19
Apparel, accessories	T	0.86	0.59	93.6	-0.30	0.18	0.20
Miscellaneous textile goods	T	0.89	0.59	18.8	-0.10	0.19	0.29
Leather, fur	T	0.97	0.63	4.6	0.44	0.13	0.14
Leather products	T	0.85	0.58	7.2	-0.20	0.24	0.24
Lumber, plywood	M	0.83	0.47	48.7	-0.42	0.12	0.16
Wood products	M	0.91	0.45	5.3	-0.01	0.23	0.32
Furniture	M	0.91	0.61	9.2	0.10	0.21	0.21
Pulp	M	0.96	0.48	3.2	0.10	0.16	0.23
Paper, paperboard	M	0.90	0.51	20.5	-0.04	0.15	0.26
Other paper products	M	0.74	0.51	11.8	-0.42	0.19	0.23
Printing, publishing	M	0.97	0.69	42.2	0.09	0.31	0.21
Rubber products	M	0.80	0.59	20.2	-0.34	0.19	0.22
Basic inorganic chemicals	M	0.78	0.46	6.7	-0.21	0.24	0.33
Basic organic chemicals	M	0.77	0.38	8.7	-0.36	0.14	0.25
Explosives	M	0.80	0.38	1.8	-0.22	0.17	0.30
Paint, printing ink	M	0.76	0.34	4.6	-0.36	0.13	0.26
Drugs	M	0.80	0.39	25.2	-0.19	0.19	0.32

Soap, surfactants	M	0.69	0.40	6.6	−0.68	0.13	0.23
Cosmetics	M	0.99	0.35	7.5	0.15	0.20	0.37
Pesticides	M	0.82	0.34	5.1	−0.24	0.15	0.31
Miscellaneous chemical products	M	0.92	0.44	41.9	0.14	0.16	0.25
Fertilizers	M	1.00	0.24	40.6	0.15	0.15	0.42
Petroleum products	M	0.73	0.22	70.5	−0.02	0.06	0.18
Coal products	M	0.95	0.48	43.6	0.11	0.15	0.20
Cement	M	0.96	0.26	44.1	0.16	0.20	0.43
Clay, concrete products	M	0.85	0.51	14.0	−0.13	0.29	0.33
Glass products	M	0.75	0.47	8.4	−0.21	0.26	0.36
Pottery	M	0.86	0.53	1.8	−0.09	0.32	0.36
Other nonmetallic products	M	0.67	0.48	6.1	−0.38	0.32	0.38
Pig iron	M	0.95	0.64	0.6	0.13	0.15	0.17
Steel ingots	M	0.90	0.53	17.1	−0.04	0.12	0.46
Steel sheet, bars	M	0.87	0.52	37.7	−0.16	0.12	0.25
Pipes, galvanized plated steel	M	0.83	0.48	10.5	−0.25	0.11	0.16
Cast, forged steel	M	0.83	0.42	5.1	−0.16	0.17	0.41
Nonferrous metals	M	0.86	0.49	7.6	−0.26	0.16	0.21
Nonferrous primary products	M	0.79	0.57	3.2	−0.17	0.12	0.22
Structural metal products	M	0.83	0.61	11.3	−0.14	0.17	0.18
Miscellaneous metal products	M	0.86	0.60	11.0	−0.07	0.20	0.22
Prime movers, boilers	M	0.91	0.60	5.8	0.01	0.25	0.23
Machine tools	M	0.95	0.63	2.7	0.10	0.26	0.22
Special industrial machinery	M	0.96	0.63	12.0	0.19	0.23	0.21
General industrial machinery	M	0.91	0.67	4.7	0.01	0.27	0.21
Office, service machinery	M	0.70	0.75	0.4	−0.42	0.29	0.16
Sewing machines	M	0.89	0.62	1.3	0.09	0.22	0.21
Machine components	M	0.81	0.61	1.9	−0.20	0.27	0.25
Electrical equipment	M	0.91	0.49	13.2	0.07	0.17	0.23
Electronics	M	0.88	0.53	39.9	0.15	0.17	0.20
Electrical products	M	0.82	0.51	11.4	0.02	0.19	0.23

Table 1.A.1 (continued)

Sector	Type	p_j	α_j	X_j^*	g_j	ℓ_j^*	k_j^*
Miscellaneous electrical equipment	M	0.81	0.38	10.4	−0.22	0.13	0.25
Shipbuilding	M	0.98	0.57	9.0	0.16	0.22	0.21
Railroad equipment	M	1.00	0.59	11.7	0.26	0.16	0.17
Motor vehicles	M	0.69	0.48	47.6	−0.37	0.15	0.20
Bicycles, carts	M	0.83	0.48	8.3	−0.14	0.16	0.23
Instruments	M	0.75	0.55	6.3	−0.52	0.19	0.20
Synthetic resin products	M	0.94	0.45	17.6	−0.03	0.18	0.28
Miscellaneous manufactures	M	0.92	0.41	66.8	0.01	0.19	0.34
South Korea, 1973							
Rice, barley, wheat	A	0.98	0.66	748.0	0.00	0.57	0.30
Pulses, cereals	A	0.98	0.81	31.5	−0.01	0.71	0.19
Vegetables	A	0.83	0.76	139.1	−0.18	0.58	0.17
Fruits	A	0.85	0.49	36.8	−0.05	0.37	0.47
Industrial crops	A	0.93	0.82	90.2	0.00	0.59	0.18
Livestock, poultry	A	0.97	0.46	298.1	1.05	0.22	0.23
Forest products	A	0.95	0.42	64.0	−0.03	0.26	0.64
Fishing	A	0.91	0.39	129.4	−0.07	0.26	0.45
Coal mining	R	0.37	0.76	30.3	−0.80	0.56	0.18
Metal ores	R	0.98	0.37	20.2	0.05	0.40	0.47
Raw salt	R	0.92	0.72	6.1	−0.07	0.43	0.44
Meat, dairy products	F	0.95	0.43	109.7	−0.01	0.09	0.17
Processed fruits, vegetables	F	0.88	0.33	14.0	−0.06	0.16	0.27
Processed seafoods	F	0.97	0.35	52.8	0.11	0.18	0.23
Grain milling	F	1.00	0.47	108.9	−0.23	0.12	0.23
Bakery, confectionery	F	0.96	0.58	77.0	0.07	0.12	0.16
Refined sugar	F	0.81	0.18	37.9	−0.12	0.04	0.23
Seasonings, oils	F	0.92	0.45	80.1	0.05	0.13	0.22

Other foods	F	0.86	0.42	86.0	−0.33	0.09	0.19
Soft drinks	F	0.70	0.55	18.6	0.04	0.13	0.21
Cotton yarn	T	0.95	0.50	98.9	0.03	0.10	0.21
Silk yarn	T	0.99	0.40	50.2	0.07	0.10	0.19
Worsted, woolen yarns	T	1.01	0.52	34.3	0.14	0.11	0.21
Hemp, flax yarns	T	1.00	0.67	2.2	0.18	0.17	0.14
Other yarns	T	0.99	0.42	99.2	0.25	0.11	0.27
Cotton fabrics	T	0.99	0.47	84.2	0.12	0.09	0.19
Silk fabrics	T	1.00	0.41	19.8	0.11	0.20	0.25
Worsted, woolen fabrics	T	1.00	0.40	43.1	0.10	0.16	0.29
Hemp fabrics	T	0.89	0.43	2.5	−0.14	0.22	0.34
Other fabrics	T	1.00	0.55	99.2	0.14	0.14	0.14
Knit products	T	1.00	0.48	165.3	0.18	0.16	0.27
Rope, fishnets	T	0.93	0.53	11.5	−0.17	0.12	0.21
Apparel, accessories	T	0.99	0.49	450.0	0.10	0.15	0.28
Miscellaneous textile products	T	0.97	0.51	55.3	−0.09	0.15	0.29
Leather, fur	T	0.99	0.38	21.7	0.04	0.13	0.23
Leather products	T	0.91	0.61	16.4	0.01	0.19	0.19
Lumber, plywood	M	0.99	0.42	211.4	0.08	0.09	0.17
Wood products	M	0.86	0.55	10.8	−0.21	0.21	0.24
Furniture	M	0.92	0.52	20.4	0.01	0.18	0.23
Pulp	M	0.94	0.79	2.8	−0.04	0.13	0.26
Paper, paperboard	M	0.92	0.39	52.0	−0.04	0.11	0.27
Other paper products	M	0.90	0.48	31.7	−0.05	0.17	0.19
Printing, publishing	M	0.96	0.72	91.1	0.05	0.28	0.20
Rubber products	M	0.84	0.51	60.8	−0.38	0.14	0.16
Basic inorganic chemicals	M	0.87	0.46	17.9	−0.07	0.19	0.36
Basic organic chemicals	M	0.90	0.39	34.7	−0.05	0.10	0.26
Explosives	M	0.77	0.35	2.1	−0.47	0.20	0.16
Paint, printing ink	M	0.83	0.30	7.5	−0.27	0.11	0.18
Drugs	M	0.75	0.33	52.1	−0.34	0.16	0.38

Table 1.A.1 (continued)

Sector	Type	p_j	α_j	X_j^*	g_j	$\hat{\ell}_j^*$	$\hat{k}_j^*$
Soap, surfactants	M	0.85	0.39	15.4	−0.30	0.10	0.24
Cosmetics	M	0.49	0.35	11.5	−0.89	0.17	0.31
Pesticides	M	0.87	0.32	10.4	−0.17	0.11	0.22
Miscellaneous chemical products	M	0.93	0.34	180.2	0.01	0.10	0.30
Fertilizers	M	1.00	0.39	52.8	0.10	0.19	0.38
Petroleum products	M	0.88	0.12	291.6	0.26	0.05	0.21
Coal products	M	0.93	0.42	87.2	0.73	0.14	0.24
Cement	M	0.85	0.22	42.9	−0.08	0.19	0.48
Clay, concrete products	M	0.90	0.57	26.9	−0.05	0.28	0.35
Glass products	M	0.83	0.52	13.2	−0.10	0.26	0.29
Pottery	M	0.93	0.69	4.3	−0.02	0.30	0.35
Other nonmetallic products	M	0.77	0.63	16.6	−0.24	0.28	0.42
Pig iron	M	0.98	0.68	1.3	0.07	0.15	0.18
Steel ingots	M	0.98	0.48	83.8	0.04	0.06	0.33
Steel sheet, bars	M	0.95	0.47	111.4	−0.05	0.06	0.18
Pipes, galvanized plated steel	M	0.88	0.41	28.9	−0.39	0.08	0.10
Cast, forged steel	M	0.92	0.45	17.3	−0.06	0.15	0.27
Nonferrous metals	M	0.94	0.45	13.4	−0.03	0.14	0.22
Nonferrous primary products	M	0.89	0.60	7.3	−0.07	0.10	0.14
Structural metal products	M	0.92	0.57	25.8	−0.09	0.16	0.15
Miscellaneous metal products	M	0.89	0.63	27.7	−0.10	0.15	0.26
Prime movers, boilers	M	0.96	0.58	7.3	0.08	0.23	0.12
Machine tools	M	0.97	0.59	6.8	0.10	0.19	0.16
Special industrial machinery	M	0.98	0.57	34.1	0.10	0.19	0.16
General industrial machinery	M	0.97	0.56	10.7	0.05	0.23	0.18
Office, service machinery	M	0.96	0.60	14.6	0.07	0.19	0.09
Sewing machines	M	0.91	0.44	2.1	−0.01	0.15	0.30
Machine components	M	0.81	0.47	4.6	−0.37	0.20	0.16

Electrical equipment	M	0.91	0.48	18.2	−0.09	0.16	0.17
Electronics	M	0.98	0.42	240.4	0.14	0.13	0.19
Electrical products	M	0.92	0.50	31.3	0.27	0.17	0.17
Miscellaneous electrical equipment	M	0.96	0.36	52.1	0.05	0.10	0.20
Shipbuilding	M	0.98	0.61	32.8	0.08	0.27	0.12
Railroad equipment	M	1.00	0.89	17.4	0.13	0.14	0.17
Motor vehicles	M	0.83	0.56	62.2	−0.07	0.17	0.13
Bicycles, carts	M	0.93	0.55	25.2	0.02	0.11	0.24
Instruments	M	0.87	0.62	18.6	−0.14	0.13	0.18
Synthetic resin products	M	0.96	0.44	55.9	0.09	0.17	0.15
Miscellaneous manufactures	M	0.97	0.52	132.7	0.06	0.19	0.26
Taiwan							
Other common crops	A	0.86	0.54	5,848	0.02	0.38	0.32
Crops for processing	A	0.91	0.71	6,083	0.10	0.52	0.22
Horticultural crops	A	0.55	0.60	5,644	−0.44	0.43	0.30
Hogs	A	0.83	0.54	14,936	0.10	0.15	0.11
Other livestock	A	0.90	0.63	7,482	0.23	0.25	0.14
Forestry	A	0.89	0.58	5,974	0.37	0.41	0.29
Fisheries	A	0.73	0.50	6,321	−0.18	0.33	0.32
Rice	A	0.94	0.48	1,790	0.18	0.47	0.29
Coal, products	R	0.92	0.81	3,009	0.18	0.58	0.18
Metallic minerals	R	0.92	0.64	244	0.11	0.35	0.23
Petroleum, natural gas	R	0.89	0.12	1,111	0.16	0.10	0.59
Salt	R	0.61	0.63	682	0.12	6.33	0.19
Sugar	F	0.55	0.46	3,831	−0.82	0.32	0.20
Canned foods	F	0.48	0.58	3,884	−4.02	0.17	0.11
Slaughtered meat	F	0.81	0.34	18,829	0.43	0.06	0.06
Monosodium glutamate	F	1.00	0.19	1,474	0.90	0.10	0.32
Wheat flour	F	0.87	0.34	1,663	−0.50	0.07	0.09
Vegetable oil	F	0.66	0.46	3,003	−1.42	0.06	0.05

Table 1.A.1 (continued)

Sector	Type	p_j	α_j	X_j^*	g_j	$\hat{\ell}_j^*$	$\hat{k}_j^*$
Nonalcoholic beverages	F	0.48	0.34	741	−0.30	0.18	0.25
Tea	F	0.40	0.52	543	−1.49	0.11	0.10
Miscellaneous food products	F	0.72	0.58	3,152	−0.46	0.15	0.11
Artificial fibers	T	0.91	0.20	10,322	0.14	0.08	0.24
Artificial fabrics	T	0.79	0.53	2,935	−0.18	0.12	0.11
Cotton fabrics	T	0.65	0.54	1,385	−0.67	0.13	0.11
Woolen, worsted fabrics	T	0.66	0.41	2,746	−0.45	0.12	0.15
Miscellaneous fabrics, apparel	T	0.52	0.78	1,621	−0.64	0.20	0.08
Leather, products	T	0.66	0.75	1,173	−0.66	0.19	0.08
Lumber	M	0.64	0.63	1,263	−0.91	0.16	0.11
Plywood	M	0.66	0.61	10,880	−0.93	0.17	0.12
Wood, bamboo, rattan products	M	0.79	0.60	10,275	0.00	0.24	0.17
Pulp, paper, products	M	0.83	0.52	12,020	0.11	0.15	0.14
Printing, publishing	M	0.94	0.69	14,287	0.21	0.34	0.17
Rubber, products	M	0.84	0.60	4,079	0.10	0.17	0.12
Chemical fertilizer	M	0.89	0.41	25,737	0.28	0.08	0.11
Medicines	M	0.75	0.61	3,077	−0.13	0.30	0.19
Plastics, products	M	0.87	0.49	6,314	0.12	0.16	0.16
Petroleum products	M	0.75	0.13	14,082	0.20	0.04	0.24
Nonedible oils	M	0.77	0.40	1,330	−0.52	0.11	0.16
Industrial chemicals	M	0.84	0.29	88,867	0.05	0.13	0.27
Miscellaneous chemical products	M	0.83	0.48	3,451	−0.05	0.15	0.15
Cement	M	0.66	0.28	4,804	0.01	0.15	0.27
Cement products	M	0.65	0.63	542	−0.31	0.28	0.15
Glass	M	0.70	0.49	962	−0.18	0.24	0.24
Miscellaneous nonmetallic minerals	M	0.73	0.66	1,986	−0.17	0.42	0.21
Steel, iron	M	0.87	0.67	6,191	−0.02	0.10	0.08
Steel, iron products	M	0.72	0.47	5,352	−0.41	0.16	0.17

Aluminum	M	0.81	0.48	1,064	-0.06	0.14	0.19
Aluminum products	M	0.92	0.54	1,363	0.29	0.18	0.17
Miscellaneous metals, products	M	0.88	0.63	2,892	0.06	0.19	0.13
Machinery	M	0.80	0.61	6,594	-0.21	0.24	0.17
Household electrical equipment	M	0.61	0.60	40,507	-0.37	0.31	0.21
Communications equipment	M	0.81	0.51	10,809	-0.23	0.15	0.14
Other electrical equipment	M	0.79	0.60	4,738	-0.12	0.24	0.17
Shipbuilding	M	0.93	0.68	2,852	0.21	0.25	0.13
Motor vehicles	M	0.68	0.53	4,838	-0.33	0.16	0.14
Other transport equipment	M	0.89	0.49	2,228	0.04	0.21	0.21
Tunisia							
Cereals, feed	A	0.87	0.69	119,486	0.00	0.54	0.25
Vegetables	A	0.76	0.78	27,545	-0.19	0.54	0.25
Horticultural crops	A	0.81	0.75	69,730	-0.04	0.57	0.25
Olive oil	A	0.60	0.40	56,760	-0.76	0.11	0.18
Forestry	A	0.96	0.83	5,070	0.19	0.72	0.14
Livestock	A	0.84	0.45	114,968	0.01	0.25	0.32
Fisheries	A	0.75	0.67	6,859	-0.14	0.80	0.27
Phosphate mining	R	0.78	0.88	9,062	-0.39	0.65	0.34
Metal mining	R	0.79	0.88	5,423	-0.18	0.54	0.21
Salt	R	0.56	0.93	972	-0.32	0.44	0.12
Crude petroleum, natural gas	R	0.99	0.02	45,395	0.02	0.04	0.91
Canned foods	F	0.69	0.38	7,623	-0.23	0.13	0.24
Cereal foods	F	0.78	0.78	42,778	-0.34	0.11	0.07
Sugar products	F	0.77	0.23	17,928	0.10	0.05	0.16
Milk, products	F	0.90	0.12	4,269	0.32	0.05	0.28
Coffee	F	0.65	0.12	1,669	-0.53	0.05	0.29
Other vegetable oils	F	0.95	0.55	15,303	0.90	0.07	0.08
Spinning (except jute)	T	0.69	0.54	5,868	-0.25	0.15	0.20
Weaving (except jute)	T	0.75	0.63	22,900	0.13	0.20	0.20

Table 1.A.1 (continued)

Sector	Type	p_j	α_j	X_j^*	g_j	$\hat{\ell}_j^*$	$\hat{k}_j^*$
Jute spinning, weaving	T	0.77	0.57	1,633	0.01	0.13	0.14
Hosiery	T	0.76	0.92	9,113	0.83	0.15	0.08
Clothing	T	0.74	0.66	10,161	0.16	0.20	0.17
Leather products	T	0.72	0.65	7,574	0.04	0.20	0.20
Oil refining	M	0.79	0.21	30,723	1.12	0.04	0.12
Cement, lime, plaster	M	0.88	0.74	8,534	0.33	0.25	0.25
Cement products	M	0.86	0.47	7,696	0.09	0.23	0.33
Ceramics	M	0.71	0.57	11,916	−0.18	0.39	0.37
Tiles, sanitary fixtures	M	0.75	0.61	2,135	0.09	0.26	0.30
Glass, products	M	0.86	0.43	2,134	0.17	0.22	0.35
Iron, steel	M	0.87	0.28	31,613	0.10	0.10	0.22
Nonferrous metals	M	1.00	0.82	5,193	1.10	0.14	0.06
Foundries, etc.	M	0.87	0.48	6,585	0.11	0.25	0.29
Iron, metal products	M	0.84	0.41	12,416	0.11	0.17	0.25
Nonferrous products	M	0.92	0.66	3,000	0.25	0.19	0.16
Electrical products	M	0.87	0.91	6,780	0.57	0.15	0.12
Motor vehicle assembly	M	0.72	0.37	5,931	−0.01	0.09	0.20
Phosphoric acid, flour products	M	0.88	0.45	2,563	−0.04	0.21	0.23
Basic chemicals	M	0.94	0.38	80	0.21	0.22	0.36
Fertilizers	M	0.87	0.57	21,658	0.13	0.15	0.14
Industrial gas, explosives, pyrotechnics	M	0.81	0.78	1,761	0.03	0.31	0.17
Paint, varnish, ink	M	0.89	0.38	4,346	0.21	0.15	0.25
Toilet products, perfumes	M	0.80	0.48	6,517	−0.24	0.21	0.41
Pharmaceuticals	M	0.97	0.38	2,220	0.04	0.24	0.43
Rubber products	M	0.75	0.32	3,842	−0.14	0.15	0.31
Plastics	M	0.82	0.49	4,863	0.22	0.15	0.17
Cork, wood	M	0.86	0.42	8,985	0.06	0.23	0.34
Paper, printing, publishing	M	0.90	0.44	15,260	0.10	0.25	0.35
Miscellaneous manufactures	M	0.81	0.24	9,129	0.04	0.15	0.44

Turkey

Agriculture	A	0.95	0.67	82,107	0.00	0.50	0.28
Animal husbandry	A	0.95	0.67	24,998	−0.04	0.43	0.25
Forestry	A	0.87	0.31	4,143	0.10	0.21	0.57
Fishing	A	0.95	0.50	856	0.06	0.39	0.44
Coal mining	R	0.88	0.81	1,688	−0.36	0.90	0.29
Crude petroleum, natural gas	R	0.19	0.06	1,038	−0.80	0.07	0.82
Iron ore mining	R	0.88	0.81	159	0.06	0.48	0.25
Nonferrous mining	R	0.83	0.81	378	−0.38	0.87	0.29
Nonmetallic mining	R	0.83	0.81	227	−0.28	0.71	0.28
Quarrying	R	0.83	0.40	606	−0.04	0.29	0.49
Meat, products	F	0.95	0.32	9,664	0.05	0.03	0.13
Canned fruits, vegetables	F	0.98	0.36	2,294	0.26	0.10	0.31
Oils, fats	F	0.87	0.37	4,486	−0.06	0.08	0.20
Grain mill products	F	0.93	0.28	3,597	−0.02	0.05	0.15
Sugar	F	0.41	0.91	2,579	−2.20	0.17	0.10
Other food products	F	0.93	0.72	14,106	0.18	0.14	0.17
Nonalcoholic beverages	F	0.93	0.57	750	0.49	0.18	0.22
Tobacco	F	0.80	0.32	9,015	0.28	0.13	0.29
Ginning	T	0.87	0.15	5,113	−0.42	0.02	0.15
Textiles	T	0.78	0.77	22,369	0.12	0.21	0.16
Apparel	T	0.67	0.31	3,362	−0.45	0.15	0.37
Leather, fur products	T	0.87	0.32	1,532	−0.08	0.11	0.34
Footwear	T	0.67	0.24	1,687	−0.37	0.15	0.53
Wood, products	M	0.74	0.39	4,406	−0.30	0.14	0.29
Wood furniture, fixtures	M	0.74	0.61	533	−0.19	0.19	0.21
Paper, products	M	0.47	0.66	1,723	−0.47	0.21	0.23
Printing, publishing	M	0.47	0.42	1,731	−0.52	0.23	0.43
Fertilizers	M	0.80	0.25	571	−0.82	0.31	0.97
Pharmaceuticals	M	0.48	0.46	1,871	−0.48	0.20	0.34
Other chemical products	M	0.46	0.44	5,636	−0.09	0.13	0.23

Table 1.A.1 (continued)

Sector	Type	p_j	α_j	X_j^*	g_j	ℓ_j^*	k_j^*
Petroleum refining	M	0.27	0.05	16,443	0.07	0.02	0.17
Petroleum, coal products	M	0.27	0.27	1,106	−0.79	0.10	0.36
Rubber products	M	0.30	0.17	1,753	−0.90	0.09	0.43
Plastic products	M	0.30	0.58	1,264	−0.83	0.15	0.24
Glass, products	M	0.83	0.61	1,669	0.19	0.26	0.25
Cement	M	0.44	0.63	1,848	−0.48	0.23	0.25
Nonmetallic mineral products	M	0.83	0.61	3,495	0.02	0.32	0.32
Iron, steel	M	0.41	0.33	8,618	−0.68	0.16	0.33
Nonferrous metals	M	0.56	0.33	2,714	−0.62	0.20	0.47
Fabricated metal products	M	0.45	0.42	5,138	−0.51	0.16	0.28
Machinery	M	0.49	0.42	4,993	−0.10	0.14	0.24
Agricultural machinery	M	0.49	0.33	2,455	−0.23	0.07	0.20
Electrical machinery	M	0.48	0.36	3,578	−0.51	0.17	0.36
Shipbuilding	M	0.45	0.87	361	−0.55	0.55	0.16
Railroad equipment	M	0.45	0.87	624	−0.64	0.45	0.11
Motor vehicles	M	0.45	0.40	7,569	−0.36	0.13	0.28
Other transport equipment	M	0.45	0.22	479	−0.52	0.15	0.55
Uruguay							
Agriculture	A	1.00	0.67	1,847	0.09	0.40	0.33
Livestock	A	1.00	0.67	2,953	0.00	0.52	0.33
Mining	R	0.40	0.49	319	−0.63	0.31	0.36
Food, beverages	F	1.05	0.43	5,633	0.20	0.18	0.27
Tobacco	F	0.84	0.11	202	−0.19	0.12	0.57
Textiles	T	0.58	0.39	1,666	−0.67	0.12	0.20
Shoes, clothing	T	0.68	0.45	504	−0.27	0.23	0.34
Leather, products	T	0.79	0.22	101	−0.31	0.13	0.39
Wood products	M	0.61	0.53	194	−0.40	0.27	0.25
Paper, printing, publishing	M	0.73	0.51	364	−0.24	0.26	0.30

Rubber	M	0.42	0.31	190	−0.66	0.19	0.41
Chemicals	M	0.89	0.46	640	−0.05	0.21	0.30
Energy	M	0.19	0.51	868	−0.85	0.26	0.31
Metal products, machinery	M	0.73	0.48	473	−0.25	0.27	0.34
Electrical machinery	M	0.63	0.36	451	−0.40	0.18	0.33
Transport equipment	M	0.30	0.69	399	−0.74	0.37	0.18
Other industries	M	0.59	0.51	231	−0.47	0.30	0.40
Belgium							
Agriculture, forestry	A	0.85	0.60	1,248	−0.21	0.35	0.25
Fisheries	A	0.91	0.53	27	0.02	0.37	0.34
Coal mining	R	0.99	0.72	256	−0.27	0.79	0.35
Nonmetallic minerals	R	0.94	0.55	135	0.11	0.40	0.34
Animal, vegetable oils	F	0.93	0.63	160	0.02	0.16	0.11
Meat, products	F	0.90	0.20	815	0.27	0.06	0.18
Dairy products	F	0.95	0.63	356	0.26	0.11	0.09
Canned fruits, vegetables	F	0.91	0.75	31	−0.09	0.26	0.13
Grain mill products	F	0.89	0.45	352	−0.04	0.17	0.20
Sugar	F	0.94	0.72	129	0.54	0.21	0.11
Chocolate, confectionery	F	0.89	0.57	124	0.03	0.21	0.18
Animal feeds	F	0.91	0.68	357	0.14	0.09	0.07
Other food products	F	0.91	0.63	84	−0.09	0.20	0.15
Yarn, cloth	T	0.96	0.78	783	0.14	0.22	0.10
Textile products	T	0.87	0.72	400	−0.08	0.26	0.13
Knitted products	T	0.84	0.74	115	−0.09	0.29	0.13
Leather	T	0.89	0.76	33	−0.01	0.22	0.11
Leather products	T	0.79	0.66	22	−0.11	0.29	0.18
Shoes	T	0.85	0.84	58	−0.03	0.40	0.10
Clothing	T	0.86	0.82	484	0.03	0.31	0.09
Coke, coal products	M	0.99	0.76	281	0.03	0.22	0.15
Petroleum refining	M	0.68	0.34	720	2.19	0.02	0.04
Iron, steel	M	0.91	0.62	292	−0.29	0.17	0.13

Table 1.A.1 (continued)

Sector	Type	p_j	α_j	X_j^*	g_j	$\hat{\ell}_j^*$	$\hat{k}_j^*$
Iron, steel products	M	0.92	0.74	2,175	0.04	0.17	0.09
Nonferrous metal products	M	0.95	0.71	783	0.05	0.17	0.10
Nonmetallic mineral products	M	0.85	0.80	85	-0.01	0.54	0.18
Cement	M	0.88	0.60	336	0.05	0.34	0.26
Glass, products	M	0.88	0.83	123	-0.01	0.52	0.16
Petrochemicals	M	0.93	0.66	73	0.09	0.30	0.19
Industrial chemical products	M	0.93	0.63	513	0.11	0.30	0.21
Synthetics	M	0.93	0.74	143	0.06	0.29	0.14
Household, government chemical products	M	0.85	0.69	211	-0.08	0.31	0.18
Foundry products	M	0.86	0.76	74	-0.04	0.47	0.21
Other metal products	M	0.88	0.71	460	-0.01	0.36	0.18
Agricultural industrial machinery	M	0.90	0.72	961	0.02	0.35	0.17
Business machines	M	0.91	0.74	18	0.01	0.34	0.15
Electrical equipment	M	0.88	0.70	773	0.00	0.38	0.18
Motor vehicles	M	0.95	0.65	86	0.12	0.16	0.10
Shipbuilding	M	0.97	0.89	114	0.11	0.56	0.10
Railroad equipment	M	0.92	0.70	78	0.04	0.36	0.18
Motorcycles, bicycles	M	0.86	0.88	12	-0.02	0.41	0.11
Aircraft	M	0.95	0.86	53	0.04	0.57	0.11
Instruments	M	0.89	0.88	37	0.02	0.54	0.13
Lumber, plywood	M	0.92	0.53	300	0.08	0.24	0.23
Wood products	M	0.86	0.49	190	-0.02	0.26	0.28
Pulp, paper	M	0.91	0.64	121	-0.13	0.28	0.20
Paper products	M	0.87	0.70	135	-0.03	0.25	0.13
Printing, publishing	M	0.91	0.68	342	0.04	0.40	0.22
Rubber products	M	0.88	0.79	53	-0.11	0.42	0.15
Plastic products	M	0.89	0.55	145	0.01	0.26	0.22
Miscellaneous manufactures	M	0.95	0.86	214	0.13	0.21	0.05

France

Agriculture, forestry	A	0.91	0.60	14,170	0.07	0.44	0.30
Fisheries	A	0.89	0.54	313	0.14	0.30	0.26
Coal mining	R	0.96	0.73	713	−0.10	0.67	0.27
Petroleum, natural gas	R	1.00	0.19	254	0.21	0.17	0.68
Iron ore mining	R	0.91	0.65	267	0.20	0.42	0.23
Other metal mining	R	0.80	0.62	39	0.03	0.27	0.18
Nonmetallic minerals	R	0.83	0.54	1,084	0.11	0.39	0.33
Animal, vegetable oils	F	0.95	0.61	593	0.33	0.18	0.12
Meat, products	F	0.91	0.64	4,997	0.82	0.06	0.05
Dairy products	F	0.88	0.55	1,908	−0.17	0.13	0.10
Canned fruits, vegetables	F	0.86	0.53	592	0.21	0.18	0.17
Grain mill products	F	0.79	0.35	2,191	−0.09	0.16	0.27
Sugar	F	0.95	0.52	910	0.49	0.16	0.15
Chocolate, confectionery	F	0.83	0.50	531	0.08	0.29	0.28
Animal feeds	F	0.98	0.63	1,010	0.70	0.08	0.05
Other food products	F	0.79	0.59	392	−0.18	0.18	0.13
Yarn, cloth	T	0.85	0.82	2,632	0.21	0.24	0.08
Textile products	T	0.74	0.64	1,657	−0.19	0.24	0.14
Knitted products	T	0.72	0.85	643	−0.12	0.31	0.08
Leather	T	0.86	0.51	665	0.25	0.17	0.15
Leather products	T	0.74	0.81	211	−0.09	0.30	0.10
Shoes	T	0.73	0.89	424	−0.09	0.30	0.08
Clothing	T	0.74	0.67	2,485	0.02	0.27	0.15
Coke, coal products	M	0.96	0.34	528	0.20	0.08	0.13
Petroleum refining	M	0.99	0.61	2,426	0.47	0.13	0.19
Iron, steel	M	0.79	0.74	362	−0.03	0.31	0.16
Iron, steel products	M	0.79	0.74	2,289	−0.03	0.31	0.16
Nonferrous metals, products	M	0.89	0.45	2,149	0.27	0.19	0.21
Nonmetallic mineral products	M	0.79	0.59	748	0.05	0.33	0.24
Cement	M	0.80	0.56	1,217	0.08	0.32	0.26

Table 1.A.1 (continued)

Sector	Type	p_j	α_j	X_j^*	g_j	$\hat{\ell}_j^*$	$\hat{k}_j^*$
Glass, products	M	0.75	0.68	386	−0.03	0.45	0.23
Petrochemicals	M	0.78	0.58	290	−0.04	0.33	0.24
Industrial chemical products	M	0.78	0.58	1,992	−0.09	0.33	0.25
Synthetics	M	0.76	0.52	705	−0.05	0.27	0.24
Household, government chemical products	M	0.77	0.73	2,594	0.05	0.28	0.13
Foundry products	M	0.73	0.79	832	−0.03	0.36	0.13
Other metal products	M	0.75	0.73	3,000	−0.02	0.34	0.15
Agricultural, industrial machinery	M	0.76	0.74	5,306	−0.01	0.33	0.14
Business machines	M	0.74	0.75	252	−0.07	0.30	0.14
Electrical equipment	M	0.74	0.79	3,426	−0.01	0.32	0.12
Motor vehicles	M	0.73	0.81	2,948	−0.05	0.28	0.09
Shipbuilding	M	1.00	0.83	280	0.00	0.58	0.15
Railroad equipment	M	0.78	0.75	480	0.03	0.26	0.11
Motorcycles, bicycles	M	0.87	0.80	289	0.28	0.27	0.08
Aircraft	M	0.91	0.77	1,206	0.33	0.35	0.12
Instruments	M	0.75	0.69	543	−0.02	0.42	0.20
Lumber, plywood	M	0.85	0.60	1,951	0.26	0.23	0.17
Wood products	M	0.75	0.84	1,189	0.03	0.31	0.11
Pulp, paper	M	0.83	0.64	1,449	0.20	0.27	0.17
Paper products	M	0.77	0.64	799	−0.12	0.20	0.13
Printing, publishing	M	0.90	0.72	2,907	0.18	0.38	0.17
Rubber products	M	0.77	0.75	1,249	0.03	0.34	0.13
Plastic products	M	0.71	0.70	692	−0.06	0.29	0.16
Miscellaneous manufactures	M	0.77	0.76	1,055	0.12	0.31	0.13
Germany							
Agriculture, forestry	A	0.85	0.60	8,749	−0.22	0.30	0.21
Fisheries	A	0.94	0.34	189	0.10	0.18	0.29
Coal mining	R	0.98	0.97	3,373	0.09	0.44	0.07

Petroleum, natural gas	R	0.76	0.35	1,381	1.21	0.08	0.11
Iron ore mining	R	1.00	0.77	40	-0.10	0.42	0.18
Other metal mining	R	1.00	0.77	33	-0.10	0.42	0.18
Nonmetallic minerals	R	0.98	0.44	1,575	0.13	0.30	0.37
Animal, vegetable oils	F	0.97	0.44	1,153	0.34	0.09	0.11
Meat, products	F	0.92	0.57	5,366	0.32	0.12	0.10
Dairy products	F	0.89	0.50	2,810	0.16	0.08	0.08
Canned fruits, vegetables	F	0.83	0.51	420	-0.12	0.18	0.17
Grain mill products	F	0.86	0.50	3,109	0.00	0.17	0.18
Sugar	F	0.78	0.35	434	-0.13	0.12	0.21
Chocolate, confectionery	F	0.85	0.59	683	-0.01	0.19	0.15
Animal feeds	F	0.95	0.57	1,042	0.28	0.11	0.10
Other food products	F	0.81	0.27	1,012	-0.20	0.10	0.23
Yarn, cloth	T	0.91	0.60	2,751	0.03	0.25	0.18
Textile products	T	0.91	0.60	3,305	0.03	0.25	0.18
Knitted products	T	0.91	0.60	1,198	0.04	0.25	0.18
Leather	T	0.93	0.86	525	0.18	0.18	0.05
Leather products	T	0.90	0.61	329	-0.02	0.30	0.20
Shoes	T	0.90	0.69	672	-0.01	0.34	0.17
Clothing	T	0.89	0.60	2,394	-0.02	0.26	0.18
Coke, coal products	M	0.98	0.97	1,382	0.09	0.44	0.07
Petroleum refining	M	0.76	0.35	3,263	1.21	0.08	0.11
Iron, steel	M	0.93	0.88	1,999	0.04	0.15	0.06
Iron, steel products	M	0.93	0.88	12,622	0.04	0.15	0.06
Nonferrous metals, products	M	0.98	0.53	3,219	0.13	0.17	0.16
Nonmetallic mineral products	M	0.92	0.68	746	-0.01	0.42	0.23
Cement	M	0.97	0.56	2,110	0.12	0.30	0.26
Glass, products	M	0.91	0.63	1,062	0.02	0.35	0.24
Petrochemicals	M	0.92	0.58	1,059	0.04	0.24	0.20
Industrial chemical products	M	0.92	0.58	3,217	0.04	0.24	0.20
Synthetics	M	0.92	0.58	1,283	0.04	0.24	0.20

Table 1.A.1 (continued)

Sector	Type	p_j	α_j	X_j^*	g_j	ℓ_j^*	k_j^*
Household, government chemical products	M	0.92	0.58	3,539	0.04	0.24	0.20
Foundry products	M	0.93	0.69	2,633	0.02	0.36	0.21
Other metal products	M	0.90	0.66	5,601	−0.03	0.34	0.19
Agricultural industrial machinery	M	0.95	0.74	7,538	−0.04	0.35	0.15
Business machines	M	0.94	0.50	566	0.01	0.34	0.34
Electrical equipment	M	0.90	0.69	5,719	−0.02	0.34	0.18
Motor vehicles	M	0.92	0.60	8,826	0.04	0.24	0.17
Shipbuilding	M	0.96	0.87	792	0.06	0.37	0.09
Railroad equipment	M	0.94	0.93	240	0.07	0.40	0.07
Motorcycles, bicycles	M	0.92	0.68	214	0.01	0.33	0.17
Aircraft	M	0.94	0.93	514	0.07	0.40	0.07
Instruments	M	0.90	0.70	1,242	−0.03	0.39	0.19
Lumber, plywood	M	0.94	0.62	5,801	0.10	0.28	0.19
Wood products	M	0.94	0.62	3,760	0.10	0.28	0.19
Pulp, paper	M	0.90	0.62	2,013	0.02	0.25	0.18
Paper products	M	0.89	0.62	1,462	0.01	0.25	0.18
Printing, publishing	M	0.96	0.61	3,769	0.10	0.34	0.24
Rubber products	M	0.91	0.64	1,544	0.01	0.32	0.19
Plastic products	M	0.90	0.80	996	−0.01	0.25	0.25
Miscellaneous manufactures	M	0.92	0.57	1,234	0.02	0.30	0.23
Italy							
Agriculture, forestry	A	0.83	0.60	8,009	−0.04	0.40	0.27
Fisheries	A	0.87	0.36	232	0.01	0.28	0.48
Coal mining	R	0.94	0.76	19	0.11	0.63	0.23
Petroleum, natural gas	R	0.95	0.27	150	0.13	0.26	0.58
Iron ore mining	R	0.95	0.87	9	0.12	0.69	0.16
Other metal mining	R	0.95	0.82	61	0.13	0.68	0.19
Nonmetallic minerals	R	0.87	0.69	666	0.14	0.52	0.26

Animal, vegetable oils	F	0.87	0.52	593	0.38	0.09	0.10
Meat, products	F	0.84	0.39	2,768	0.34	0.07	0.11
Dairy products	F	0.86	0.50	1,485	0.18	0.11	0.11
Canned fruits, vegetables	F	0.80	0.61	232	-0.13	0.24	0.18
Grain mill products	F	0.93	0.48	3,735	0.35	0.10	0.11
Sugar	F	0.52	0.48	358	-0.53	0.14	0.14
Chocolate, confectionery	F	0.76	0.63	294	-0.16	0.24	0.17
Animal feeds	F	0.81	0.32	199	-0.02	0.07	0.14
Other food products	F	0.91	0.32	699	0.48	0.08	0.16
Yarn and cloth	T	0.93	0.74	1,801	0.15	0.26	0.13
Textile products	T	0.87	0.68	1,114	-0.01	0.29	0.15
Knitted products	T	0.89	0.64	445	-0.01	0.27	0.19
Leather	T	0.87	0.66	320	0.09	0.20	0.12
Leather products	T	0.81	0.56	114	-0.14	0.25	0.20
Shoes	T	0.96	0.66	740	0.24	0.32	0.19
Clothing	T	0.82	0.46	1,350	-0.10	0.18	0.22
Coke, coal products	M	0.95	0.58	258	0.40	0.18	0.14
Petroleum refineries	M	0.78	0.38	3,808	3.50	0.05	0.06
Iron, steel	M	0.94	0.65	565	0.03	0.14	0.10
Iron, steel products	M	0.94	0.71	3,894	0.18	0.20	0.12
Nonferrous metals, products	M	0.94	0.65	956	0.18	0.26	0.18
Nonmetallic mineral products	M	0.79	0.71	406	-0.09	0.46	0.22
Cement	M	0.88	0.56	820	0.06	0.32	0.26
Glass, products	M	0.87	0.67	433	0.07	0.34	0.19
Petrochemicals	M	0.91	0.50	517	0.14	0.20	0.19
Industrial chemical products	M	0.91	0.50	2,616	0.15	0.20	0.19
Synthetics	M	0.91	0.60	982	0.14	0.31	0.22
Household, government chemical products	M	0.90	0.58	1,525	0.16	0.27	0.21
Foundry products	M	0.80	0.80	305	-0.16	0.36	0.13
Other metal products	M	0.91	0.68	1,481	0.03	0.36	0.21
Agricultural industrial machinery	M	0.87	0.73	2,618	0.05	0.36	0.16

Table 1.A.1 (continued)

Sector	Type	p_j	α_j	X_j^*	g_j	$\hat{\ell}_j^*$	$\hat{k}_j^*$
Business machinery	M	0.89	0.76	284	0.05	0.46	0.17
Electrical equipment	M	0.87	0.74	1,810	0.00	0.35	0.15
Motor vehicles	M	0.83	0.72	1,506	−0.15	0.28	0.13
Shipbuilding	M	0.97	0.90	228	−0.01	0.47	0.10
Railroad equipment	M	0.93	0.92	267	0.08	0.63	0.08
Motorcycles, bicycles	M	0.88	0.82	128	−0.02	0.35	0.12
Aircraft	M	0.88	0.64	130	−0.01	0.28	0.17
Instruments	M	0.91	0.72	327	0.08	0.37	0.16
Lumber, plywood	M	0.90	0.47	1,210	0.14	0.23	0.26
Wood products	M	0.88	0.42	797	0.11	0.24	0.32
Pulp, paper	M	0.89	0.62	702	0.09	0.25	0.17
Printing, publishing	M	0.75	0.67	264	−0.13	0.26	0.14
Rubber products	M	0.96	0.72	1,261	0.23	0.38	0.17
Plastic products	M	0.89	0.67	659	0.05	0.34	0.19
Miscellaneous manufactures	M	0.95	0.70	489	0.26	0.26	0.12
	M	0.82	0.61	332	−0.08	0.33	0.23

*Less than 0.05.

Appendix D: Computational Procedure

A two-factor application of the model for South Korea has 326 constraints and 680 variables including the shadow prices. At first glance solution appears formidable. However, an iterative procedure was developed that greatly simplifies solution. South Korea solutions, for example, required less than twenty seconds of central processor time on the University of Minnesota CDC Cyber 74 computer. The procedure is described here in terms of computational steps. The matrix notation is defined in Appendix A.

Initial Steps

Step 1. The following data are read into the computer: A (input-output coefficients), ℓ^0 and k^0 (vectors of value-added labor and capital coefficients), p_T and p_{n+1} (international prices), X_T^0 (base-year output levels), C_H^0 (home goods final consumption levels), L^0 and K^0 (labor and capital endowments), and δ (output change coefficient).

Step 2. The home goods inverse matrix $(I - A_{HH})^{-1}$ is computed.

Step 3. Equations (28) and (29) are used to compute Cobb-Douglas coefficients.

Step 4. Equations (7) and (A1) are used to compute the direct and indirect IVA coefficients (the $\hat{z}_j$).

Step 5. A vector, $\hat{C}_H$, of the direct and indirect home goods output requirements to meet the home goods final demands is computed:

$$\hat{C}_H = (I - A_{HH})^{-1} C_H^0.$$

Step 6. A vector $X_{T(\min)}$ of minimum output levels for international goods is computed as $X_{T(\min)} = (1 - \delta) X_T^0$, and a vector, D_T of differences between maximum and minimum levels as $D_T = 2\delta X_T^0$.

Step 7. An initial value for the wage/capital price ratio, $R = w/c$, is set. A convenient, but not necessary, initial value is $R = 1$, which corresponds to the base-year solution.[16]

Iterative Steps

Step 8. The equilibrium condition

$$-\frac{dK_j}{dL_j} = \frac{\alpha_j}{(1 - \alpha_j)} \frac{k_j}{\ell_j} = R \qquad (j = 1, \ldots, n)$$

is invoked. Dividing (1) by X_j,

$$A\ell_j^{\alpha_j} k_j^{1-\alpha_j} = 1. \qquad (j=1, \ldots, n)$$

These equations are solved for

$$\ell_j = \left(\frac{\alpha_j}{(1-\alpha_j)}\right)^{1-\alpha_j} R^{\alpha_j - 1}/A \text{ and } k_j = \frac{(1-\alpha_j)}{\alpha_j} \ell_j R.$$

these labor and capital service per unit output coefficients are constants that correspond to cost minimization as long as R is constant.

Step 9. Equation (A7) is used to construct the vectors, $\hat{\ell}_T$ and $\hat{k}_T$, of direct and indirect labor and capital coefficients for international goods.

Step 10. The factor endowments are redefined as $\bar{L}^0$ and $\bar{K}^0$, which are net of the requirements for the minimum output levels for international goods, and the home goods output levels to meet the home goods final demands:

$$\bar{L}^0 = L^0 - \ell_T X_{T(\min)} - \ell_H \hat{C}_H^0$$
$$\bar{K}^0 = K^0 - \hat{k}_T X_{T(\min)} - k_H \hat{C}_H^0.$$

Step 11. The g_j coefficients as given by (22) are computed for each of the international goods with $w = R$ and $c = 1$ and are ranked from highest to lowest. Note that the ranking is invariant with respect to the choice of $w > 0$ as long as $w/c = R$.

Step 12. The vector D_T gives the maximum amounts by which the international goods outputs can be increased going from minimum to maximum levels. The output of the good with the highest g_j is increased until one factor service quantity becomes zero or until it reaches its maximum limit, whichever happens first. The factor service requirements are deducted from $\bar{L}^0$ and $\bar{K}^0$, and the process is repeated for the second highest g_j, the third highest, and so on until the residual quantity of one of the factor services becomes zero.

Step 13. If both residual factor service quantities become zero at the same time, the iterations are complete and computations shift to the final step. If the residual quantity of one is positive, another iteration is made beginning at step 8 for a new value of R. If capital is left over, R is increased to increase the capital/labor service ratio in every industry. If labor services are left over, R is decreased to decrease the capital/labor service ratios. For the present applications, the absolute value of the changes of R was $(0.1)(0.9)^I$, where I is the sequential number of the iteration.

Final Step

Step 14. An optimal solution has been obtained when the residual quantities of both factor services become zero. The reader may verify that constraints (14.5) through (14.10) are satisfied. Determination of optimal values for shadow prices and home goods output levels that satisfy (14.1) through (14.4) is straightforward.

Convergence

In fifteen of sixteen two-factor applications, convergence took place and was rapid. Some thirty-five iterations were required for South Korea 1970, with 118 sectors. Factor quantities less than 0.000001 were treated as zero. South Korea 1973 did not converge. The computations shifted back and forth between excess labor and excess capital services. Examination revealed that two sectors alternated being marginal, one corresponding to excess labor services and the other to excess capital services. An optimal solution was obtained by letting both sectors be marginal and adjusting their outputs so that both residual factor quantities became zero.

Notes

1. An alternative approach is provided by Vittorio Corbo and Patricio Meller, "The Substitution of Labor, Skill, and Capital: Its Implications for Trade and Employment," chapter 5 of this volume.

2. Input-output data often show international trade for service sectors that are treated as home goods. Such observed trade is included in the C_i^0, but no expansion or contraction of international trade in home goods is allowed.

3. These do not include home goods input requirements for the traded goods inputs necessary to produce the home goods final demands. Since international prices and input-output coefficients are both constants, these inputs have a fixed international value (see Appendix A) that is assumed to be deducted from maximal IVA before final consumption levels are determined for international goods.

4. Point D is near, but not on, the X_2 axis. For Cobb-Douglas transformation curves $-dX_2/dX_1 \to 0$ as $X_1 \to 0$, and $-dX_2/dX_1 \to -\infty$ as $X_2 \to 0$. Consequently, complete specialization would not occur in the absence of output constraints if $\hat{z}_1$ and $\hat{z}_2$ were both positive.

5. This follows from the existence of the nonoptimal interior solutions given by base-year observations.

6. This is not strictly true. In an unusual case all goods might be at limits. No such cases were encountered in the empirical applications. Consequently, the tedious explanation of how to handle such cases is omitted.

7. These are properties of optimal solutions for the model. Observed profits are often positive as a consequence of existing distortions for sectors for which the model indicates negative rents.

8. The applications include a few home goods sectors that use only one of the two factors. These are easily accommodated by omitting either (17) or (18).

9. It is assumed that $\hat{z}_j = 0$ for all marginal goods. This is the case for all of the applications described in section 1.5. If this assumption is not satisfied, a country can increase its total IVA by leaving some of both factors unemployed, and optimal factor prices are both zero.

10. A necessary condition for z_j to be negative is that r_j is positive, that is, the lower limit constraint on output j is binding.

11. See Johnson (1960).

12. Indirect covers the factor service quantities necessary to produce the home goods to support a unit of international good j. See Appendix A.

13. This measure is similar to DRC (domestic resource cost). See Krueger (1966).

14. There are two for South Korea for 1973.

15. Equation (28) follows because input-output data have base-year labor and capital prices equal to one. Consequently, ℓ_j (k_j) equals both the labor (capital) services used per unit of output and the expenditure upon labor (capital) per unit of output.

16. The Cobb-Douglas factor production functions are the only nonlinear element of the model. Once R is set, labor and capital service coefficients per unit output are determined, then the problem becomes one of solving a linear program. The iterative steps below exploit the particular properties of the present model to obtain linear programming solutions.

References

Johnson, Harry G. 1960. The cost of protection and the scientific tariff. *Journal of Political Economy* 68:327–45.

Hadley, George. 1962. *Linear programming*. Reading, Mass.: Addison-Wesley.

Krueger, Anne O. 1966. Some economic costs of exchange control: The Turkish case. *Journal of Political Economy* 74:466–80.

———. 1977. *Growth, distortions and patterns of trade among many countries*. Princeton Studies in International Finance no. 40. Princeton: Princeton University Press.

Krueger, Anne O.; Lary, Hal B.; Monson, Terry; and Akrasanee, Narongchai, eds. 1981. *Trade and employment in developing countries*. Vol. 1. *Individual studies*. Chicago: University of Chicago Press for National Bureau of Economic Research.

2   Effective Protection and the Distribution of Personal Income by Sector in Colombia

T. Paul Schultz

2.1   Introduction

The high level of effective protection in many low-income countries and the wide dispersion in levels of protection across industries leads one to expect that these trade regimes pull considerable domestic resources into suboptimal patterns of production and trade. The structure of protection may also affect the relative prices of labor and capital, and the relative wages of skilled and unskilled labor, inducing firms to adopt techniques of production that employ factors in proportions that do not make the most efficient use of the country's resources. From a policy perspective, the distributional effects of protection among factors, sectors, firms, and persons are as important as the static effects of these distortions on the productivity of domestic resources (valued at world prices) or the more elusive dynamic consequences of these distortions on economic growth (Corden 1975). But the literature on effective protection that has grown rapidly after the initial contributions of Johnson, Corden, and Balassa in the mid-1960s has not proposed an empirical measure of these distributional consequences of protection on factor returns, sectoral incomes, or personal incomes. The NBER project on alternative trade strategies and employment documented factor proportions in categories of traded goods and compared rankings of these sectors by their factor content and

T. Paul Schultz is associated with Yale University.

This paper was prepared for the NBER project on alternative trade strategies and employment sponsored by the United States Agency for International Development and directed by Anne O. Krueger. The computational assistance of Ruth Daniel has been most valuable, and the careful typing of the paper by Lois Van de Velde is appreciated. Helpful comments were given by C. Díaz-Alejandro, A. Fishlow, T. Hutcheson, A. O. Krueger, P. Krugman, H. Lary, R. E. Lipsey, R. Olsen, S. Polachek, G. Ranis, and M. Rosenzweig. Any errors that remain are my own responsibility.

trade status as predicted by the Heckscher-Ohlin-Samuelson (HOS) factor proportions trade theory as extended by Krueger (1977). This study derives a measure of the quasi rents that accrue to factors of production in Colombia associated with variation in effective protection. As in most schemes designed to measure market distortions or quasi rents that do not have a clear allocative function, one can also attribute unexplained variation in factor returns to qualitative differences in the factors, such as labor's productive skills, or to differences in managerial efficiency, or to the distribution of complementary untraded factors of production. But until these additional explanations for sectoral variation in factor returns are conceptualized, empirically measured, and jointly analyzed with data on effective protection, analyses of the sort presented below provide a prima facie case for a connection between effective protection and factor returns. The method proposed here is to analyze incomes of individuals as reported in the 1973 Colombian census 4 percent sample, by sex, age, education, job type, and sector of employment. Sectoral deviations in individual standardized incomes are then matched with trade and census of manufacturing sectoral data to estimate the partial association between effective protection and personal incomes.

The analysis is restricted by available data in several ways. Less highly aggregated industrial sectors would strengthen the empirical work, as would improved information on wage rates, earnings, and wealth for the individual workers in the census sample. A match between the characteristics and income of the individual worker and the characteristics of the production unit employing the worker, such as the firm's capital stock and other inputs, outputs, and trade relations, would greatly augment the range of questions one might study. Additional studies would help confirm the causal and intertemporal character of the association found here across industries in wages and protection. I would like to be able to evaluate the consequences *over time* of effective protection on factor returns and conversely to study factor mobility as a mechanism for eroding over time quasi rents among groups distinguished by their sectoral attachment, skills, and ownership of other productive factors. But protection estimates for Colombia are available for only one year, 1970. Another check on the evidence that emerges from this study would involve comparing the industrial structure of protection and worker incomes across a sample of low-income countries that presumably face similar technological options. Would special features of Colombian protection be associated with unusual deviations in the Colombian industrial structure of wages, holding constant other variables prescribed by theory? From this initial study, based on a single cross section from a single country, the evidence suggests that workers receive notably higher wages in sectors of the economy that are effectively protected, and the proportional increment to personal incomes that is associated with effective protection is slightly greater for Colombian employers than it is for Colombian employees.

The paper is organized as follows. First the concept of effective protection is outlined and the reasons are stated for the expectation that effective protection increases primarily the returns to capital. Second, the trade and tax regime of Colombia is described, as are the data sources for this study. Empirical evidence is then reported, first derived from regressions across individual workers, and subsequently across sectors. Finally, the character of the evidence is discussed and the problems with its causal interpretation are stated with the aim of identifying issues for further research.

2.2 Effective Protection

The incentive effects of trade policies, and perhaps also tax and subsidy policies, on specific economic activities in a country are often summarized in a single index of effective protection. In a trade regime of only tariffs that are sufficient to account for the divergence of domestic and foreign supply prices, the effective rate of protection is the nominal tariff on output minus the weighted average of the tariff on its inputs, expressed as a proportion of the value added per unit of output measured at world prices (Corden 1975). Different schemes for the treatment of nontraded inputs have been proposed, and here I follow Corden's convention of combining the primary factor content of nontraded inputs with value added and treating traded input content of nontraded inputs with directly traded inputs (Corden 1977).[1]

When quotas and import licensing controls are used to achieve protection, as in Colombia, nominal tariff rates no longer bear a necessary relation to effective protection (Musalem 1970). Under such a complex trade regime, comparisons between domestic and world prices must be collected to obtain implicit rates of protection, and these become the starting point for the calculation of rates of effective protection. When these price comparisons were performed for Colombia in 1969, domestic/world price ratios are not correlated, to a statistically significant degree, with the nominal tariff rates on the books (Hutcheson 1973).

But there are many reasons to be wary of calculated rates of effective protection, whether derived from direct tariff information or from price comparisons, and the most serious stem from the limitations of this partial equilibrium framework.[2] There are clear theoretical arguments why substitutability between primary inputs and (imported) intermediate inputs could reverse sectoral rankings according to effective protection and according to the actual incentive effects of tariff structures. Also, in a multicommodity world a higher tariff sector does not necessarily call forth resources from a lower tariff sector (Jones 1971). From an empirical point of view, compromises in the matching of aggregate sectoral data from a variety of sources introduce more than the usual problems of heterogeneity within sectors, and cascading errors may arise as one takes account of indirect input requirements of sectors. Nonetheless, without a viable alternative, rates of effective protection can be highly useful as a rough indicator of the sectoral incentives created by trade, tax, and subsidy policies. Rates of effective protection do not indicate, however, how much the structure of production is thereby altered; for an understanding of the magnitude of the response to any system of incentives, one must know at a minimum the domestic elasticities of factor supplies.

It was commonly argued in support of the import substitution policies adopted by many developing countries during the 1950s and 1960s that protection was justified because the shadow value of labor was below the market wage in manufacturing.[3] Although subsequent analyses indicate it may be preferable to subsidize the agricultural wage (Bhagwati and Srinivasan 1974), the case for protection given domestic labor market distortions led to the consideration of a uniform rate of effective protection *for labor*, calculated by assigning the nonlabor share of value added to traded inputs (Corden 1974). A divergence between the private wage and the social shadow wage might then be eliminated by setting the level of effective protection *for labor* uniformly across sectors, to favor industries in proportion to their labor share in value added. In the Colombian case, on the contrary, effective protection appears to favor industries with above-average capital intensity and with a larger proportion of skilled and educated workers.[4]

Protection may be needed to induce production where domestic costs of production are higher than elsewhere. If protection exceeds this cost margin, this "excess" effective protection should be associated with quasi rents accruing to factors in the industry.[5] In the short run, factor mobility across sectors may determine how the quasi rents are allocated within the sector, whereas in the longer run the monopoly position of the industry and the specific character of the factor and its supply elasticity would modify the persistence and factoral distribution of the quasi rent associated with the "excess" effective protection.

In the two-factor case, without intermediate good inputs, labor might be assumed to be mobile and competitively supplied, whereas capital is perfectly inelastically supplied across industries. In this instance capital returns would be increased by the margin of "excess" effective protection divided by the share of income received by capital. The owners of equity capital have the residual claim on rents in a capitalist economy where labor is supplied competitively. Such reasoning may have guided Hutcheson and Schydlowsky's (1977) analysis of Colombian effective protection, for they attributed all the gains of sectoral protection to capital.[6]

Conversely, one might assume that capital and entrepreneurship were mobile across sectors but that labor supplies were inelastically supplied (i.e., restricted) to the protected sectors, perhaps through unionization and sheltered government arrangements. In this situation, labor incomes might be expected to increase by the margin of effective protection divided by labor's share in factor income. If labor's share were about half, the elasticity of wages with respect to "excess" effective protection (net of higher domestic costs) could range from zero to two. Conversely, the comparable elasticity of capital returns with respect to effective protection could range from two to zero. Although it is practically impossible to adjust (by industry) for the domestic cost premium required to sustain Colombian production, the empirical objective of this study is more modest. It is to estimate the relationship between labor income and effective protection and thereby shed some light on how the quasi rents generated or sustained by protection are currently distributed among the factors of production.

There are at least two reasons one might find no relationship between labor incomes and effective protection by sector, controlling for other productive characteristics of workers. Effective protection may only offset higher production costs, and therefore generate or sustain no clear pattern of factor quasi rents at the level of aggregation studied. Alternatively, the sectoral advantage associated with effective protection may have been appropriated by capital, with labor mobility bidding away any quasi rents going to workers. To test the latter hypothesis, one can examine personal incomes of self-employed workers and employers who should stand to share in some of the quasi rents received by capital. If the incomes of these "capitalist" groups are also independent of whether they work in a relatively protected sector, then the empirical evidence would support the null hypothesis that the pattern of effective protection is not responsible for redistributing personal income by sector.[7] Before proceeding to the empirical analysis, the next section reviews the evolution and liberalization of Colombian postwar trade policies.

2.3 Colombian Trade Regime

During the Great Depression, Colombia, like many other countries in Latin America, instituted foreign exchange and trade controls. Postwar periods of increasing coffee prices encouraged domestic expansion and permitted some liberalization of this inherited trade regime; periods of falling coffee prices tightened the restrictive aspects of the system. The overriding features of the early period are summarized by Díaz-Alejandro: "Before 1968, there were not only severe restrictions on the importation of capital goods, but also erratic stop-go fiscal and monetary policies, with expansionary binges being followed by restrictive policies.

Austerity in fiscal and monetary matters, when applied, did help the balance of payments, but at the cost of slowing GNP expansion and generating excess capacity even in sectors where direct and indirect demand for imported inputs was small, such as construction" (1976, p. 237). Beneath this pattern of foreign-exchange-constrained growth and stagnation, Colombia pursued from at least the late 1950s to 1967 a policy of import substitution. The new tariff of 1959 was higher and less uniform than that of 1950, and reforms in 1962 added further to dispersion in tariff rates. Although the tendency was for final manufactured products to be more protected than intermediate goods, and for primary products to be least protected, this generalization has to be amended to recognize that substantial disparities existed between final manufactured goods.[8]

Imports were controlled by three instruments: tariffs, which were often redundant; variable advanced deposits on imports, which added only about 2 percent as much as did tariff revenues to the direct cost of imports but were far more restrictive when credit was rationed; and import licensing, which had the greatest restrictive effect on Colombian trade. Import tax exemptions for intermediate goods imports were exchanged for assurances that output would be exported, and import duty exemptions were also extended broadly to the government and the church. Multiple exchange rates taxed exports of coffee, oil, and sugar, whereas capital subsidies accrued to all who could secure government-controlled credit in which nominal interest rates were less than inflation rates. Overall, the structure of incentives up to 1967 penalized agriculture and oil and sheltered manufacturing unevenly; effective protection on finished goods tended to exceed that on unfinished goods, and the dispersion in rates of protection on intermediate goods was substantial. Finally, certain major capital goods projects were undertaken with government support or participation and were heavily subsidized. The degree of concentration of investment and growth in capital-intensive activities is reflected in the fact that a quarter of total investment in manufacturing from 1962 to 1967 occurred in the chemical and petrochemical sectors (Thoumi 1980).

With the shift from a fixed and chronically overvalued exchange rate to a creeping-peg system in 1967, a systematic effort began to redress the imbalance between incentives for import substitution and those for export promotion. A 15 percent subsidy (Certificado de Abono Tributario) was granted on "nontraditional" exports, and credit arrangements were established for exporters. Price controls in the domestic market and taxes on exports also introduced an added divergence between the protection levels in the domestic and export market for a sector; consequently, an average of the two is analyzed here. By 1970, when the most detailed estimates of Colombian effective protection are available, the ratio of the Corden index of effective protection to value added is negative in agriculture and mining, is less than $+10$ percent in construction materials and processed food, $+10$ to 20 percent in intermediate goods (and processed food without sugar), and ranges from $+20$ to 40 percent in beverages, tobacco, durable and nondurable consumer goods, and machinery, to over 100 percent in transport equipment (Hutcheson and Schydlowsky 1977, table 2A).

Examining factor proportions and trade status of Colombian industries in 1970 and 1973, Thoumi (1977) finds evidence that by 1973 export-oriented manufacturing industries had become more labor-intensive and less skill-intensive than those sectors that were classified as either importing or import-competing. Thus the pattern of Colombian trade in 1973, six years after the start of the export-oriented trade liberalization program, appears to be explained fairly well by the factor intensity trade theory of comparative advantage.[9] But Thoumi's analysis of labor inputs and its skill composition is restricted to manufacturing and to the distinction between blue- and white-collar workers. Also, data from the manufacturing census and DANE's (Departamento Administrativo Nacional de Estadística) sample of firms tend to reflect developments in larger firms and to underrepresent small firms that employ on average less modern and more labor-intensive technologies. These standard data sources, therefore, do not adequately describe what is often called the "craft" or "informal" sector. To analyze in greater detail the incomes and characteristics of all Colombian workers by industry, a 4 percent sample of the 1973 census of population is considered in the next section. Representative of all private households in the twenty-two departments of Colombia plus the special district of Bogotá, this census sample reflects more accurately the balance of employment in small and large firms but provides less information on industry categories.

2.4 Empirical Evidence

In this section Colombian data on individual incomes reported in the population census are analyzed by sector to determine whether industry specific income levels are associated with the sector's level of effective protection. I shall return later to a discussion of the difficulties that stem from using a single cross section on incomes and protection and to how one is to interpret such an association, if one exists. To obtain an estimate of the elasticity of labor income with respect to effective protection, one among several restrictions must be imposed on a simple interindustry model of an income-generating function.

2.4.1 A Statistical Model: Alternative Restrictions

The income-generating function of years of schooling and years of postschooling experience has been used to describe cross-sectional variation in the logarithms of worker incomes in many countries and in many time periods. Though this specification of the income-generating function has its origins in the human capital framework (Mincer 1974), it is used here as a set of controls for the schooling, skills, and maturity of workers that might be presumed to influence worker productivity and thereby affect labor incomes among workers in a competitive market. The model fitted is of the following form:

$$(1) \qquad \ln Y_i = \alpha_0 + \alpha_1 S_i + \alpha_2 X_i + \alpha_3 X_i^2 + e_i, \quad i = 1, 2, \ldots, N$$

where $\ln Y_i$ is the natural logarithm of the ith individual worker's monthly income, S_i is his years of schooling, X_i is his years of postschooling experience proxied by his age minus schooling minus 7, (i.e., age of school entry), and X_i^2 is the experience variable squared (and generally divided by 100). The αs are estimated by ordinary least squares over a sample of N workers, and the es are assumed to be well-behaved independent, constant-variance disturbances. Two restrictions implicit in this specification are (1) that proportionate increase in income associated with an additional year of schooling is constant across educational levels, and (2) that the quadratic in "experience" adequately captures the cross-sectional life-cycle variation in income. Both of these functional restrictions are considered and accepted by Fields and Schultz (1977) in their analysis of these census data. This very parsimonious three-parameter function for individual incomes fits the Colombian census data nearly as well as an unrestricted analysis of variance model, within which the parsimonious model is nested, with its many additional fitted parameters. Only about a third of the logarithmic variance of incomes is accounted for by the three variables, yet this level of explanatory power when working with individual data is somewhat higher than noted in similar exercises performed with census data from the United States and other countries.

To this conventional income function (1) an additional variable is added for the percentage of effective protection, P_j, in the jth sector employing the individual. The estimated coefficient on this sector-specific protection variable is then interpreted as an estimate of the elasticity of labor incomes in a sector with respect to effective protection. All the variables in the conventional income-generating function relate to individual characteristics of workers supplying labor. Now a sectoral characteristic of the firm that demands labor has also been included. If labor markets are geographically separated or institutionally insulated from one another by distortions or long-term commitments, different premiums may be attached at any moment in time to schooling and experience in different industries. In this situation, the parameters to the initial income function may differ across industries, and one would like to estimate the following equation:

(2) $$\ln Y_i = \alpha_{0j} + \alpha_{1j}S_i + \alpha_{2j}X_i + \alpha_{3j}X_i^2 + \alpha_4 P_j + u_i,$$

$$i = 1, 2, \ldots, N$$
$$j = 1, 2, \ldots, J$$

where the α_{0j}, α_{1j}, α_{2j}, and α_{3j} differ across J industrial sectors.

Since P takes on only J different values, a linear combination of the industry-specific constant terms, α_{0j}, could equal P_j, and thus equation (2) is singular and cannot be estimated directly; too much information is being asked of the data. If one knew how the parameters to the conventional income functions varied across industries, or which groups of sectors shared a common income function, this added information might be imposed as restrictions on the specification of equation (2). I lack a satisfactory basis for imposing these restrictions.

Three approaches to estimating the parameter α_4 are followed here. The first is to assume that the conventional income function parameters, α_0 through α_3, are identical across industries, as is the common practice in the literature on labor market behavior and human capital; that is, $\alpha_{kj} \equiv \alpha_k$, $k = 0, 1, 2, 3; j = 1, 2, \ldots, J$. There is no problem, then, with estimation, but one cannot examine directly how sectoral incomes differ, in order to determine if anomalous sectoral observations are associated with peculiar factor demands, regional location, ownership, capital intensity, or trade status. It is possible, nonetheless, to add other characteristics of the firms demanding labor in the sector, such as capital intensity, yet these indicators of industrial characteristics do not have a clear theoretical interpretation in an income-generating function, and they are employed here largely to test the robustness of the estimate of α_4 with respect to the inclusion of other potentially collinear features of the sector.

The second approach estimates a set of unrestricted industry-specific intercepts in the income-generating function and then regresses these on protection levels by sector. First, estimates are obtained for the following equation:

(3) $$\ln Y_i = \alpha_1 S_i + \alpha_2 X_i + \alpha_3 X_1^2 + \sum_{j=1}^{I} \delta_j D_{ji} + u_i,$$

$$i = 1, 2, \ldots, N$$

where D_{ji} is one if the ith worker is in sector j and otherwise zero, and δ_j represents the level of the logarithmic income function for each of the $j = 1, 2, \ldots, I$ sectors (for the benchmark individual with no schooling or experience). Second, the estimated values of δ are regressed on the sector's level of effective protection:

(4) $$\hat{\delta}_j = \beta_0 + \beta_1 P_j + \omega_j, \quad j = 1, 2, \ldots, I$$

where β_1 is a second estimate of the elasticity of incomes with respect to sectoral effective protection. Since the errors in (4) are probably heteroskedastic across the different-sized sectors, generalized least-squares estimates are more efficient than the unweighted ordinary least-squares estimates. The working hypothesis adopted here is that the error in (4) is due to estimation error of δ in (3), or, in other words, $\omega_j = \hat{\delta}_j - \delta_j$.[10] In the individual regressions it is assumed that each worker observation is subject to an independent, constant-variance error, u_i. If the allocation of workers by sector is independent of this error, the variance of a sector's error is inversely proportional to the square root of the number of workers observed in the sector $1/\sqrt{n_j}$. This weight for ω_j is therefore initially assumed to be this simple function of the number of "workers" in the sector when aggregate second-stage estimates are obtained. A better procedure appears to be to use the variance/covariance matrix of the coefficient estimates of δ in (3), which provides information on the precision of the sector intercept estimates used as the dependent variable in (4). This weighting procedure is referred to as the "covariance" matrix weights. The first set of estimates across individuals, and the second covariance two-stage estimates across sectors, should yield similar estimates for α_4 and β_1, respectively, if protection is not correlated with u_i and the assumed structure of ω_j is correct.

If parameters of the income-generating function differed markedly from industry to industry, a third hybrid model might document the shortcomings of the previous schemas, though the third model necessitates aggregate comparisons of incomes based on the average characteristics of a representative worker. The parameters of the income-generating function are first estimated by ordinary least squares *within* each industrial sector:

(5) $$\ln Y_{ij} = \alpha_{0j} + \alpha_{1j}S_i + \alpha_{2j}X_i + \alpha_{3j}X_i^2 + e_i.$$

$$i = 1, 2, \ldots, N$$
$$j = 1, 2, \ldots, J$$

In the second stage, a predicted wage is calculated by cross-multiplying the industry-specific estimates and the mean worker characteristics of the entire sample, denoted by the bars:

$$\widehat{\ln Y_j} = \hat{\alpha}_{0j} + \hat{\alpha}_{1j}\bar{S} + \hat{\alpha}_{2j}\bar{X} + \hat{\alpha}_{2j}\bar{X}^2. \qquad j = 1, 2, \ldots, J$$

The predicted sectoral income is then regressed on the sectoral level of effective protection,

(6) $$\widehat{\ln Y_j} = \gamma_0 + \gamma_1 P_j + v_j. \qquad j = 1, 2, \ldots, J$$

Again, one anticipates that the error, v_j, will be heteroskedastic. As a simple approximation, the "worker weights" of each sector are used to increase the efficiency of the estimate γ_1 of the elasticity of labor incomes with respect to effective protection.

2.4.2   Data: Sectoral Aggregates and Types of Workers

Matching industries across three data sources—(1) the 1973 population census sector-of-employment (DANE), (2) the effective protection indexes (Hutcheson and Schydlowsky 1977), and (3) trade status indexes (Thoumi, 1978)—involves an inevitable loss of sectoral detail and undoubtedly some mismatching as well as the creation of broad heterogeneous categories of production. The 1973 population census 4 percent sample distinguishes some forty-four industrial sectors that contain more than seventy male employees reporting the personal variables examined here. Appendix table 2.A.3 reports the logarithmic income function estimates for male employees allowing for the level of income to vary independently across each of these forty-four industry categories. To match with the protection series, the census sectors are reaggregated into thirty-eight sectors (reported in appendix table 2.A.4), losing primarily the ability to distinguish among activities in mining: coal, oil and gas, metals, others, and not specified elsewhere.[11] Of these thirty-eight sectors, protection indexes are available for only thirty-five, which requires the omission of plastics, pottery, and glass products. Three small categories are also omitted as probably unreliable for this exercise, because most of the workers in these census industry categories report the residual code "not specified elsewhere," whereas the subsectors for which protection and trade data are most applicable are specified elsewhere in the census codes.[12] Of these thirty-two consistently defined sectors, six are treated as untradables in the protection and trade data. Five of these untradables are clearly justified—electricity and water-related utilities, construction, personal services, and professional and business services—but printing and publishing is called an untradable in the protection series, perhaps for lack of comparable world and domestic price series. I am left, therefore, with a sample of twenty-six sectors producing tradable commodities, of which twenty-two are manufacturing. But the sectors omitted for lack of good matching data employed less than 4 percent of the male employee labor force, according to the 1973 census sample. The sectors classified as producing untraded goods, on the other hand, contained about one-sixth of the male employees.

Two sectors warrant special attention, the first small and readily overlooked, the second large and defying generalizations. The first case is the refining sector, which employs ninety-one men and nine women in the sample. Entirely government-operated and highly capital-intensive, the refining sector is sheltered by an oil export tax, which creates a subsidized market for domestic consumption of oil products. This small sector pays its employees 50 to 80 percent more than is common elsewhere in the Colombian economy and is predictably an outlier in any intersectoral comparison of personal incomes, regardless of sex or level of education.

The second outlying sector is agriculture, but it includes more than half of male employees and therefore dominates any weighted comparison of sectoral incomes and protection. The negative effective protection afforded Colombian agriculture represents a large transfer of resources from agricultural producers to others in the economy. This is predominantly a reflection of the tax on coffee exports that reduces by some 50 percent the peso equivalent obtained per dollar of f.o.b. value exported. Aside from coffee, Colombian agriculture receives about 14 percent effective protection on exports and a 2 percent level of protection in the domestic market. When broader redistributive policies are considered, such as the direct taxation system and credit subsidies, the margin of effective protection plus subsidies received by agricultural commodities other than coffee sums to 24 percent of value added of exports and 2.6 percent on the domestic market (Hutcheson and Schydlowsky 1977, table 2d).

It is impossible here to distinguish between wages received in different segments of agriculture subject to these contrary incentives.[13] Regional differences could be explored, but the distinction would be blurred even in coffee-producing regions, because many landless and landowning agricultural workers earn only a small fraction of their income from coffee production, and the possibilities of substitution among agricultural activities cannot be ignored. A major uncertainty in such an investigation is whether agriculture, with its heterogeneity, can be usefully analyzed here. If agriculture is excluded, then the smaller loss of forestry, fishing, and mining leaves one with the residual sample of much less variability for which all sectors are represented in the DANE manufacturing survey, with its energy utilization and value added per worker proxies for capital stock.

Three samples of sectors are therefore considered in the following analysis. The first includes all thirty-two traded and untraded sectors. The second includes the twenty-six traded sectors, and the third sample is restricted to the twenty-two manufacturing sectors, most importantly excluding agriculture. The analysis relies on the 1973 Colombian census of population, from which a 4 percent sample has been prepared by the National Statistical Office (DANE). Several groups of workers can be distinguished, but the most useful are male employees between the ages of fifteen and sixty-five reporting last month's income.[14] It would be desirable to eliminate unearned income and divide the earned income by the time worked (during the month) to obtain a proper wage rate, but the data do not permit either adjustment to be performed. Later analysis turns to the much smaller group of male employers, to determine if this group, with its greater returns from entrepreneurship and capital, is also affected by sectoral levels of protection.[15] There are only 14 percent as many female as male employees in the census sample, and their sectoral concentration is sufficient to yield high-variance estimates of incomes for many sectors. Male and female employee income levels are strongly positively correlated across sectors, but for several reasons analysis is restricted here to males.[16]

2.4.3   Empirical Findings

Estimates of the first model are reported in table 2.1, where the units of observation are male employees. Since proxies for capital stock per worker are available only for manufacturing, the first four regressions are for the quarter of the employees in manufacturing, and the last two regressions include all male employees in traded sectors, including primarily the addition of agriculture. Regressions (1) and (5) show the conventional income-generating functions that reveal similar returns to schooling in both samples, that is, 20 percent, but more steeply sloped experience-income profiles in manufacturing.

Table 2.1   **Income Function Estimates for Male Employees with Proxies for Capital Stock per Worker in Manufacturing**

Explanatory Variables	Twenty-two Manufacturing Sectors				All Twenty-six Traded Sectors	
	(1)	(2)	(3)	(4)	(5)	(6)
Schooling	.200	.195	.194	.191	.197	.163
	(94.4)	(91.2)	(90.6)	(88.5)	(126.)	(95.7)
Experience	.0897	.0889	.0880	.0867	.0563	.0528
	(50.5)	(50.2)	(49.8)	(49.1)	(56.0)	(53.7)
(Experience squared)/100	− .126	− .124	− .123	− .121	− .0776	− .0723
	(37.2)	(36.9)	(36.7)	(36.2)	(46.3)	(44.2)
Corden index of		.339	.384	.323		1.24
effective protection		(10.7)	(12.0)	(10.2)		(45.1)
Horsepower 1969 per			.0190			
worker			(9.91)			
(Value added 1969 per				.190		
worker)/100				(13.1)		
Constant term	4.89	4.91	4.86	4.85	5.00	5.33
	(203.)	(204.)	(198.)	(200.)	(355.)	(341.)
R^2	.473	.478	.483	.487	.308	.342
Standard error of of the estimate	.689	.686	.683	.681	.828	.807
Sample size	10,919	10,919	10,919	10,919	38,547	38,547

NOTE: Dependent variable is the natural logarithm of the monthly income variable from the 1973 census of population sample.

The central issue of this study is the estimate on the Corden index of effective protection in regressions (2) and (6). Across all traded sectors the estimated elasticity of male employee incomes with respect to effective protection is 1.24, whereas across only the manufacturing sectors the elasticity estimate is one-fourth as large, or 0.34, but both estimates are far from zero.[17]

Within the more restricted range of the manufacturing sector, it might be thought that higher incomes would accrue to workers employed in more capital-intensive sectors, because of imperfections in labor markets or the greater selectivity of employers in these sectors. The two proxies available for capital stock per worker are a measure of installed horsepower capacity and value added (see table 2.A.2).[18] These data, however, come from the DANE survey of manufacturing establishments, which may not sample the full range of smaller firms that should be represented in the population census. The measure of horsepower capacity, for all its conceptual inadequacies, is also weakly correlated from year to year across sectors, suggesting to me that it may be subject to substantial sampling variability. Value added per worker, on the other hand, includes payments for wages and salaries, which are likely to be correlated with productive characteristics of the sector's work force, such as education and postschooling experience. Adding the horsepower capacity variable in regression (3) increases the coefficient on protection by 13 percent, and including the value added per worker variable in regression (4) decreases it 5 percent. Though only poorly specified proxies for the capital stock are available in Colombia, the magnitude of the partial relationship between employee incomes and sectoral protection does not appear very sensitive to the inclusion of these types of capitallike variables.

It is also noteworthy that the "returns" to schooling are not greatly affected by sectoral levels of protection across manufacturing (18.9 versus 18.5 percent), whereas given the lower educational attainment of workers in agriculture the protection variable does depress the partial association between schooling and employee incomes across all traded sectors, from 22.2 to 19.8 percent.

One can decrease the dependence of these estimates of the effect of protection on the inclusion or exclusion of agriculture by adding to the income function an "effect" for distinctly different levels of income in rural and urban areas. This could be justified if the prevalence of non-monetized income payments were greater in the rural sector, such as the provision of food and shelter, and the general cost of living were lower in rural than in urban areas, closing the apparent difference between reported money income and *real* incomes. Including such a rural/urban residence dummy variable in regression (6) in table 2.1 confirms that rural male employee money incomes are some 20 percent lower than urban, and allowing for this difference the estimate on the protection variable decreases a third from 0.0124 to 0.0084.[19] But this procedure would be warranted only if one believed that rural and urban *real* incomes in Colombia were similar for male employees, given their education, experience, and sector of employment. The historical and continuing pace of rural/urban migration and the widely documented evidence of differences in real incomes between the rural and urban sectors of the Colombian economy indicate, on the contrary, that the above adjustment blurs rather than sharpens our capacity to measure the magnitude of the real differential in incomes between the agricultural and nonagricultural sectors, and hence this adjustment of the income function leads to an underestimate of the slope of the partial relationship between real incomes and effective protection. Later estimates of the second and third formulation of the model, based on aggregate sectoral data, will clarify how the extreme situation of agriculture alters the relationship. In sum, the choice of sectors for inclusion in the study sample has a marked and unavoidable effect on the final estimates; given the other factors depressing agricultural incomes, it may be reasonable to concentrate our attention on the more homogeneous sample of manufacturing sectors.

2.4.4 Employers and Self-Employed: Additional Evidence

Here I advance for testing the hypothesis that a portion of the variation in returns to factors across sectors and employment groups can be linked to the incentive effects of effective protection. Examining the incomes of population groups other than employees may add to our understanding of this relationship. The self-employed represent about a fifth of the male labor force in Colombia, but disparate groups are included in this category. They are predominantly small-scale farmers, both landowners and probably tenant farmers, whose excess demands for labor are largely satisfied within the family. Without a basis for imputing a share of the self-employed incomes to unpaid family workers and to owned land and capital, reported incomes are a mixture of factor returns.[20] In nonagricultural sectors self-employed are engaged in a variety of activities, but since they do not by definition employ other workers, their incomes are likely to be predominantly returns to their own labor and entrepreneurship.[21]

Employer income is also a mixture of returns to labor, capital, and entrepreneurship, but this group may be more comparable across sectors. No information, however, is available on the capitalization of employers in their own activity, not even information on firm size or employer capitalization by sector. Thus, interpretation of the partial association between employer incomes and sectoral levels of effective protection must still be approached with considerable caution. This appears, nonetheless, to be one indicator of the returns to a mixture of entrepreneurial factors, whereas the relation with employee incomes is a purer indicator of the effect of protection on labor incomes only.

The same regressions as reported in table 2.1 for male employees are reported for male employers in table 2.2. A strong positive partial association is again found between the level of personal incomes and effective protection in the sector of employment. For employers the elasticity estimate is higher than for employees, 1.98 across all traded sectors, and 0.49 across manufacturing sectors. Adding the available proxies for sectoral capital intensity increases the income effect of protection in the case of installed capacity and decreases the effect for value added. Though the samples are much smaller and the levels of statistical significance on the effect of protection are less for employers than employees, the pattern of sectoral variation in employer incomes suggests that they benefit proportionately by a larger margin than do employee incomes by the incentive effects of effective protection.

2.4.5   Returns to Schooling and Protection

The educational coefficient is not particularly sensitive to the inclusion of the protection variable (compare regressions 1 and 2, table 2.1), suggesting that sectoral levels of protection are not closely associated

Table 2.2   **Income Function Estimates for Male Employers with Proxies for Capital Stock per Worker in Manufacturing**

Explanatory Variables	Manufacturing Sectors				All Traded Sectors	
	(1)	(2)	(3)	(4)	(5)	(6)
Schooling	.189	.185	.182	.180	.222	.198
	(22.6)	(21.7)	(21.2)	(20.9)	(45.3)	(38.3)
Experience	.0475	.0485	.0487	.0483	.0335	.0347
	(5.28)	(5.39)	(5.43)	(5.40)	(7.06)	(7.42)
(Experience squared)/100	.0639	.0648	.0656	−.0647	−.0346	−.0352
	(4.79)	(4.87)	(4.94)	(4.89)	(5.46)	(5.65)
Corden index of		.494	.540	.379		1.98
effective protection		(2.06)	(2.25)	(1.58)		(13.)
Horsepower 1969 per			.0251			
worker			(2.32)			
(Value added 1969 per				.351		
worker)/100				(3.70)		
Constant term	5.83	5.85	5.78	5.72	5.36	5.78
	(36.2)	(36.3)	(35.6)	(35.0)	(61.4)	(63.1)
R^2	.330	.333	.336	.341	.295	.317
Standard error of of the estimate	1.006	1.005	1.003	.999	1.118	1.100
Sample size	1,160	1,160	1,160	1,160	5,108	5,108

NOTE: Dependent variable is the natural logarithm of the monthly income variable from the 1973 census of population sample.

Table 2.3   **Income Function Pooled for Male Employees and Employers**
                   (Colombia 1973, All Twenty-six Traded Sectors)

	Employee (1)	Employer (2)
Explanatory variable		
Schooling	.195	.175
	(49.)	(33.)
Experience	.0303	.0284
	(8.55)	(7.99)
(Experience squared)/100	−.0298	−.0272
	(6.33)	(5.76)
Corden index of effective	1.98	2.79
protection	(17.)	(15.)
Corden index × education		.124
		(5.72)
Constant Term	5.87	6.06
	(82.)	(77.)
Employee interaction		
Schooling	−.0334	−.0147
	(7.66)	(2.59)
Experience	.0223	.0241
	(6.03)	(6.50)
(Experience squared)/100	−.0424	−.0447
	(8.46)	(8.90)
Corden index of effective	−.740	−1.46
protection	(6.27)	(7.79)
Corden index × education		.108
		(4.73)
Constant term	−.532	−.709
	(7.28)	(8.78)
R^2	.3508	.3514
Standard error of the estimate	.846	.845
Sample size	43,655	43,655

with the returns to schooling *within* a sector. Direct calculations, however, indicate that sectors with a larger proportion of their labor force
above primary school level tend to be sectors with above-average effective protection.[22] To consider the interaction between schooling and
effective protection directly, and also test for differences in the income
generating functions of male employees, employers and self-employed,
pooled regressions for these groups are reported in table 2.3. All the
coefficients in the income-generating function are allowed to differ between the employment groups. Hence, regression (1) in table 2.3 is
literally a combination of regressions (6) from tables 2.1 and 2.2. For
example, the elasticity of employer income with respect to effective
protection is 1.98 and employees 1.24 (i.e., 1.98 − .74). Regression (2)

introduces an interaction variable between the return to schooling and the level of protection. For employees it is negligible ($-.124 + .108$), whereas for employers it appears negative. The evidence is again that sectoral protection does not alter the relative levels of employee incomes by education but does shift demands generally to skill-intensive sectors that should indirectly augment the premium schooling receives in the overall labor market.

2.4.6   Aggregate Sectoral Comparisons

Estimates for the first stage of the second model represented in equation (3) are shown in table 2.4. Regressions for all traded sectors and for only manufacturing are reported for male employees in columns 3 and 4 and for male employers in columns 6 and 7. The sample employment weights of the sectors are reported for male employees and employers in columns 3 and 5, respectively. The industry-specific coefficients represent the natural logarithm of the monthly wage of a worker in that sector with no schooling or postschooling experience. Differences between sectoral coefficients reflect proportional differences in the levels of incomes in the two sectors, for example, in column 3 male employees in refining report monthly incomes 35 percent ($6.395 - 6.042$) higher than those in industrial chemicals. The direct inclusion of industry dummy variables clearly depresses the schooling and experience variables, since for some workers entry into particular sectors may depend in part on precisely these characteristics.

Regressing the estimated industry deviation in income level from table 2.4 on the Corden index of effective protection, one obtains estimates of equation (4) shown in table 2.5. Various samples of sectors are examined, both unweighted (panel A), and with "worker" (panel B) and "covariance" (panel C) weights. The covariance weighted estimates are the preferred estimates analogous to those obtained in tables 2.1 and 2.2 based directly on the individual data. For male employees across all traded sectors the elasticity of incomes with respect to effective protection is the same as with the first formulation, 1.24, and across only the manufacturing sectors it is 0.35 compared with the previous estimate of 0.34. For male employers the aggregate estimates in panel C of table 2.5 imply an elasticity of incomes with respect to effective protection of 1.92 and 0.49 across all traded and manufacturing sectors, respectively, which are also quite close to the individual estimates reported in table 2.2.

Employee income estimates are plotted against the levels of effective protection by sector in figure 2.1. The small weights assigned to several outlying sectors, such as refining (19) and transport equipment (31), improve the fit of the weighted regression. Figure 2.1 also indicates how the inclusion of the heavily weighted agricultural (1) sector increases the

Table 2.4 Income Functions for Male Employees and Employers with Unrestricted Shifts Associated with Twenty-six Census Sectors of Employment That Can Be Matched with Trade and Protection Indexes

Sector	ISIC Category (1)	Number of Employees (2)	Employee Regressions		Number of Employers (5)	Employer Regressions	
			All Traded Sectors (3)	Manufacturing Sectors (4)		All Traded Sectors (6)	Manufacturing Sectors (7)
Agriculture	11	26,816	5.078		3,870	5.324	
Forestry	12	194	5.360		18	5.490	
Fishing	13	90	5.522		17	5.597	
Mining	2	618	5.514		45	5.880	
Food processing	311	2,379	5.557	4.947	267	5.959	5.895
Other food	312, 31–	102	5.635	4.981	26	5.816	5.789
Beverages	313	500	5.977	5.253	11	6.104	6.147
Tobacco	314	103	5.751	5.057	5	6.408	6.306
Textiles	321	1,486	5.972	5.256	68	5.968	5.924
Apparel	322	509	5.569	4.920	146	5.912	5.843
Leather	323	225	5.625	5.002	38	5.834	5.792
Footwear	324, 32–	806	5.415	4.807	123	5.820	5.728
Wood	331, 33–	538	5.492	4.888	78	5.730	5.688
Furniture	332	740	5.476	4.872	156	5.836	5.778
Paper	341, 34–	218	5.955	5.234	11	6.500	6.437
Industrial chemicals	351	161	6.042	5.300	8	6.079	6.070
Other chemicals	352	386	5.996	5.240	25	6.217	6.188
Refining	353	91	6.395	5.575	4	7.087	7.036
Rubber	355	138	5.984	5.263	6	6.273	6.189
Nonmetallic minerals	369	712	5.561	4.948	56	5.878	5.842
Basic iron, steel	371	318	5.931	5.210	21	6.319	6.263
Nonferrous metals	372, 37–	100	5.830	5.183	4	6.114	6.077

Table 2.4 (continued)

Sector	ISIC Category (1)	Number of Employees (2)	Employee Regressions		Number of Employers (5)	Employer Regressions	
			All Traded Sectors (3)	Manufacturing Sectors (4)		All Traded Sectors (6)	Manufacturing Sectors (7)
Fabricated metals	381	562	5.656	5.017	71	6.037	5.963
Machinery	382	211	5.866	5.180	21	5.966	5.907
Electrical equipment	383	293	5.935	5.226	14	6.339	6.301
Transport equipment	384	251	5.960	5.268	5	5.943	5.893
Schooling			.134	.181		.191	.179
			(75.)	(80.)		(36.)	(20.)
Experience			.0486	.0839		.0325	.0477
			(50.)	(48.)		(6.96)	(5.22)
(Experience squared)/100			−.0665	−.116		−.0323	−.0630
			(41.)	(35.)		(5.19)	(4.66)
R^2			.370	.497		.328	.342
Standard error of the estimate			.788	.673		1.09	1.01
Sample size			38,547	10,919		5,108	1,160

NOTE: Matching of sectors is described in appendix table 2.A.1 and associated notes. Income functions estimated with thirty-eight census sectors defined, including sectors without estimates of effective protection are reported in appendix table 2.A.2. The maximum number of census sectors is forty-four, which are used in appendix table 2.A.3 regressions.

Table 2.5   **Aggregate Association between Worker Incomes and Effective Protection by Sector**

	Male Employees		Male Employers	
Weighting Scheme of Regression	All Twenty-six Traded Sectors (1)	Twenty-two Manufac- turing Sectors (2)	All Twenty-six Traded Sectors (3)	Twenty-two Manufac- turing Sectors (4)
A. Unweighted				
Corden index of effective	.421	.233	.178	.0311
protection	(2.18)	(1.67)	(.68)	(.13)
Constant	5.71	5.10	6.01	6.05
	(109.)	(128.)	(85.)	(87.)
R^2	.165	.123	.019	.0008
B. Weighted by number of workers by sector from table 2.4, cols. 2 and 5				
Corden index of effective	1.44	.388	2.01	.546
protection	(6.36)	(2.55)	(7.83)	(2.25)
Constant	5.50	5.04	5.85	5.88
	(104.)	(152.)	(103.)	(187.)
C. Weighted using covariance matrix of sectoral coefficients				
Corden index of effective	1.24	.350	1.92	.494
protection	(5.20)	(2.35)	(6.98)	(1.98)
Constant	5.34	4.91	5.78	5.85
	(39.)	(41.)	(33.)	(34.)

NOTE: Sectoral regression coefficients from columns 3, 4, 6, and 7 of table 2.4 are regressed on the sectoral index of effective protection from table 2.A.2.

slope of the overall income relationship with respect to effective protection.

The final empirical exercise is a two-stage procedure based on estimates of income-generating functions *within* sectors (equation 5) that are reported in appendix table 2.A.8. Multiplying these within-sector estimates by the average schooling and experience characteristics of all employees (table 2.A.9), a sector-predicted income estimate is obtained (table 2.A.10). This prediction of employee income is then regressed on the effective protection by sector, and these estimates of equation (6) are reported in table 2.6. Panel A presents the unweighted results and panel B the "worker" weighted results. The protection effects are very similar to those reported in table 2.5, panel B, with the same weighting scheme: 1.36 and 0.39 for all traded sectors and manufacturing, versus 1.44 and 0.39. The third and fourth regressions exclude the atypical government-operated refining sector and the large outlying agricultural sector to

Fig 2.1 Plot of relative male employee income against effective protection, by sector (weighted regression line provided for reference).

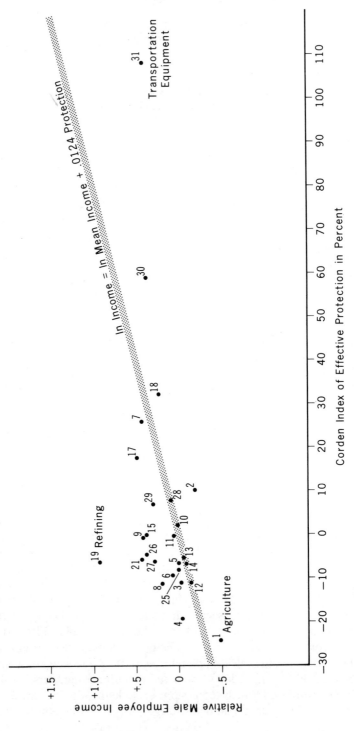

Source: Corden index of effective protection and sectoral code numbers from table 2.A.1.

Table 2.6   Aggregate Regression of Within-Sector Predicted Male Employee
                   Income on Corden Index of Effective Protection

Weighting Scheme and Explanatory Variable	Sample Composition			
	All Traded Sectors (1)	Manufac- turing Sectors (2)	Traded Sectors Less Refineries (3)	Traded Sectors Less Refineries and Agriculture (4)
	A. *Unweighted*			
Corden index of effective	.342	.221	.389	.304
protection	(2.04)	(1.41)	(3.02)	(2.82)
Constant	6.67	6.72	6.64	6.67
	(147.)	(150.)	(186.)	(222.)
R^2	.148	.090	.284	.265
Standard error of the estimate	.228	.202	.175	.142
F	4.18	1.99	9.12	7.95
(Degrees of freedom)	(1,24)	(1,20)	(1,23)	(1,22)
Sample size	26	22	25	24
	B. *Weighted by Number of Employees by Sector* *Table 2.4, Column 2*			
Corden index of effective	1.36	.385	1.35	.407
protection	(6.33)	(2.66)	(6.41)	(3.33)
Constant	6.46	6.66	6.46	6.64
	(129.)	(211.)	(131.)	(252.)
Standard error of the estimate	7.07	3.25	6.95	2.83
F	40.1	7.08	41.1	11.1
(Degrees of freedom)	(2,24)	(2,20)	(2,23)	(2,22)
Sample size	26	22	25	24

NOTE: The logarithm of the individual income is regressed within each sector on schooling
and a quadratic in postschooling experience (appendix table 2.A.8). These sector-specific
parameters are multiplied by the overall sample mean values of the explanatory variables
(table 2.A.9) to obtain a sector predicted logarithmic income. These sector predicted
income levels are then regressed on the Corden index, without and with worker weights. In
weighted regressions R^2 is not comparable.

confirm that the omission of refining does not alter the results (compare
regressions 1 and 3) and that most of the difference between all traded
sectors and manufacturing is due to the omission of agriculture (compare
regressions 2 and 4).

2.5 Conclusions

All three statistical formulations of the interactions between the parameters of the income-generating function and the level of effective
protection have yielded parallel findings. The individual and the aggregate two-stage estimates suggest that in examining all traded sectors of

the economy one obtains a very high elasticity estimate on the order of 1.24 for male employees, but this large value is clearly a function of the inclusion of agriculture. Given the reservations expressed earlier regarding any interpretation of the effect of protection on agriculture in Colombia, it is preferable here to rely on the smaller elasticity estimate across only the manufacturing sectors of between 0.34 and 0.35. In the case of manufacturing, effective protection of 30 percent is associated with male employee incomes' being 10 percent higher. Among male employers in the manufacturing sectors, a 30 percent level of sectoral effective protection is associated with 15 percent more income.

Two interpretations can attach to this strong association between levels of effective protection and levels of employee and employer incomes. Without speculating on the original reason for more protected industries to pay employees higher incomes, one may assume that once such pay differentials are established, the protected industries attract better than average workers within the rough schooling/experience categories held constant here. Competitive pressures of labor and product markets are assumed, under this interpretation, to create offsetting differentials in unobserved quality and productivity of workers by sector to justify the historically given intersectoral pay differentials. This explanation is then consistent with a stable equilibrium in factor markets and an absence of distortions or factor quasi rents.

I prefer a second interpretation, which assumes that intersectoral differentials to some degree represent real distortions in the labor market that sustain "excess" factor returns above the level needed to retain the services of the factor. As I indicated earlier, the best way to discriminate between these two explanations of the sectoral pattern in income and protection that are documented here is to examine changes in the Colombian economy over time. Are factors drawn to the sectors incurring "excess" returns? Or are trade restrictions on imported investment goods administered to prevent factor markets from responding to "excess" returns, at least when capacity in the sector is thought to be underutilized (Díaz-Alejandro 1976)? Do new changes in the structure of effective protection generate shifts in factor returns across sectors? Although these avenues for empirical research cannot be followed in this chapter, it is interesting to examine how sectoral income levels are related to trade status by sector.

Trade status is summarized for a particular sector by a T index defined as the quantity of imports minus exports expressed as a share of domestic consumption. Table 2.7 reports unweighted and weighted regressions of the male employee income levels on trade status by sector. There is a positive association, suggesting that, where employee incomes are unusually high, Colombia is on balance not an exporter but an importer. Conversely, where incomes are relatively low, Colombia tends to be

Table 2.7   **Regressions of Male Sectoral Income Levels on Sectoral Trade Status Index**

	Sample Composition		
Regression	Traded Sectors Only (A)	Traded Sectors Less Refineries (B)	Traded Sectors Less Refineries and Agriculture (C)
Unweighted regression			
Trade index, T	.593	.708	.626
	(2.43)	(4.15)	(3.71)
Constant	1.17	1.12	1.14
	(20.)	(27.)	(28.)
R^2	.180	.399	.355
Standard error of the estimate	.294	.204	.195
F	5.92	17.2	13.8
(Degrees of freedom)	(1,27)	(1,26)	(1,25)
Sample size, N	29	28	27
Weighted regression[a]			
Trade index, T	1.52	1.51	.685
	(6.77)	(7.08)	(3.07)
Constant	1.01	1.00	1.14
	(22.)	(23.)	(28.)
Standard error of the estimate[b]	6.59	6.26	4.48
F	45.8	50.1	9.42
(Degrees of freedom)	(2,27)	(2,26)	(2,25)
Sample size, N	29	28	27

NOTE: The trade index, T, is defined as the sector's (imports-exports)/(domestic consumption). Source is Thoumi (1978), reported in table 2.A.1.

[a]Regression weighted by the number of male employees in the sector in the 1973 census sample. The dependent variable is the relative wage effects for the thirty-eight census sectors obtained from regression 1, table 2.A.4.

[b]This is an estimate of σ where the model is $Y_i = \beta X_i + \varepsilon_i$ is normally distributed, $N(0, \sigma^2 1/n_i)$, and n_i is the number of the employees in the ith industry. To obtain estimated standard deviation of the wage for an individual in the ith industry, the reported SEE should be multiplied by $\sqrt{n_i}$.

capable of exporting domestic production. As one would expect, the magnitude of the relationship is again sensitive to whether agriculture is included or excluded in the sample of sectors analyzed.

The country studies volume associated with this NBER project (Krueger et al. 1981) indicates how effective protection and comparative advantage interact to influence the allocation of domestic resources and the trade status of sectors as exporting, import-competing, or predominantly importing. No simple correlations or ranking among sectors according to factor returns, protection, factor proportions, and trade status can confirm causal relations; nonetheless, the sectoral patterns among these variables are suggestive. Import substitution policies in the 1950s and early 1960s led to substantial and uneven levels of effective protection. Where economies of scale or market structure inhibited the development of competitive pressures in the protected domestic market, high levels of effective protection appear to have resulted in quasi rents for factors employed in the more protected sectors.

Low or negative levels of effective protection are associated with lower employee incomes across the groups of sectors arranged by trade status in table 2.8; the less protected sectors also tend to be labor-intensive activities where Colombia's comparative advantage for exports may lie. In the 1970s these less protected sectors were Colombia's export sectors, and they were also relatively labor-intensive, according to Thoumi (1977). Protection in Colombia has therefore favored in its structure more capital-intensive sectors, and, as I observed earlier, it has provided more protection for sectors using a more educated labor force. But within protected and unprotected sectors the proportionate variation in incomes associated with years of schooling does not appear to behave systematically.

To summarize the overall magnitude of the distributional effects associated with the structure of protection, it is useful to construct two measures, though they are only illustrative given the partial equilibrium framework used in this investigation. The first measure is called the *gross* distributional effect and the second the *net* effect, which would allow sectors with decreased income to offset sectors with increased income.

Table 2.8   **Male Employee Wages and Effective Protection by Trade Status of Sector**

Trade Status of Sectors[a] (Number of Sectors)	Net Corden Effective Protection[b]	Relative Wage Deviation[c]
Exports, all (16)	-11.6	-.0608
Excluding refining and and agriculture (14)	-3.95	.135
Import-competing (11)	+16.0	.324
Imports (5)	+58.2	.356
Untraded (6)	—	.152

[a]Groups defined in terms of a trade status index, T, defined by Thoumi (1978) as the sector's (imports-exports)/(domestic consumption): exports $T<0$; import-competing $0<T<0.4$; imports $.4<T<1.0$. See table 2.A.1, col. 4.
[b]Net Corden protection index, Table 2.A.1, weighted by domestic price value added.
[c]Relative wage effects by industry derived from regression 1, table 2.A.4 weighted by domestic price value added.

The distributional effects are approximated by multiplying the level of effective protection in each manufacturing sector by the estimated elasticity of employee incomes with respect to protection, or 0.34 (table 2.1, regression 2), and weighting it by the share of manufacturing male employees in that sector. The sectoral income weights could also be adjusted to accord with average schooling and experience levels in each sector, but for simplicity employees are treated equally here.[23] These sectoral weighted income effects are then summed, without regard to sign, to obtain the total *gross* shift of resources in 1973 associated with the structure of effective protection in 1970. In manufacturing this gross redistributional effect in Colombia is 3.9 percent of male employee income, whereas the *net* effect is an increase in male employee incomes of 1.0 percent. If the same elasticity of employee income-to-protection is also applied to the traded sectors outside of manufacturing, primarily agriculture and mining, the gross redistributional effect increases to 7.0 percent, and the net effect of protection is to decrease male employee incomes by 5.5 percent. The empirical evidence suggests that the effects are somewhat larger for male employers (table 2.2), and markedly larger if the estimates obtained across all traded sectors including agriculture are accepted at face value. As already noted, however, this appears to attribute too much of the responsibility for the depressed state of agricultural incomes in Colombia to the policies restraining free trade in agricultural commodities.[24]

In most studies of labor markets and trade policies, it is not possible to analyze wage and income variation across sectors, except at the aggregate level or sometimes by gross classifications of workers into blue- and white-collar jobs and into production and nonproduction employment. This study has sacrificed the international comparative aspect to deal with individual income data by sector in greater detail, but from only one country: Colombia. Since workers differ in formal education and post-schooling experience, it is appropriate that at least these productive features of the work force be "held constant" when measuring intersectoral income differences. Employment type and sex are also straightforward bases for stratification. Undoubtedly, more satisfactory measures of the quasi rents accrued by labor owing to their sector of employment can be fashioned in the future, standardizing perhaps for other generally productive characteristics of workers, such as their investments in job-related skills, ability, and motivation: variables that are unfortunately difficult to measure and unavailable for study here. When large and visible rents are to be earned in a society, one may also presume that economic and political resources will be expended to appropriate them (Krueger 1974). Nonetheless, the close relationship found here between levels of effective protection and unexplained variation in labor incomes provides a prima facie case that development and trade policies have played a role in generating or at least maintaining intersectoral differences in factor incomes that look like quasi rents.

Because the structure of protection is a political manifestation of a balance struck between private interest groups and broader developmental goals of a society, it is not clear what economic and social consequences would follow from the systematic removal of protection barriers. Would newfound efficiencies and the loss of quasi rents that now serve no allocative function leave resources allocated as they are today? Certainly it cannot be argued that jobs would be lost if labor can be substituted between sectors, for the structure of protection in Colombia in 1970 favored capital-intensive sectors. Protection may have increased the returns to both labor and capital in the more protected sectors, but the proportionate gains for employers exceed those received by employees, and the absolute gains are even more highly skewed toward employers. With both of these biases in the distributional consequences of protection, it seems reasonable to conclude that the structure of effective protection in Colombia in 1970 increased the inequality in personal income distribution, induced a misallocation in factors of production among sectors, and stimulated rent-seeking activity that is commonly associated with a deadweight loss to the society.

Appendix

Table 2.A.1 Sources and Data Used in Constructing Compatible Measures of Incomes: Trade Status (*t*) and Net Effective Protection by Industry

Title from Census	Hutcheson Code and Description (1)	ISIC Code and Description (2)	Domestic Price Value Added (3)	Sector Share of Value Added (4)	Trade Status (*t*) (5)	Net Nominal Effective Protection Index — Balassa (6)	Net Nominal Effective Protection Index — Corden (7)
1 Agriculture and hunting	1 Coffee	11– Agriculture and hunting	5335	.31	-.212	-24.6[a]	-24.2[a]
	2 Agriculture and cattle-raising		24290	.69	-.212	-56.3	-56.0
2 Forestry and logging	3 Forestry	12– Forestry and logging	376		-.004	-20.3	-9.8
						10.4	10.2
3 Fishing	4 Fishing	130 Fishing	406		-.048	-12.1	-11.2
4 Mining and quarrying	5 Mining	2– Mining and Quarrying	262		-.223	-20.6	-19.4
5 Food processing	6 Meat preparation	3111 Meat preparation	93		-.090	-8.4	-6.9
	7 Milk products	3112 Dairy products	746		.127	-6.4	-5.0
	8 Canning fruits and vegetables	3113 Canning fruits and vegetables	67		-.002	-1.3	-1.0
	9 Canning and preserving fish products	3114 Canning and preserving fish products	8		-.004	20.7	15.2
					-1.574	-3.9	-1.7
	10 Milling	3116 Mill products	20		-.004	6.1	4.3

Table 2.A.1 (continued)

Title from Census / Hutcheson Code and Description (1)	ISIC Code and Description (2)	Domestic Price Value Added (3)	Sector Share of Value Added (4)	Trade Status (t) (5)	Net Nominal Effective Protection Index — Balassa (6)	Net Nominal Effective Protection Index — Corden (7)
11 Baked goods	3117 Baked goods	193		.000	−24.7	−14.4
12 Sugar refining	3118 Sugar refining	879		−.246	−19.6	−17.4
13 Candy	3119 Confectionery	444		−.006	3.6	2.9
	3115 Vegetable and animal oils			.059		
6 Food processing not specified above				.024[b]	−17.7	−9.5
14 Diverse food	3121 Other food	341		.012	−17.7	−9.5
	3122 Animal feed			.036		
7 Beverage industries						
15 Spiritous beverages	3131 Spirits	985		.053	30.6	25.8
16 Wine-making	3132 Wine industry	20		.051	30.7	26.1
97 Breweries	3133 Malt liquors			.157	24.3	15.0
98 Soft drinks	3134 Soft drinks					
8 Tobacco manufactures						
17 Cigarettes and cigars	3140 Tobacco manufactures	754		.118	−13.0	−11.5
9 Manufacture of textiles				−.047	.3	−.6
18 Spinning industry	3211 Spinning, weaving, finishing textiles	267		−.059[c]	−1.5	−1.1
21 Cotton textiles		1739			−7.0	−5.8
22 Wool textiles		133			−8.2	−4.1
23 Artificial fibers		251			34.4	19.8

Division	Item	ISIC category	N			
	31 Nonclothing textile products	3212 Nonclothing textile products	25	.016	−18.5	−11.8
	19 Knitting mills	3213 Knitting mills	348	−.002	22.1	15.4
	25 Other textiles	3214 Carpets and rugs	13	−.001	−22.6	−8.6
	20 Rope	3215 Cordage, rope, twine	126	.030	−5.5	−4.6
	24 Hard textile fabrics	3219 Other textiles	8	−.011	9.8	5.7
	25 Other textiles		13		−22.6	−8.6
10 Manufacture of wearing apparel		3220 Wearing apparel		−.004	2.3	1.8
	27 Men's clothing		699	−.004	3.7	2.8
	28 Women's clothing		59		−6.0	−3.0
	29 Children's clothing		42		2.5	1.8
	30 Hat-making		20		−15.2	−12.1
	32 Other clothing		13		−8.7	−6.1
11 Manufactured leather and leather products	43 Tanneries	3231 Tanneries	176	−.166	−.6	−.4
		3232 Fur dressing and dyeing		−.194	−2.2	−1.6
	44 Leather products	3233 Leather products, except footwear	26	−.013	8.0	6.2
	45 Leather industrial products		4		10.6	8.1
	46 Leather sporting goods		1		9.4	6.6
12 Manufacture of footwear	26 Shoemaking	3240 Footwear manufacture	91	−.079	−15.7	−11.2
13 Manufacture of wood and wood products	33 Wood preparation	3311 Wood mills	130	−.043	−8.8	−5.8
	34 Wood for construction		19	−.054	−8.9	−5.7
		3312 Cane ware		.000	−7.4	−4.6
	35 Wood toys	3319 Wood and cork products	6	.019	−13.9	−8.2

Table 2.A.1 (continued)

Title from Census	Hutcheson Code and Description (1)	ISIC Code and Description (2)	Domestic Price Value Added (3)	Sector Share of Value Added (4)	Trade Status (t) (5)	Net Nominal Effective Protection Index	
						Balassa (6)	Corden (7)
	36 Toothpicks		4			−7.2	−5.9
	37 Other wood products		4			−8.0	−6.3
	38 Cork products		12			−9.0	−6.9
14 Manufacture of wood furniture	39 Wood furniture 100 Bamboo furniture	3320 Wood furniture	97		−.006	−10.8	−7.2
15 Manufacture of pulp and paper products	40 Pulp and paper 42 Cardboard 41 Paper goods	3411 Pulp and paper 3412 Paper boxes 3419 Paper products	538 142 122		.226 .301 .011 .144	−.6 1.6 2.0 −13.5	−.2 .9 1.4 −6.8
16 Printing, publishing, and allied industries	101 Printing 102 Photogravure 103 Bookbinding 104 Other graphic arts 105 Matches	3420 Printing and publishing			.148	—[d]	—[d]
17 Manufacture of industrial chemicals	51 Chemical products	3511 Basic industrial chemicals	1381	.56	.390[e] .455	23.0 23.0	17.4 17.4

Industry group	ISIC code	National product					
18 Manufacture of other chemicals							
	3512 Fertilizers and pesticides		.30		.152		
	3513 Resins and plastics		.14		.640		
	3521 Paints and lacquers	55 Paints		214	.123	47.3	32.1
	3522 Drugs and medicines	53 Drugs		1341	.168	55.3	32.6
	3523 Soap and cosmetics	54 Soap		475	.138	65.3	45.4
	3529 Other chemical products					-8.3	-5.5
		56 Glues and waterproofing		29	.030	36.1	24.1
		57 Other chemical products		5	.550	162.8	38.0
19 Petroleum refineries							
	3530 Petroleum refining					-9.3	-6.6
		58 Petroleum refining		510	-.058	-9.8	-6.9
		52 Fats and oils		51	-.058	-4.5	-3.4
20 Products of petroleum and coal							
	3540 Products of petroleum and coal				-.889	-1.2	-1.0
		60 Coke and other coal and oil derivatives		7	-.889	-3.4	-2.5
		59 Asphalt		18		-.4	-.4
21 Manufacture of rubber products							
	3551 Tires and tubes	47 Tires and tubes		655	.043	-6.5	-5.7
	3592 Other rubber products					-8.8	-7.6
		48 Shoes and household goods		144	-.007	-5.4	-4.8
		49 Industrial products		34	.216	25.3	20.6
		50 Sporting goods		10		17.8	14.3
22 Manufacture of plastic products							
	3560 Plastic products				.014		
23 Manufacture of pottery, china and earthenware							
	3610 Pottery, china, earthenware				-.002		

Table 2.A.1 (continued)

Title from Census	Hutcheson Code and Description (1)	ISIC Code and Description (2)	Domestic Price Value Added (3)	Sector Share of Value Added (4)	Trade Status (t) (5)	Net Nominal Effective Protection Index — Balassa (6)	Net Nominal Effective Protection Index — Corden (7)
24 Manufacture of glass and glass products		3620 Glass and glass products			-.018		
25 Manufacture of other nonmetallic minerals	107 Bricks	3691 Structural clay products	331	.08	.001[f]	-11.1	-8.1
	63 Cement	3692 Cement, lime, and plaster	267	.47	.060	-13.9	-10.4
	64 Asbestos and cement products	3699 Other nonmetallic mineral products		.45	-.085	-11.2	-8.1
	65 Other nonmetallic mineral products		15		.080	54.6	42.7
26 Iron and steel basic industries		3710 Iron and steel basic industries			.437	16.8	-4.7
	66 Basic iron and steel		86		.437	6.4	4.1
	67 Manufactures of iron and steel		268			20.2	-7.5
27 Nonferrous metals basic industries		3720 Nonferrous metal basic industries			.405	-21.4	-6.1
	68 Basic nonferrous metals		1		.405	17.5	11.1
	69 Manufactures of nonferrous metals		20			-23.4	-7.0

Domestic classification	Count	ISIC classification	Ratio		
28 Manufacture of fabricated metal products					
71 Hand tools and knives	87	3811 Cutlery, hand tools, and general hardware	.093	11.4	7.7
			.173	15.0	12.3
72 Cutlery	72			-1.3	-1.1
73 Kitchenware	54			14.4	11.2
		3812 Metal fixtures and furniture	.073		
76 Foundry products	144	3813 Structural metal products	.098	-9.8	-7.1
70 Tin plate manufactures	305	3819 Other fabricated metal products	.076	38.3	27.9
74 Aluminum articles	164			6.7	4.7
75 Wire products	214			-.1	-.1
77 Diverse metal products	320			1.5	1.1
78 Other metal manufactures	21			92.0	18.2
29 Manufactures of machinery not electrical					
79 Motor-driven machinery	7	3821 Engines and turbines	.717	9.9[h]	6.9[h]
80 Agricultural machinery	115	3822 Agricultural machinery	.930	35.0	20.6
81 Industrial machinery	110	3823 Metal and woodworking machinery	.729	-.8	-.6
			.941	10.0	7.1
		3824 Industrial machinery	.832		
83 Other machinery	80	3825 Office machinery	.425	38.2	38.1
		3829 Other	.478		
82 Parts for machinery	28			-29.9	-8.5
30 Manufacture of electrical equipment					
84 Electrical machinery	243	3831 Electrical industrial machinery	.363	143.1[h]	59.2[h]
			.702	29.6	17.9

Table 2.A.1 (continued)

Title from Census	Hutcheson Code and Description (1)	ISIC Code and Description (2)	Domestic Price Value Added (3)	Sector Share of Value Added (4)	Trade Status (t) (5)	Net Nominal Effective Protection Index — Balassa (6)	Net Nominal Effective Protection Index — Corden (7)
	85 Radio and television apparatus	3832 Radio, television, and communication apparatus	142		.485	296.2	52.6
	95 Phonograph records		71			−2.6	−2.3
	86 Electrical appliances	3833 Electrical appliances	102		.471	77.3	46.0
	87 Wire and cable	3839 Other electrical supplies	169		.063	−113.8	−3417.8
	88 Light bulbs		16			−21.9	−10.8
	89 Other electrical		213			210.8	97.8
31 Manufacture of transport equipment					.528[h]	160.7[h]	108.1[h]
	110 Ship repair	3841 Ship building and repair		.07	.616		
	111 Railroad equipment repair	3842 Railroad equipment manufacturing		.03	.779		
	90 Auto and truck assembly	3843 Motor vehicles	758	.83	.472	164.9	112.0
	112 Auto repair						
	91 Bicycle manufacture	3844 Motorcycle and bicycle manufacturing	16	.04	.178	47.5	25.4
	113 Airplane repair	3845 Aircraft		.12	.891		
		3849 Other transport equipment		.01	.335		

Sector		ISIC				
32 Manufacture of scientific and professional instruments	92 Medical and scientific equipment	3851 Professional and scientific equipment	33	.710	−21.0	−16.2
	93 Optical goods	3852 Photographic and optical goods	13	.764	−12.2	−10.8
		3853 Watches and clocks		.978		
33 Other manufacturing industries	94 Jewelry	3901 Jewelry	34	−.001	−13.9	−12.0
		3902 Musical instruments		.653		
	96 Diverse industries	3903 Sporting goods	619	.727	74.5	49.6
		3909 Other industries				
34 Electricity, gas and steam	119 Electricity, gas, and water	410 Electricity, gas, and steam		*Untraded Sectors* values not relevant or calculated.		
35 Waterworks and supply	119 Electricity, gas and water	420 Waterworks and supply				
	106 Compressed gases					
36 Construction	116 Construction	500 Construction				
37 Trade, transport and communication, financing, business, community, and social services	117 Transportation	710 Transportation				
	118 Communications	720 Communication				

Table 2.A.1 (continued)

Title from Census	Hutcheson Code and Description (1)	ISIC Code and Description (2)	Domestic Price Value Added (3)	Sector Share of Value Added (4)	Trade Status (*t*) (5)	Net Nominal Effective Protection Index	
						Balassa (6)	Corden (7)
	120 Banks and insurance	800 Financing, insurance, real estate, and business services					
	121 Commerce, professional services and artisans	900–949 Community and social services					
		600 Commerce					
38 Personal services	114 Watch repair	95 Personal services					
	115 Dental laboratories						
	99 Shoe repair						

SOURCES

Column 3: Domestic price value added from Hutcheson's computer output table labeled annex table 2, VDSTAR.

Column 5: F. Thoumi's "Colombian *t* values by ISIC II codes" (1978) defined as (imports-exports)/domestic consumption.

Columns 6 and 7: Net nominal effective protection to value added (average of exports and domestic); Hutcheson and Schydlowsky (1977), annex table 5c.

NOTE: The Colombian census of 1973 reports employment sector according to three-digit ISIC II codes. If only the two digits are reported, the individual is allocated to the "not specified elsewhere" category, which is indicated by a dash in the final code column. This treatment of individuals with missing third codes casts some doubt on the information content of three sectors that include mostly such unspecified activities: coal and oil derivatives (20), scientific equipment (32), and other manufacturing (33). Several sectors were aggregated to match trade and protection series: mining (4) agriculture (1), and wood products other than furniture (13). The nontraded categories, following Thoumi (1977) and Hutcheson (1973), are printing and publishing (16), electricity, gas, and steam (34), waterworks and supply (35), construction (36), trade and professional services (37), and personal services (38). Hutcheson's (1973) protection figures that are the starting point for the protection estimates used here did not include three sectors: plastics, pottery and china, and glass. These sectors were therefore not used in the subsequent analysis of protection effects, but are included in the income functions for male employees in table 2.1. Balassa and Corden effective protection indexes and trade status figures were often aggregated to correspond with the broader sectoral categories reported in the 1973 population census. The weights for aggregation were generally drawn from Hutcheson's computer output for detailed sectoral breakdowns on "domestic price value added" (column 3). When these figures are not available or inappropriate, alternative bases for weights are shown in column 4 and their source is explained in the subsequent notes.

[a]In agriculture the value-added weights at domestic prices are roughly 5.3 for coffee to 24.3 for cattle and all else, whereas at world price the value-added weights are 11.0 and 24.4, respectively. The latter weights are used because of the international trade importance of coffee. The data source in both instances is Hutcheson's computer output.

[b]In other foods and animal feed, ISIC categories 3121 and 3122, no estimates of value added were obtained, and a simple average was used.

[c]In textiles Thoumi's worksheet for ISIC category 3211 (spinning, weaving, and finishing) reports two trade status t values: $-.093$ and $-.023$. An average of these is used here.

[d]Treated as a home good.

[e]In basic chemicals the t values of the components are weighted by "value added in factor prices" 1970 from the *U.N. Yearbook of Industrial Statistics, 1975*, volume 1, (New York, 1977), p. 96; basic industrial chemicals—459; fertilizers and pesticides—246; resins—114.

[f]In nonmetallic minerals the t values are weighted by "valor agregado bruto," *Industria Manufacturera Nacional, 1969* (Bogotá, Colombia: DANE, n.d.), table 1: (in 100,000 pesos) structural clay products—616; cement, lime, and plaster—3,765; other nonmetallic mineral products—3,617.

[g]In transport equipment the t values are weighted from the source cited in note 5: shipbuilding—450; railroad equipment, construction, and repair—182; construction of automobiles—3,142; construction of bicycles—222; repair of automobiles and bicycles—1,555; construction and repair of airplanes—75; other—33.

[h]In machinery other than electrical, electrical equipment, and transport equipment the Corden and Balassa figures were not calculated as weighted averages but were obtained directly from Hutcheson and Schydlowsky (1977), table 5c.

Table 2.A.2   Colombian Estimates of Effective Protection and Proxies for Capital Stock per Worker by Sector, 1969–70

Traded Sectors	Corden Index of Effective Protection (%) (1)	Value Added per Worker in 1969 (1,000 Pesos) (2)	Horsepower Energy Capacity per Hundred Workers in 1969 (3)
1 Agriculture	−24.2	n.d.	n.d.
2 Forestry	10.2	n.d.	n.d.
3 Fishing	−11.2	n.d.	n.d.
4 Mining	−19.4	n.d.	n.d.
5 Food processing	−6.9	55.1	53.0
6 Other foods	−9.5	84.9	164.0
7 Beverages	25.8	157.5	300.1
8 Tobacco	−11.5	229.3	32.0
9 Textiles	−.6	52.2	353.7
10 Apparel	1.8	27.2	7.5
11 Leather	−.4	378.0	61.7
12 Footwear	−11.2	18.9	5.5
13 Wood	−5.8	26.9	75.0
14 Furniture	−7.2	25.9	20.0
15 Paper	−.2	83.9	651.2
17 Industrial chemicals	17.4	121.2	819.2
18 Other chemicals	32.1	86.5	69.0
19 Refining	−6.6	380.2	5997.0
21 Rubber	−5.7	69.1	444.0
25 Nonmetallic minerals	−8.1	38.1	163.4
26 Basic iron and steel	−4.7	77.2	242.1
27 Nonferrous metals	−6.1	64.2	166.9
28 Fabricated metals	7.7	41.0	114.1
29 Machinery	6.9	34.9	69.9
30 Electrical equipment	59.2	57.5	82.4
31 Transport equipment	108.1	27.8	33.6

SOURCE: Col. 1, table 2.A.1, col. 7; cols. 2 and 3, Departamento Administrativo Nacionale de Estadistica, *Industria, Manufacturera Nacionale 1969*, Bogotá.

NOTE: n.d. means no data available for nonmanufacturing sectors.

Table 2.A.3   Relative Wage Effects Associated with
Forty-four Industrial Sectors Distinguished in 1973 Census:
Semilogarithmic Regression for Male Employees

Industry Number	ISIC Category	Description	Number of Individuals in Regression	Regression Coefficients[a]	
				(1)	(2)
1	111	Agriculture and livestock production	25,984	− .474	− .349
2	112, 113, 11–	Agricultural services and hunting	828	− .237	− .152
3	12	Forestry and logging	194	− .194	− .0978
4	13	Fishing	90	− .0273	.0069
5	21	Coal mining	172	− .0374	.0605
6	22	Crude petroleum and natural gas production	70	.810	.803
7	23	Metal ore mining	108	− .332	− .292
8	29	Other mining	173	− .126	− .100
9	2–	Mining, not further specified	95	− .222	− .141
10	311	Food processing	2,379	0	0
11	312, 31–	Other food processing not specified above	102	.0715	.0635
12	313	Beverage industries	498	.403	.378
13	314	Tobacco manufactures	103	.182	.158
14	321	Manufacture of textiles	1,486	.400	.381
15	322	Manufacture of wearing apparel	508	.0064	− .0147
16	323	Manufacture of leather and leather products	225	.0662	.0471
17	324, 32–	Manufacture of footwear	806	− .142	− .171
18	331	Manufacture of wood products	457	− .0704	− .0744
19	332	Manufacture of wood furniture	740	− .0807	− .105
20	33–	Other wood manufacturing, not specified	81	− .0320	− .0477
21	341, 34–	Manufacture of paper and paper products	218	.382	.361
22	342	Printing, publishing, and allied industries	494	.319	.294
23	351	Manufacture of industrial chemicals	161	.466	.449

Table 2.A.3 (continued)

Industry Number	ISIC Category	Description	Number of Individuals in Regression	Regression Coefficients[a]	
				(1)	(2)
24	352	Manufacture of other chemicals	385	.418	.399
25	353	Petroleum refineries	91	.809	.787
26	354, 35–	Manufacture of coal and oil derivatives; chemical manufactures not further specified	90	.455	.440
27	355	Manufacture of rubber products	138	.411	.391
28	356	Manufacture of plastic products	153	.277	.252
29	361, 36–	Manufacture of pottery, china, and earthenware	159	.104	.102
30	362	Manufacture of glass and glass products	164	.278	.258
31	369	Manufacture of other nonmetallic mineral products	712	.0044	− .0011
32	371	Iron and steel basic industries	318	.358	.353
33	372, 37–	Nonferrous metal basic industries	100	.268	.239
34	381	Manufacture of metal products except machinery and equipment	562	.0948	.0654
35	382	Manufacture of machinery except electrical	211	.298	.274
36	383	Manufacture of electrical equipment	293	.364	.340
37	384	Manufacture of transport equipment	251	.391	.366
38	385, 38–	Manufacture of scientific equipment; manufacture of metals not further specified	163	.321	.295
39	39, 3–	Other manufacturing industries, manufacturing not further specified	1,003	.142	.118
40	41	Electric, gas, steam	449	.400	.382
41	42	Waterworks and supply	178	.334	.324
42	50	Construction	5,408	− .0663	− .0860

Table 2.A.3 (continued)

Industry Number	ISIC Category	Description	Number of Individuals in Regression	Regression Coefficients[a]	
				(1)	(2)
43	600–949	Trade, transportation and communication, finances, professional, miscellaneous	766	.342	.329
44	95	Personal services	302	− .492	− .460

Other conditioning variables (and t-statistics)

Experience (age − schooling − 7)				.0526 (61.)	.0524 (61.)
(Experience squared)/100				− .0717 (50.)	− .0720 (50.)
Years of education				.141 (95.)	.138 (92.)
Rural/urban zone of residence (rural = 1)					− .195 (.18)
Constant				5.479 (275.)	5.529 (275.)
R^2				.415	.419
Standard error of the estimate				.771	.768
F				738.	734.
(Degrees of freedom)				(46,47821)	(47,47820)
Sample size			47,868		

[a]Food processing (ISIC–311) sector is omitted; sectoral coefficients represent, therefore, the proportionate deviation of wages in the specific sector from those received in food processing, holding constant for the proportionate effects of years of schooling completed, postschooling experience, experience squared, and, in regression 2, rural/urban zone of residence. The choice of food processing as the numeraire is arbitrary and has no effect on the estimated differentials. The food processing sector is a large industry with about average incomes for male employees.

Table 2.A.4   **Relative Wage Effects Associated with**
Thirty-eight Aggregated 1973 Census Sectors
Matched to Trade and Protection Categories:
Semilogarithmic Regression for Male Employees

Industry Number	ISIC Category	Description	Number of Individuals in Regression	Regression Coefficients[a]	
				(1)	(2)
1	11	Agriculture and hunting	26,812	−.463	−.334
2	12	Forestry	194	−.193	−.0924
3	13	Fishing	90	−.0252	.0103
4	2	Mining	618	−.0460	.0095
5	311	Food processing	2,379	0	0
6	312, 31–	Other food processing, not specified above	102	.0693	.0612
7	313	Beverage industries	498	.398	.373
8	314	Tobacco manufactures	103	.178	.153
9	321	Manufacture of textiles	1,486	.395	.376
10	322	Manufacture of wearing apparel	508	.0031	−.0185
11	323	Manufacture of leather and leather products	225	.0646	.0448
12	324, 32–	Manufacture of footwear	806	−.143	−.174
13	331,33–	Manufacture of wood products	538	−.0651	−.0711
14	332	Manufacture of wood furniture	740	−.0820	−.107
15	341, 34–	Manufacture of paper and paper products	218	.377	.356
16	342	Printing, publishing, and allied industries	494	.314	.288
17	351	Manufacture of industrial chemicals	161	.459	.442
18	352	Manufacture of other chemicals	385	.410	.391
19	353	Petroleum refineries	91	.800	.779
20	354, 35–	Manufacture of coal and oil derivatives; chemical manufactures not further specified	90	.448	.433
21	355	Manufacture of rubber products	138	.406	.386
22	356	Manufacture of plastic products	153	.271	.246

Table 2.A.4 (continued)

Industry Number	ISIC Category	Description	Number of Individuals in Regression	Regression Coefficients[a]	
				(1)	(2)
23	361, 36–	Manufacture of pottery, china, and earthenware	159	.104	.101
24	362	Manufacture of glass and glass products	164	.275	.251
25	369	Manufactures of other, nonmetallic mineral products	712	.0046	−.0012
26	371	Iron and steel basic industries	318	.354	.349
27	372, 37–	Nonferrous metal basic industries	100	.265	.235
28	381	Manufacture of metal products, except machinery and equipment	562	.0920	.0616
29	382	Manufacture of machinery except electrical	211	.292	.268
30	383	Manufacture of electrical equipment	293	.358	.334
31	384	Manufacture of transport equipment	251	.386	.360
32	385, 38–	Manufacture of scientific equipment; manufacture of metals, not further specified	163	.317	.291
33	39, 3–	Other manufacturing, manufacturing not further specified	1,003	.138	.114
34	41	Electric, gas, steam	449	.395	.377
35	42	Waterworks and supply	178	.330	.320
36	50	Construction	5,408	−.0661	−.0867
37	600–949	Trade, transportation and communication, financial, professional, miscellaneous	766	.337	.324
38	95	Personal services	302	−.489	−.457

Table 2.A.4 (continued)

Industry ISIC Number Category Description	Number of Individuals in Regression	Regression Coefficients[a]	
		(1)	(2)
Other conditioning variables (and t-statistics)			
Experience (age − schooling − 7)		.0528	.0526
		(61.)	(62.)
(Experience squared)/100		− .0720	− .0722
		(50.)	(50.)
Years of education		.143	.140
		(96.)	(94.)
Rural/urban zone of residence			− .204
(rural = 1)			(19.)
Constant		5.469	5.523
		(274.)	(275.)
R^2		.413	.417
Standard error of the estimate		.772	.769
F		841.	836.
(Degrees of freedom)		(40,47827)	(41,47826)
Sample size	47,868		

[a]Food processing (ISIC–311) sector is omitted; sectoral coefficients represent, therefore, the proportionate deviation of wages in the specific sector from those received in food processing, holding constant for the proportionate effects of years of schooling completed, postschooling experience, experience squared, and, in regression 2, rural/urban zone of residence. The choice of food processing as the numeraire is arbitrary and has no effect on the estimated differentials. The food processing sector is a large industry with about average incomes for male employees.

Table 2.A.5 **Relative Wage Effects Associated with Thirty-eight Aggregated 1973 Census Sectors Matched to Trade and Protection Categories: Semilogarithmic Regression for Female Employees**

Industry Number	ISIC Category	Description	Number of Individuals in Regression	Regression Coefficients[a]	
				(1)	(2)
1	11	Agriculture and hunting	758	−.321	−.0562
2	12	Forestry	7	−.124	−.126
3	13	Fishing	9	.344	.387
4	2	Mining	48	−.632	−.506
5	311	Food processing	434	.000	.000
6	312, 31–	Other food processing, not specified above	37	.0779	.109
7	313	Beverage industries	83	.430	.428
8	314	Tobacco manufactures	129	−.193	−.212
9	321	Manufacture of textiles	686	.221	.230
10	322	Manufacture of wearing apparel	1,421	−.0117	−.0125
11	323	Manufacture of leather and leather products	58	.0913	.0868
12	324, 32–	Manufacture of footwear	159	.106	.0966
13	331,33–	Manufacture of wood products	27	−.183	−.177
14	332	Manufacture of wood furniture	40	.236	.221
15	341, 34–	Manufacture of paper and paper products	58	.334	.325
16	342	Printing, publishing, and allied industries	197	.157	.151
17	351	Manufacture of industrial chemicals	36	.507	.506
18	352	Manufacture of other chemicals	246	.263	.262
19	353	Petroleum refineries	9	.768	.776
20	354, 35–	Manufacture of coal and oil derivatives; chemical manufactures not further specified	30	.474	.470
21	355	Manufacture of rubber products	38	.525	.517
22	356	Manufacture of plastic products	88	.227	.217

Table 2.A.5 (continued)

Industry Number	ISIC Category	Description	Number of Individuals in Regression	Regression Coefficients[a]	
				(1)	(2)
23	361, 36–	Manufacture of pottery, china, and earthenware	43	.197	.224
24	362	Manufacture of glass and glass products	21	.350	.339
25	369	Manufactures of other, nonmetallic mineral products	45	.0846	.0740
26	371	Iron and steel basic industries	20	.448	.465
27	372, 37–	Nonferrous metal basic industries	10	−.211	−.180
28	381	Manufacture of metal products, except machinery and equipment	71	.276	.269
29	382	Manufacture of machinery except electrical	27	.538	.541
30	383	Manufacture of electrical equipment	76	.302	.298
31	384	Manufacture of transport equipment	27	.464	.484
32	385, 38–	Manufacture of scientific equipment; manufacture of metals, not further specified	28	.262	.262
33	39, 3–	Other manufacturing, manufacturing not further specified	373	.162	.161
34	41	Electric, gas, steam	46	.426	.434
35	42	Waterworks and supply	18	.475	.482
36	50	Construction	142	.391	.394
37	600–949	Trade, transportation and communication, financial, professional, miscellaneous	324	.301	.309
38	95	Personal services	1,026	−.354	−.373

Table 2.A.5 (continued)

Industry ISIC Number Category Description	Number of Individuals in Regression	Regression Coefficients[a]	
		(1)	(2)
Other conditioning variables (and t-statistics)			
Experience (age − schooling − 7)		.0567	.0553
		(24.)	(24.)
(Experience squared)/100		− .0923	− .0895
		(19.)	(19.)
Years of education		.172	.165
		(48.)	(47.)
Rural/urban zone of residence			− .442
(rural = 1)			(11.)
Constant		5.020	5.077
		(109.)	(110.)
R^2		.476	.486
Standard error of the estimate		.704	.698
F		155.	158.
(Degrees of freedom)		(40,6854)	(41,6853)
Sample size	6,895		

[a]Food processing (ISIC–311) sector is omitted; sectoral coefficients represent, therefore, the proportionate deviation of wages in the specific sector from those received in food processing, holding constant for the proportionate effects of years of schooling completed, postschooling experience, experience squared, and, in regression 2, rural/urban zone of residence. The choice of food processing as the numeraire is arbitrary and has no effect on the estimated differentials. The food processing sector is a large industry with about average incomes for male employees.

Table 2.A.6   **Relative Wage Effects Associated with
Thirty-eight Aggregated 1973 Census Sectors
Matched to Trade and Protection Categories:
Semilogarithmic Regression for Male Employers**

Industry Number	ISIC Category	Description	Number of Individuals in Regression	Regression Coefficients[a]	
				(1)	(2)
1	11	Agriculture and hunting	3,870	−.641	−.140
2	12	Forestry	18	−.477	.0854
3	13	Fishing	17	−.369	−.0720
4	2	Mining	45	−.0786	.0349
5	311	Food processing	267	0.00	0.00
6	312, 31–	Other food processing, not specified above	20	−.131	−.115
7	313	Beverage industries	11	.182	.367
8	314	Tobacco manufactures	5	.450	.359
9	321	Manufacture of textiles	68	.0189	.0162
10	322	Manufacture of wearing apparel	146	−.0435	−.0911
11	323	Manufacture of leather and leather products	38	−.120	−.188
12	324, 32–	Manufacture of footwear	123	−.143	−.306
13	331,33–	Manufacture of wood products	78	−.226	−.211
14	332	Manufacture of wood furniture	156	−.129	−.262
15	341, 34–	Manufacture of paper and paper products	11	.549	.524
16	342	Printing, publishing, and allied industries	62	.417	.368
17	351	Manufacture of industrial chemicals	8	.145	.173
18	352	Manufacture of other chemicals	25	.273	.210
19	353	Petroleum refineries	4	1.14	1.09
20	354, 35–	Manufacture of coal and oil derivatives; chemical manufactures not further specified	2	.0286	.220
21	355	Manufacture of rubber products	6	.310	.162
22	356	Manufacture of plastic products	16	.120	.100

Table 2.A.6 (continued)

Industry Number	ISIC Category	Description	Number of Individuals in Regression	Regression Coefficients[a]	
				(1)	(2)
23	361, 36–	Manufacture of pottery, china, and earthenware	88	− .876	− .783
24	362	Manufacture of glass and glass products	4	.619	.545
25	369	Manufactures of other, nonmetallic mineral products	56	− .0758	− .0836
26	371	Iron and steel basic industries	21	.369	.292
27	372, 37–	Nonferrous metal basic industries	4	.173	.301
28	381	Manufacture of metal products, except machinery and equipment	71	.0823	− .0459
29	382	Manufacture of machinery except electrical	21	.0181	− .0359
30	383	Manufacture of electrical equipment	14	.399	.357
31	384	Manufacture of transport equipment	5	.0021	− .0138
32	385, 38–	Manufacture of scientific equipment; manufacture of metals, not further specified	16	.0673	− .0761
33	39, 3–	Other manufacturing, manufacturing not further specified	129	.213	.157
34	41	Electric, gas, steam	15	− .0247	− .0511
35	42	Waterworks and supply	3	− .544	− .452
36	50	Construction	277	− .0479	− .0927
37	600–949	Trade, transportation and communication, financial, professional, miscellaneous	134	.473	.502
38	95	Personal services	3	− .437	− .456

Table 2.A.6 (continued)

Industry ISIC Number Category Description	Number of Individuals in Regression	Regression Coefficients[a]	
		(1)	(2)
Other conditioning variables (and t-statistics)			
Experience (age − schooling − 7)		.0353	.0312
		(8.44)	(7.69)
(Experience squared)/100		− .0371	− .0345
		(6.54)	(6.28)
Years of education		.187	.155
		(41.)	(33.)
Rural/urban zone of residence			− .863
(rural = 1)			(20.)
Constant		5.94	6.36
		(58.)	(63.)
R^2		.406	.445
Standard error of the estimate		1.08	1.04
F		98.	112.
(Degrees of freedom)		(40,5736)	(41,5735)
Sample size	5,777		

[a]Food processing (ISIC–311) sector is omitted; sectoral coefficients represent, therefore, the proportionate deviation of wages in the specific sector from those received in food processing, holding constant for the proportionate effects of years of schooling completed, postschooling experience, experience squared, and, in regression 2, rural/urban zone of residence. The choice of food processing as the numeraire is arbitrary and has no effect on the estimated differentials. The food processing sector is a large industry with about average incomes for male employees.

Table 2.A.7   **Relative Wage Effects Associated with Thirty-eight Aggregated 1973 Census Sectors Matched to Trade and Protection Categories: Semilogarithmic Regressions for Male Self-Employed**

Industry Number	ISIC Category	Description	Number of Individuals in Regression	Regression Coefficients[a]	
				(1)	(2)
1	11	Agriculture and hunting	6,136	−.573	−.177
2	12	Forestry	97	−.0982	.292
3	13	Fishing	218	−.306	−.128
4	2	Mining	177	−1.64	−1.32
5	311	Food processing	229	0.0	0.0
6	312, 31–	Other food processing, not specified above	10	.0601	.0443
7	313	Beverage industries	18	.120	.0552
8	314	Tobacco manufactures	0	NA	NA
9	321	Manufacture of textiles	60	−.629	−.470
10	322	Manufacture of wearing apparel	269	−.160	−.162
11	323	Manufacture of leather and leather products	43	.321	.274
12	324, 32–	Manufacture of footwear	174	−.178	−.236
13	331,33–	Manufacture of wood products	196	−.0740	−.0241
14	332	Manufacture of wood furniture	273	−.0766	−.0832
15	341, 34–	Manufacture of paper and paper products	11	−.575	−.629
16	342	Printing, publishing, and allied industries	33	.312	.261
17	351	Manufacture of industrial chemicals	6	.0800	.0556
18	352	Manufacture of other chemicals	20	−.468	−.453
19	353	Petroleum refineries	3	−.210	−.121
20	354, 35–	Manufacture of coal and oil derivatives; chemical manufactures not further specified	1	−.172	−.096
21	355	Manufacture of rubber products	11	.616	.543
22	356	Manufacture of plastic products	12	.676	.655

Table 2.A.7 (continued)

Industry Number	ISIC Category	Description	Number of Individuals in Regression	Regression Coefficients[a] (1)	(2)
23	361, 36–	Manufacture of pottery, china, and earthenware	18	−.213	−.239
24	362	Manufacture of glass and glass products	4	.140	.078
25	369	Manufactures of other, nonmetallic mineral products	49	−.184	−.185
26	371	Iron and steel basic industries	9	.577	.528
27	372, 37–	Nonferrous metal basic industries	3	.508	.465
28	381	Manufacture of metal products, except machinery and equipment	91	.242	.229
29	382	Manufacture of machinery except electrical	12	.145	.128
30	383	Manufacture of electrical equipment	6	.845	.823
31	384	Manufacture of transport equipment	8	−.073	−.122
32	385, 38–	Manufacture of scientific equipment; manufacture of metals, not further specified	15	.500	.467
33	39, 3–	Other manufacturing, manufacturing not further specified	130	.225	.220
34	41	Electric, gas, steam	6	.336	.273
35	42	Waterworks and supply	4	.650	.550
36	50	Construction	952	.0694	.0339
37	600–949	Trade, transportation and communication, financial, professional, miscellaneous	167	.543	.525
38	95	Personal services	18	−.386	−.304

Table 2.A.7 (continued)

Industry ISIC Number Category Description	Number of Individuals in Regression	Regression Coefficients[a] (1)	(2)
Other conditioning variables (and t-statistics)			
Experience (age − schooling − 7)		.0495	.0475
		(16.)	(16.)
(Experience squared)/100		− .0617	− .0605
		(14.)	(14.)
Years of education		.157	.138
		(30.)	(26.)
Rural/urban zone of residence			− .610
(rural = 1)			(18.)
Constant		5.43	5.63
		(58.)	(61.)
R^2		.2191	.2443
Standard error of the estimate		1.19	1.17
F		66.	74.
(Degrees of freedom)		(40,9448)	(41,9447)
Sample size		9,489	9,489

[a]Food processing (ISIC–311) sector is omitted; sectoral coefficients represent, therefore, the proportionate deviation of wages in the specific sector from those received in food processing, holding constant for the proportionate effects of years of schooling completed, postschooling experience, experience squared, and, in regression 2, rural/urban zone of residence. The choice of food processing as the numeraire is arbitrary and has no effect on the estimated differentials. The food processing sector is a large industry with about average incomes for male employees.

Table 2.A.8   Within-Sector Semilogarithmic Income Function for Male Employees

Industry Number	ISIC Category	Description	Number of Male Employees	Experience	(Experience Squared)/100	Years of Education	Constant	R^2	Standard Error of the Estimate
1	11	Agriculture and hunting	26,816	.0351 (30.)	−.0491 (26.)	.0885 (32.)	5.34 (336.)	.059	.813
2	12	Forestry	194	.0254 (1.67)	−.0226 (.88)	.187 (10.)	5.42 (27.)	.362	.758
3	13	Fishing	90	.0203 (1.14)	−.0194 (.70)	.128 (4.68)	5.84 (24.)	.205	.767
4	2	Mining	618	.0776 (7.75)	−.110 (6.56)	.209 (.18)	4.89 (35.)	.387	.950
5	311	Food processing	2,379	.0808 (21.)	−.110 (16.)	.180 (35.)	4.98 (99.)	.388	.699
6	312, 31–	Other food processing, not specified above	102	.101 (4.65)	−.158 (4.13)	.187 (8.92)	4.84 (16.)	.455	.745
7	313	Beverage industries	500	.0729 (9.23)	−.0856 (5.46)	.164 (19.)	5.41 (48.)	.452	.574
8	314	Tobacco manufactures	103	.0761 (3.33)	−.0692 (1.47)	.239 (12.)	4.63 (18.)	.628	.740
9	321	Manufacture of textiles	1,486	.0952 (19.)	−.137 (14.)	.197 (35.)	5.04 (69.)	.461	.622
10	322	Manufacture of wearing apparel	509	.0735 (8.27)	−.102 (6.01)	.168 (13.)	5.11 (39.)	.288	.740
11	323	Manufacture of leather and leather products	225	.115 (8.57)	−.171 (6.40)	.181 (11.)	4.71 (28.)	.445	.655
12	324, 32–	Manufacture of footwear	806	.0983 (15.)	−.151 (12.)	.162 (14.)	4.79 (51.)	.312	.722
13	331, 33–	Manufacture of wood products	538	.0706 (10.)	−.100 (8.68)	.158 (13.)	5.15 (48.)	.288	.713

	SIC	Industry	n						
14	342	Manufacture of wood furniture	740	.0676 (11.)	−.0923 (8.20)	.140 (11.)	5.23 (55.)	.225	.714
15	341, 34–	Manufacture of paper and paper products	218	.0745 (6.19)	−.0784 (3.38)	.216 (16.)	4.99 (28.)	.548	.656
16	342	Printing, publishing, and allied industries	494	.0822 (13.)	−.104 (8.22)	.161 (17.)	5.32 (57.)	.493	.564
17	351	Manufacture of industrial chemicals	161	.101 (6.02)	−.141 (4.35)	.229 (15.)	4.76 (20.)	.609	.621
18	352	Manufacture of other chemicals	386	.0857 (8.37)	−.110 (4.98)	.207 (27.)	4.98 (41.)	.656	.624
19	353	Petroleum refineries	91	.0714 (3.67)	−.0883 (2.07)	.148 (7.71)	5.94 (20.)	.428	.510
20	354, 35–	Manufacture of coal and oil derivatives; chemical manufactures not further specified	90	.0819 (4.38)	−.106 (2.53)	.213 (15.)	5.03 (23.)	.719	.544
21	355	Manufacture of rubber products	138	.0769 (4.30)	−.101 (2.93)	.181 (11.)	5.32 (22.)	.475	.670
22	356	Manufacture of plastic products	153	.0903 (5.63)	−.117 (3.45)	.178 (11.)	5.07 (24.)	.466	.667
23	361, 36–	Manufacture of pottery, china and earthenware	159	.0941 (5.62)	−.149 (4.72)	.135 (6.53)	5.18 (23.)	.275	.662
24	362	Manufacture of glass and glass products	164	.0823 (7.54)	−.0903 (4.20)	.210 (15.)	4.93 (32.)	.604	.544
25	369	Manufacture of other nonmetallic mineral products	712	.0805 (9.73)	−.111 (7.02)	.179 (19.)	4.99 (49.)	.363	.748
26	371	Iron and steel basic industries	318	.0731 (7.63)	−.105 (5.69)	.176 (18.)	5.40 (39.)	.496	.541
27	372, 37–	Nonferrous metal basic industries	100	.0829 (4.07)	−.0998 (2.30)	.160 (7.07)	5.24 (20.)	.389	.549

Table 2.A.8 (continued)

Industry Number	ISIC Category	Description	Number of Male Employees	Experience	(Experience Squared)/100	Years of Education	Constant	R^2	Standard Error of the Estimate
28	381	Manufacture of metal products, except machinery and equipment	562	.0856 (12.)	−.129 (9.28)	.171 (16.)	5.09 (48.)	.369	.677
29	382	Manufacture of machinery except electrical	211	.0889 (8.47)	−.132 (6.33)	.169 (13.)	5.24 (35.)	.493	.508
30	383	Manufacture of electrical equipment	293	.0853 (8.70)	−.0962 (4.34)	.175 (16.)	5.17 (39.)	.532	.534
31	384	Manufacture of transport equipment	251	.0946 (7.61)	−.137 (5.07)	.186 (16.)	5.14 (34.)	.541	.598
32	385, 38–	Manufacture of scientific equipment; manufacture of metals, not further specified	38	.0889 (5.38)	−.111 (2.95)	.180 (12.)	5.14 (27.)	.522	.583
33	39, 3–	Other manufacturing, manufacturing not further specified	1,003	.0995 (17.)	−.151 (12.)	.193 (30.)	4.86 (67.)	.507	.631
34	41	Electric, gas, steam	449	.0695 (9.41)	−.0967 (7.01)	.151 (20.)	5.60 (50.)	.482	.485
35	42	Waterworks and supply	178	.0660 (5.16)	−.0832 (3.66)	.169 (14.)	5.44 (29.)	.537	.585
36	50	Construction	5,408	.0610 (24.)	−.0818 (18.)	.153 (40.)	5.25 (146.)	.256	.744
37	600–949	Trade, transportation and communication, financial, professional, miscellaneous	769	.0769 (12.)	−.111 (9.05)	.190 (32.)	5.25 (62.)	.577	.634
38	95	Personal services	298	.0777 (6.93)	−.113 (5.60)	.164 (7.78)	4.70 (37.)	.241	.757

**Table 2.A.9   Variable Means and Standard Deviation
for 1973 Census Sample of Employees**

Explanatory Variable	Male	Female	Both Sexes
Number of persons	47,875	6,895	54,770
Years of schooling	3.13 (3.02)	4.81 (3.13)	3.34 (3.09)
Years of experience (age − schooling − 7)	21.8 (14.2)	15.8 (11.5)	21.0 (14.1)
(Experience squared)/100	6.76 (8.31)	3.83 (5.56)	6.39 (8.07)
Actual wages (pesos per month)	980.5 (1624.)	909.4 (981.5)	971.5 (1558.)
Actual wages urban sector	1,469 (2139.)	965.8 (1010.)	1,363
Actual wages rural sector	512.3 (577.3)	390.3 (386.7)	572.3
Percentage of employees in urban sector	48.9	90.2	54.1

Table 2.A.10   **Relative Wage Effect of Schooling within Sectors and Predicted Sectoral Wage for Representative Worker**

Industrial Sector Code	Schooling Coefficient within Industries[a]		Wage Predicted within Industry[b]	
	Male	Female	Male	Female
1	.08852	.17587	429.00	359.94
2	.18668	.27611	626.97	100.25
3	.12822	.18225	711.30	1625.9
4	.20848	.46057	672.39	168.19
5	.17985	.17331	714.97	490.14
6	.18717	.16219	720.26	463.76
7	.16352	.17698	1032.4	771.78
8	.23859	.22335	722.52	416.88
9	.19721	.19189	920.05	570.87
10	.16811	.14593	707.77	473.73
11	.18063	.22539	751.65	524.55
12	.16207	.13227	625.79	618.85
13	.15799	.20308	681.34	340.43
14	.13995	.15618	685.89	641.91
15	.21555	.19271	874.78	657.35
16	.16068	.14895	1010.2	622.76
17	.22912	.17002	852.05	971.31
18	.20662	.19807	872.31	586.38
19	.14752	.20534	1583.7	752.22
20	.21344	.17076	884.81	922.89
21	.18129	.11218	984.77	1031.1
22	.17757	.14791	912.27	611.57
23	.13540	.17964	782.11	623.31
24	.20950	.13416	885.50	936.39
25	.17929	.21194	716.54	456.08
26	.17623	.17272	944.22	762.06
27	.15961	.24480	969.50	677.72
28	.17126	.20819	764.56	635.53
29	.16846	.20245	923.34	841.23
30	.17481	.13625	1022.0	845.44
31	.18599	.17218	964.43	817.39
32	.18043	.23588	991.89	239.85
33	.19275	.17557	755.39	593.20
34	.15085	.06676	1042.6	1345.1
35	.16878	.22564	947.88	573.55
36	.15300	.16992	679.68	730.42
37	.19029	.18411	890.23	611.67
38	.16408	.10981	475.34	330.49

[a]Obtained from within-industry regressions of logarithm of monthly income on schooling and quadratic in postschooling experience. See appendix table 2.A.8.
[b]Coefficients from within-industry male income functions reported in appendix table 2.A.8 are multiplied by sample mean characteristics for both men and women reported in appendix table 2.A.9 to obtain industry predicted wage for males. Underlying income functions for women not reported.

Notes

1. Balassa (1965) incorporates tariffs on traded inputs that are contained in nontraded inputs. Appendix table 2.A.1 reports the level of Colombian effective protection as of 1970 according to both the Corden and the Balassa procedures. The Corden index is somewhat less variable than the Balassa index, though industry orderings are very similar. The regression results reported are based on the Corden index as indicated in the text.

2. Input-output coefficients required to infer the indirect requirements per unit of output are often insufficiently disaggregated or matched to the categories available in trade and tariff schedules (Corden 1974). Moreover, some degree of averaging of tariffs across heterogeneous sectors is unavoidable, preferably with domestic production weights, with potentially serious error (Tumlir and Tilly 1971). Finally, of course, the method is essentially a partial equilibrium approach. The only alternative is to specify, often from very limited data, a vastly more complex general equilibrium system to evaluate the consequences of trade distortions or perhaps employ a disaggregated programming model that also neglects substitution possibilities with fixed factor proportions (Evans 1971: Henderson, this volume, chap. 1).

3. The "best solution" is free trade without domestic distortions, but in the presence of certain domestic distortions it is often preferable to subsidize the factor whose market price exceeds its shadow price (Corden 1974). An exception is the Todaro (1969) model in which rural/urban migration and urban unemployment leads to a rejection of manufacturing wage subsidy argument. In this domestic distortion framework, with urban unemployment providing the clearing mechanism between the rural and urban wage differential, the best solution becomes a subsidy to agricultural wage (employment) that reduces the social loss of urban unemployment (Bhagwati and Srinivasan 1974; Corden and Findlay 1975).

4. One might anticipate that industries with effective protection rates on labor above a uniform rate on labor should contract in the long run as a more uniform rate is adopted, and that those currently below the uniform rate should expand. But this is far from certain, given the general equilibrium relations that are neglected in the effective protection formulation. In addition to the composition of tradables adapting to the structure of incentives provided by effective protection rates across industries, the relative returns to factors are also likely to change, if the factor proportions in the more protected industries differ from the average. A uniform rate of effective protection on labor is justified on the basis of encouraging disproportionately industries with greater labor content in their value added. This protection strategy provides an inducement for using more labor-intensive techniques within industries as well as for shifting the composition of tradables toward the more labor-intensive sectors (Corden 1974).

5. There is no obvious way to determine how much effective protection is required to establish domestic production in the face of domestic handicaps such as small scale, skill constraints, technology, and limitations of management. Thus there is no way to estimate the residual amount of "excess" effective protection remaining as an incentive to reallocate factors of production. Better data than are available here might permit one to develop a dynamic "infant industry" framework that would estimate factor supply elasticities and the sources of changing total factor productivity by sector, and hence the time dimension to production costs or a learning-by-doing accumulation of expertise. A more finely disaggregated breakdown of industry would, of course, facilitate such an analysis, and information on the size of firms might serve as a useful proxy for the continuum of modern to traditional technologies that coexist in many sectors of the Colombian economy (Nelson, Schultz, and Slighton 1971).

6. Because Hutcheson and Schydlowsky (1977) did not have reliable capital stock figures by sector for Colombia, they calculated the incentive effects of effective protection relative to sectoral cash flow, their choice of the best proxy available for current value of capital stock.

7. Such distributional effects are *thought* to be important in Colombia. Hutcheson and Schydlowsky (1977), among others, cite evidence that trade, tax, and subsidy policies were on balance responsible for reducing substantially the cost of capital, particularly capital imports, and raising the cost of labor. Díaz-Alejandro (1976) reports that these factor price distortions caused Colombia in the 1960s to export capital-intensive commodities.

8. This can be seen in the last columns of appendix table 2.A.1.

9. Berry and Díaz-Alejandro (1977) express doubt that the "new" Colombian exports have proved to be labor-intensive and to have contributed to a reduction in income inequality.

10. It might be more realistic to assume that ω embodies both the estimation error of δ and a stochastic error. In this case the appropriate weight would be the inverse of the sum of the variance of the estimation error of δ (used here) and the variance of the stochastic error. Following the simpler error specification set forth in the text, round-off errors in computation are reduced by partitioning the variance/covariance matrix of the estimated coefficients from equation (3) as follows: $X'X = \begin{pmatrix} A & B \\ B' & D \end{pmatrix}$, where A is the three-by-three matrix corresponding to the coefficients on education, experience, and experience squared variables in X, D is the I-by-I diagonal matrix corresponding to the number of persons in each of the I industries, and B and B' are the remaining matrixes of dimension 3-by-I and I-by-3, respectively. The "covariance" matrix of weights used here is expressed as $(D - B'A^{-1}B)^{-1}$. If the covariances between the industry dummies and the education, experience, and experience squared variables, $B'A^{-1}B$, is sufficiently small, the "worker" weights, D^{-1}, provide satisfactory estimates (compare panels B and C in table 2.5).

11. Also, agriculture is no longer divided into livestock and crops versus hunting and agricultural services (3 percent of the agricultural total), and wood products other than furniture no longer distinguishes a residual "not-specified-elsewhere" group (15 percent of wood products other than furniture).

12. These three sectors are coal and oil derivatives; other chemicals, scientific equipment, etc.; and a sizable miscellaneous grouping of manufactured products.

13. The International Coffee Agreement, subscribed to by Colombia, could be used to discourage coffee production. This policy could be premised on the assumption that the world price for Colombian coffee will increase by a greater proportion than the proportion by which exports are restricted, increasing export revenues. The tax on coffee producers is rationalized in terms of judgments on the elasticity of world coffee demand and supply schedules, which are beyond the scope of this investigation. Although the export tax on coffee is a distortion in the static sense that contributes to the low level of factor returns in agriculture, negative protection is not the only reason for low labor incomes in Colombian agriculture.

14. Between 75 and 90 percent of male employees in various age groups reported a monthly income. Nonresponses are omitted from the sample. Eight male employees out of 47,868 were eliminated from the file for reporting unreasonably large incomes. The rule applied was that those with more than 20,000 pesos monthly incomes and no more than a primary education were dropped from the file, as was any employee with a monthly income over 50,000 pesos. No employers or self-employed workers were eliminated, since capital income might explain their response.

15. The self-employed are a much more heterogeneous group than employers or employees, particularly when rural and urban sectors are combined. Only a few illustrative regressions were calculated for male self-employed (see table 2.4 and table 2.A.7).

16. The simple unweighted correlation between the male and female sectoral income effect obtained from estimating equation (3) as reported in appendix tables 2.A.5 and 2.A.6 is 0.78, based on the following regression:

ln female income = .22 + .84 ln male income $R^2 = .61$
                          (1.56) (7.48)   sample size 38

where t ratios are reported beneath the regression coefficients in parentheses. The female employee income data would be less suited to our purposes even if women were more numerous, since women more often work part time than do men, and the monthly income reported in the census does not take account of this. Also, the postschooling experience variable (i.e., age-schooling-7) may be a reasonable proxy for accumulated labor market experience across men, but it introduces much noise for women, whose attachment to the labor force is more often interrupted over the life cycle.

17. Because the dependent variable is the logarithm of the income variable and the effective protection variable is the percentage of value added, the elasticity is the regression coefficient multiplied by one hundred. The confidence intervals around the point estimates are very narrow. For all traded sectors, two standard deviations above and below the point estimate should include the "true" value with 95 percent probability. This range is from 1.30 to 1.18. For the manufacturing sectors alone, the analogous range is from .402 to .276.

18. The measure of installed horsepower per worker has a variety of limitations, in addition to its partial representation of multifaceted capital stock. By not reflecting how much time the capital stock is actually used, a firm with several shifts of workers would report much lower "capital stock" per worker than a comparable firm working only a single shift. If depreciation and obsolescence of the capital stock were independent of its rate of utilization, then installed capacity might still be a defensible proxy for the opportunity cost of capital per worker. Conversely, if the opportunity cost of capital increased proportionately with its rate of utilization, then installed capacity would misrepresent capital costs across firms with different numbers of shifts of workers. The former assumption is closer to reality than the latter. Installed horsepower capacity per worker may not adequately convey differences in capital available per worker at a moment in production that is associated with technology. Value added per worker, on the other hand, mixes returns to physical and human capital into a more comprehensive measure of "inputs" employed per worker. But, in the current study, this combination of human and physical capital blurs the distinction on which the analysis is based. The direct standardization of the labor force by its human capital characteristics makes it even less clear what value added per worker measures in this context.

19. For example, the simple correlation between the industry effects, that is the δs in model 2, estimated with and without allowing for the rural/urban shift in incomes are correlated across sectors at .99 (table 2.A.4, regressions 1 and 2). The rankings of sectors are therefore not particularly sensitive to the inclusion of the rural/urban dummy variable, but the magnitude of the slope coefficient in a subsequent regression on effective protection is reduced by its inclusion. Specifically, agricultural incomes are 46 percent lower than food processing (the omitted category in table 2.A.4) when the rural/urban dummy is excluded, but only 33 percent lower when it is included. The average absolute magnitude (unweighted) of the industry coefficients is reduced by 8 percent when the rural/urban dummy is included.

20. Small "self-employed" farmers often hire additional labor in peak periods of seasonal demand and work for wages off-the-farm at other times during the year. They do not, therefore, fit neatly into one category of "employment type" as provided on the census questionnaire. How they categorize themselves is unclear, though most who rely on family unpaid labor to meet their swings in excess demand for labor probably are counted as independent self-employed. Tenant and sharecropping farmers may also fail to assign themselves consistently to this self-employed category.

21. The heterogeneity of the self-employed category of workers is reflected in the tendency for self-employed to have a higher income than employees in the urban sector, but a lower income than employees in the rural sector of the Colombian economy. More generally, the simple correlation of incomes of male employees and employers by sector is high, .78 for the full sample of thirty-two traded and untraded sectors. But for employees and self-employed, the correlation by sector is only .32, and for employers and self-employed it falls to .14. Thus, little effort is expended here to account for the variation in self-employed incomes.

22. The simple correlation between a measure of the education intensity of a sector's

male labor force and its Corden index of effective protection is .47 across the twenty-six traded sectors. The measure of education intensity used here is the proportion of the male employees with at least some secondary schooling divided by the national average, that is, 0.2478.

23. For example, the work force in the electrical equipment manufacturing sector had a better than average education, and therefore the pesos increase in employee incomes in that sector associated with its 59.2 percent level of effective protection would be greater than the same level of protection would elicit in a sector with a less educated labor force. All workers are treated equally in this illustrative calculation of summary effects. If a general equilibrium framework were available, the net distributional effect for all employment groups and sectors in the population should approach zero, but within portions of the economy for portions of the work force, no such aggregation constraints are even suggested.

24. The male employee income elasticity estimated directly for all traded sectors is 1.24 (table 2.1, regression 6). This parameter estimate would imply that the structure of protection in Colombia was associated in 1970–73 with a gross redistribution of 24 percent of male employee incomes, with a net effect of decreasing male employee incomes by one-fifth.

References

Balassa, B. 1965. Tariff protection in industrial countries: An evaluation. *Journal of Political Economy* 73:573–94.

Basevi, G. 1971. Aggregation problems in the measurement of effective protection. In *Effective tariff protection*, ed. H. G. Grubel and H. G. Johnson. Geneva: GATT and Graduate Institute of International Studies.

Berry, R. A., and Díaz-Alejandro, C. F. 1977. The new Colombian exports: Possible effects on the distribution of income. Yale University. Mimeographed

Bhagwati, J. N., and Srinivasan, T. N. 1974. On reanalyzing the Harris-Todaro model: Policy rankings in the case of sector specific sticky wages. *American Economic Review* 64:502–8.

Corden, W.M. 1966. The structure of a tariff system and the effective protection rate. *Journal of Political Economy* 74:221–37.

———. 1971. *The theory of protection*. Oxford: Clarendon Press.

———. 1974. *Trade policy and economic welfare*. Oxford: Clarendon Press.

———. 1975. The costs and consequences of protection: A survey of empirical work. In *International trade and finance*, ed. P. B. Kenen, pp. 51–92. Cambridge: Cambridge University Press.

Corden, W. M., and Findlay, R. 1975. Urban unemployment, intersectoral capital mobility, and development policy. *Economica* 42:59–78.

Departamento Administrativo Nacional de Estadística (DANE). N.d. *Industria manfacturera nacionale 1969*. Bogotá: DANE.

Díaz-Alejandro, C. F. 1976. *Foreign trade regimes and economic development: Colombia*. New York: National Bureau of Economic Research.

Evans, H. S. 1971. The empirical specification of a general equilibrium model of protection in Australia. In *Effective tariff protection*, ed. H. G. Grubel and H. G. Johnson. Geneva: GATT and Graduate Institute of International Studies.

Fields, G. S., and Schultz, T. P. 1977. Sources of income variation in Colombia: Personal and regional effects. Discussion Paper no. 262. Economic Growth Center, Yale University.

Grubel, H. G., and Johnson, H. G., eds. 1971. *Effective tariff protection*. Geneva: GATT and Graduate Institute of International Studies.

Hutcheson, T. 1973. Incentives for industrialization in Colombia. Ph.D. diss., University of Michigan.

Hutcheson, T., and Schydlowsky, D. M. 1977. Incentives for industrialization in Colombia. Boston University. Mimeographed.

Johnson, H. G. 1965. The theory of tariff structure, with special reference to world trade and development. In *Trade and development*, ed. H. G. Johnson and P. Kenen. Geneva: Librairie Droz.

Jones, R. W. 1971. Effective protection and substitution. *Journal of International Economics* 1:59–82.

Krueger, A. O. 1966. Some economic cost of exchange control: The Turkish case. *Journal of Political Economy* 74:466–80.

———. 1974. The political economy of the rent-seeking society. *American Economic Review* 64:291–303.

———. 1977. *Growth, distortions, and patterns of trade among many countries*. Graham Lectures, Princeton Studies in International Finance, no. 40. Princeton: International Finance Section, Princeton University.

Krueger, A. O.; Lary, H. B.; Monson, T.; and Akrasanee, N., eds. 1981. *Trade and employment in developing countries*. Vol. 1. *Individual studies*. Chicago: University of Chicago Press for National Bureau of Economic Research.

Kuznets, S. 1971. *Economic growth of nations: Total output and production structure*. Cambridge: Harvard University Press.

Little, I.; Scitovsky, T.; and Scott, M. 1970. *Industry and trade in some developing countries*. London: Oxford University Press.

Mincer, J. 1974. *Schooling, experience and earnings*. New York: Columbia University Press for National Bureau of Economic Research.

Musalem, A. R. 1970. Demand for money and balance of payments: The experience of Colombia, 1950–1967. Economic Development Report no. 117. Cambridge: Harvard University.

Nelson, R. R.; Schultz, T. P.; and Slighton, R. L. 1971. *Structural change in a developing economy: Colombia's problems and prospects*. Princeton: Princeton University Press.

Schultz, T. P. 1971. Rural-urban migration in Colombia. *Review of Economics and Statistics*, vol. 53.

Thoumi, F. E. 1977. International trade strategies, employment and income distribution in Colombia. Inter-American Development Bank. Mimeographed.

———. 1978. Colombian *t* values by ISIC codes. Worksheets for NBER Project on Alternative Trade Strategies and Employment.

———. 1980. Industrial development policies during the National Front years. In *Politics of compromise: Coalition government in Colombia*, ed. R. A. Berry, R. Hellman, and M. Soluan, pp. 327–40. New Brunswick, N.J.: Transaction Books.

Todaro, M. P. 1969. A model of labor migration and urban unemployment in less developed countries. *American Economic Review* 59:138–48.

Tumlir, J., and Tilly, L. 1971. Tariff averaging in international comparison. In *Effective tariff protection*, ed. H. G. Grubel and H. G. Johnson. Geneva: GATT and Graduate Institute of International Studies.

3 Brazilian Export Growth: Estimating the Export Supply Response, 1955–74

José L. Carvalho and Cláudio L. S. Haddad

3.1 Introduction

That there was a rapid increase in Brazil's exports from the mid-1960s onward may be seen from table 3.1. Total exports, which were $1.4 billion in 1955, were only marginally above that level in 1965, and manufactured exports constituted only 16 percent of total exports. By contrast, export growth "took off" over the following decade. By 1975, total export earnings were $7.9 billion, almost five times their 1965 level, and manufactured exports had risen sharply to $2.4 billion, increasing at an average annual rate of 33.4 percent. Not only manufactured exports, but many natural resource based (NRB) commodities shared in the export boom,[1] while earnings from traditional exports, notably coffee, grew only slowly.

In analyzing the trade strategy–employment relationship, the Brazil study in this project took as a given the rapid expansion of Brazil's exports in the late 1960s and early 1970s (Carvalho and Haddad 1978). It is the purpose of this chapter to analyze the degree to which that boom was a function of the policy changes undertaken in the late 1960s. The export promotion strategy began haltingly in 1965, and it gained momentum over the next several years. By 1968, incentives for exporting had been raised significantly. The strategy was based on two main policy instruments: fiscal incentives and the mini-devaluations. The strategy

José L. Carvalho and Cláudio L. S. Haddad are associated with the Escola de Pós-Graduação em Econômica, Fundação Getúlio Vargas, Brazil.

We would like to thank Anne O. Krueger and Hal B. Lary for comments, suggestions, and encouragement. This paper is a condensed version of the second part of chapter 4 of *Foreign Trade Strategies and Employment in Brazil*, research under the NBER project on alternative trade strategies and employment. Financial support was provided by NBER, through a grant by the United States Agency for International Development, and by the Brazilian Ministry of Finance.

Table 3.1   **Brazilian Exports, Broad Commodity Categories, 1955–74**
                           (F.o.b., Millions of U.S. Dollars)

Year	Total	Coffee	Noncoffee	Manufactures	NRB[a]
			Exports		
1955	1,423	844	579	51	528
1956	1,482	1,030	452	52	400
1957	1,392	846	546	64	482
1958	1,243	688	555	67	488
1959	1,282	744	538	81	457
1960	1,269	713	556	72	484
1961	1,403	710	693	104	589
1962	1,214	643	571	83	488
1963	1,406	747	659	84	575
1964	1,430	760	670	132	538
1965	1,595	707	888	263	625
1966	1,741	764	977	197	780
1967	1,654	705	949	248	701
1968	1,881	775	1,106	263	843
1969	2,311	813	1,498	361	1,137
1970	2,739	939	1,800	527	1,273
1971	2,904	773	2,131	663	1,468
1972	3,991	989	3,002	1,044	1,958
1973	6,199	1,244	4,955	1,528	3,427
1974	7,951	864	7,087	2,360	4,727

SOURCE: Carvalho and Haddad 1978, appendix table.

[a]NRB = total exports minus coffee exports minus exports of manufactures.

received additional support from the import liberalization measures taken in 1966 and 1967 (Carvalho and Haddad 1978, chaps. 2, 3, and 4).

In this chapter we present and discuss new estimates of Brazilian export supply functions, trying to measure the effect of the main policy instruments, as well as the other exogenous variables, on export growth. Although there are some very good earlier analyses of the impressive export performance,[2] they cover a relatively short period. We therefore decided to estimate new regressions, for manufactures and noncoffee NRB goods, covering the period 1955–74. First we will make some general comments regarding the estimation of export supply functions, then we will analyze the independent variables included in the estimates.

3.2 Some Aspects of the Estimation of Export Supply Functions

Specifying an export supply function poses some special problems, because the supply of exports is an excess supply, equal to the difference between the total domestic supply and the total domestic demand for the particular product. Hence the supply of exports is affected by forces that influence both domestic supply and domestic demand. But in a general equilibrium framework, which is relevant once we estimate an aggregate supply function, forces that affect demand also affect supply, and conversely. Thus a proper specification of an export supply function is especially difficult, particularly for Brazil because of data limitations.

There is yet another problem involving the estimation itself. If the so-called small-country hypothesis is accepted, foreign prices would be exogenous, and the structural form of the model could be estimated by ordinary least squares. But then why should we include a proxy for the volume of world trade, like total world imports, in the estimates? When we do so we are assuming, implicitly, that shifts in foreign demand affect Brazilian exports. But, given the small-country hypothesis, foreign demand would influence Brazilian exports only through the indirect effect upon world prices, which would theoretically be captured by the real exchange rate or another price variable. So there would be no room to include the level of world trade, given the assumption of an infinitely elastic foreign demand.

When included in the estimates, however, the level of world imports always turns up highly significant. Furthermore, that is in accord with the feelings and statements of most policymakers and businessmen in Brazil. On the other hand, to abandon the small-country hypothesis does not seem very sensible. Except for coffee, and in recent periods soybeans, it is very hard to see how Brazil could significantly influence the world prices of her other major NRB goods, not to mention manufactures. So how can we reconcile the empirical results and general intuition with the fact that Brazil is essentially a price taker in foreign markets? We do not have a definite answer to this question, but a possible explanation lies in terms of short run versus long run. The idea is that in the short run foreign demand may be relatively price inelastic (in the very short run it is certainly vertical) although it is perfectly elastic in the long run. This explanation, advanced by Harberger (1972), can be rationalized in two ways: first, by recognizing the existence of transaction and information costs that delay the response of foreign demand to changes in prices; second, by assuming that, though perfectly elastic in the long run, foreign demand would be subject to volume limitations. This would be the case if quotas were imposed abroad limiting the quantity of Brazilian products imported. The quotas could be either institutional barriers, government contracts, or ad hoc, as, for instance, the reluctance of importers to change drastically the share of each of their foreign suppliers.[3] In any of those cases, the expansion of world trade would have also an expansionary effect on Brazilian exports.

Therefore the export supply functions that were estimated are taken as reduced forms of a model we do not attempt to specify fully. But some comment is needed on the variables included and on the expected and realized signs of the coefficients. The independent variables normally included in the estimates are discussed below.

3.2.1   Real Exchange Rate

The real exchange rate should incorporate the price effect on exports. For manufactures it is defined in two alternative ways: gross and net of subsidies to exports. The index of fiscal incentives was obtained from Tyler (1976, p. 220). We also introduced separately the real exchange rate and the subsidy index. Normally we should expect that the coefficients of the two variables would be similar to each other, since for the exporters an increase in the exchange rate should be the same as an equivalent increase in the subsidy rates. However, some factors may account for the difference in the coefficients: errors of measurement in the subsidy index; or the fact that, since imported inputs are used in export activities, a 10 percent increase in the nominal subsidy may have a more powerful effect than a devaluation of 10 percent, and, on the other hand, the higher administrative costs and the discretionary effects associated with the subsidies as compared with the devaluation.

The real exchange rate for manufactures is here defined as the product of the nominal rate received by exporters and the wholesale price index in the United States divided by a similar index in Brazil. For NRB goods we will substitute, alternatively, an index of dollar prices of noncoffee exports for the wholesale price index in the United States. Both rates are presented in table 3.2. Since fiscal incentives were granted only for manufactures, that variable was not included in the NRB equations.

3.2.2   The Variation of the Real Exchange Rate

As we mention elsewhere (Carvalho and Haddad 1978, chap. 4), one of the deterrents to export expansion until 1968 was the high risk involved in export activities owing to infrequent massive devaluations, common to countries under fixed exchange rate regimes and subjected to high rates of inflation. Supplicy (1976) handled this problem by introducing in his equations the annual average of absolute changes in the real exchange rate. Since what should matter is the relative and not the absolute risk, however, we decided to use instead the coefficient of variation (the standard deviation divided by the average) of the monthly real exchange rates during the year. The coefficient of variation of the real average export exchange rate is presented in table 3.2.

3.2.3   World Imports

We have already commented upon the role played by this variable and the possible rationales for it. In the estimates, world imports are the total dollar amount (c.i.f.) of imports of the United States, the United Kingdom, Japan, France, Germany, Italy, and the Netherlands deflated by the wholesale price index in the United States.

Table 3.2   Real Exchange Rate and Its Coefficient of Variation, 1955–74

Year	Real Exchange Rate for Manufactures[a] (1)	Real Exchange Rate Including Fiscal Incentives[b] (2)	Coefficient of Variation of Rate 1[c] (3)	Real Exchange Rate for NRB Products[d] (4)
1955	2,850	2,850	.1074	3,236
1956	3,398	3,398	.1245	2,457
1957	2,187	2,187	.1299	2,359
1958	3,315	3,315	.1124	3,292
1959	2,815	2,815	.0761	2,668
1960	2,600	2,600	.0761	2,613
1961	2,647	2,647	.0670	2,613
1962	2,517	2,517	.0867	1,982
1963	2,122	2,122	.0867	1,718
1964	2,583	2,589	.1666	2,197
1965	2,552	2,675	.0588	2,063
1966	2,190	2,426	.0922	1,821
1967	2,080	2,527	.0458	1,850
1968	2,216	2,852	.0346	1,948
1969	2,319	3,102	.0243	1,918
1970	2,272	3,166	.0187	1,864
1971	2,224	3,458	.0105	1,890
1972	2,215	3,678	.0076	1,971
1973	2,241	3,720	.0174	2,473
1974	2,287	3,797	.0403	2,732

[a]Export exchange rate times the wholesale price index in the United States (IMF, *International Financial Statistics*) divided by the wholesale price index in Brazil (column 12, *Conjuntura Econômica*).

[b]Column 1 divided by the index of fiscal incentives to exports of manufactures computed by Tyler (1976, p. 220). See note 4.

[c]Coefficients of variation computed within each year from monthly observations of the real exchange rate of column 1.

[d]Computed in the same way as rate 1, substituting the dollar price of noncoffee Brazilian exports (*Conjuntura Econômica*) for the wholesale price index in the United States. Both indexes are equal to 100 in 1970, therefore rates 1, 2, and 4 are comparable.

3.2.4   Domestic Income

Since exports are the difference between domestic supply and domestic demand, they should be affected by the growth in domestic income. However, when the country grows, both domestic demand and domestic supply are shifted, and therefore the expected overall effect of growth on exports is ambiguous. The variable included in the estimates is an index of Brazilian gross domestic real output.

3.2.5   Short-Run Changes in Income

Besides being affected by the level of income, which enters the estimates as a scale factor, exports might be affected by short-run expansion or contraction in domestic output above or below its normal trend. This is the so-called capacity-utilization variable used in previous studies. The sign of the coefficient of this variable is ambiguous, since it depends on whether the cause of the disturbance originates on the demand side or the supply side. The capacity variable used was computed as the ratio between real output (with three alternative definitions) and its long-run geometric trend estimated by least squares.

3.3   The New Estimates

In table 3.3 we present our best estimates concerning exports of manufactures and of NRB goods other than coffee. Alternative (and less satisfactory) models are also presented in Carvalho and Haddad (1978).

The estimates of manufactures yielded very good results. In equation (i) we separate the real exchange rate from the fiscal incentives, although in equation (ii) they are combined in an "effective exchange rate." We can see from equation (i) that the price elasticity due exclusively to the real exchange rate is about 1.2 and the elasticity of fiscal incentives is near 0.6, or about half.[4] Therefore, according to our estimates, a simple devaluation would be more stimulative to exports of manufactures than the same percentage increase in fiscal incentives. Bureaucracy and redundancy may explain that result.[5] In equation (ii) the combined price elasticity is equal to one. The coefficients of the real exchange rate are significantly different from zero at 1 percent significance in both equations.

The coefficient of variation of the real exchange rate enters with a negative sign, implying that the higher the exchange rate risk the lower would be the volume of exports. Its coefficient is not, however, statistically different from zero at 10 percent significance.

As mentioned above, the world imports variable has also a positive and highly significant coefficient in both equations. Real GDP does not turn up significant, but if we estimate equation (ii) without the world imports variable the GDP coefficient becomes equal to 2.26 with a t-value of 11.50. That is, we need a scale factor in our model, and that role is played by either world imports or GDP.[6] When both are included, however, the world imports variable captures most of the explanation of the variance of manufacturing exports, which indicates that the overall growth in world trade is in fact an important variable explaining annual changes in Brazilian exports of manufactures. Finally, the capacity utilization variable appears with a negative coefficient,[7] which indicates that, on average, excess capacity in industry favored increased exports of manufactures.[8]

As a test of whether there was a "structural change" in the export supply function in the mid-1960s, we performed a Chow test for the periods 1955–64 and 1965–74. The F statistic was 3.586 for the hypothesis that the two periods belong to the same structure, with a critical F for 95

Table 3.3   Estimates of Export Supply Functions: Annual Data, 1955–74

Dependent Variable	Independent Variables and t – Coefficients											
	Constant	LREX	LFIX	L(REX/FIX)	LREX1	CVREX	LGDP	LWM	CAPI	R^2	F	DW
Manufactures												
LMANEX (i)	-11.248	1.246	-0.580			-0.0002	-1.204	2.825	-0.576	0.998	179.1	1.58
	(5.87)	(3.37)	(-0.77)			(-1.21)	(-1.44)	(3.93)	(-0.76)			
LMANEX (ii)	-10.608			1.050		-0.0001	-0.756	2.292	-0.732	0.998	229.0	1.72
	(3.65)			(3.65)		(-0.82)	(-1.04)	(4.22)	(-1.44)			
NRB noncoffee												
LNRBNC (iii)	-5.031				0.258	-0.0001	0.345	0.753		0.974	140.0	2.05
	(-7.73)				(2.01)	(-1.10)	(0.76)	(2.22)				

NOTES:
L before a variable means logarithm on base e.

MANEX = exports of manufactures in real dollars; deflator used: wholesale price index in the United States.

NRBNC = exports of noncoffee NRB goods in real dollars; deflator used: index of dollar prices of Brazilian noncoffee exports.

REX = real exchange rate for manufactures; deflators used: wholesale price indexes in Brazil and United States.

FIX = index of fiscal incentives, equal to the inverse of total incentives given to manufactures.

REX1 = real exchange rate substituting the dollar prices of Brazilian noncoffee exports for the wholesale price index in the United States.

CVREX = coefficient of variation of REX during the year; computed from monthly observations.

GDP = Brazilian gross domestic product in real terms (index).

WM = imports of the United States, Germany, United Kingdom, Japan, France, Netherlands, and Italy in real dollars; deflator used: wholesale price index in the United States.

CAPI = ratio of the industrial product index to its long-run trend.

percent confidence level of 3.64. The test therefore marginally accepts the hypothesis of no structural changes.

These results enable one to attempt an estimate of the extent to which changes in the real exchange rate contributed to the spectacular expansion of Brazilian exports. The average real exchange rate in the period 1955–59 was 22.3 percent below its level in 1970–74, as can be seen from table 3.2. From the regression results in table 3.3, the elasticity of Brazilian exports with respect to the exchange rate is estimated to be 1.050. Combining these numbers would imply that Brazil's manufactured exports might have been about 23 percent less than they were in the early 1970s had the real exchange rate been kept at its level of the 1950s. To be sure, it is inconceivable that other export promotion policies would have been pursued without an alteration in exchange rate policy, and it may be inappropriate to attempt to estimate the contribution of one factor to export growth. Nonetheless, the results suggest that the altered real exchange rate was an important factor in Brazil's successful export growth of the late 1960s and early 1970s.

The estimate of supply of noncoffee NRB exports also shows good statistical results, though not as good as for manufactures. Since the changes in relative dollar prices of NRB goods are very important in determining their growth, and since those changes are very well correlated with the movement of wholesale prices in the United States, we substituted an index of dollar prices of Brazilian exports for the latter index, both in the deflation of the dollar amounts of exports and in the computation of the real exchange rate received by exporters.

As can be seen, the estimated price elasticity in equation (iii) is about 0.26, much lower than the corresponding estimates for manufactures. The estimated coefficient is different from zero at 5 percent (one-tail). The elasticity of world imports in constant dollars is 0.75, indicating that, as in the case of manufactures, that variable is important in explaining the growth of NRB exports, though less important than in the former case. On the other hand, the coefficient of real GDP does not appear significantly different from zero in any of the three models. Again, this is probably due to its collinearity with the world imports variable, which indicates that the scaling role may be played by either of the two.

Summing up our findings regarding the estimates of supply functions of noncoffee exports:

1. The real exchange rate received for exports is estimated to have played an important role in fostering the growth of exports of manufactures. Based on the model estimates, we would tend to place the price elasticity of supply of those goods near unity.

2. For NRB exports, the supply appears quite inelastic, confirming, in a sense, the expectations of policymakers in the fifties. However, though low (about 0.25), the elasticity is significantly different from zero, show-

ing that a devaluation would still have had a positive effect on NRB exports. We note that export quotas and other restrictions placed on exports of NRB goods over the period of this analysis may account for the low value of the elasticity.

3. Another variable that appears to have been important in explaining the growth of Brazilian exports is the level of world trade, defined as the volume of imports in real terms of several leading developed countries. This variable seems particularly important in explaining the success of the export promotion strategy in recent periods, especially with regard to manufactures. However, owing to the high correlation between that variable and the Brazilian real GDP, we cannot completely separate the effects of the two variables. Hence the importance of the growth in world trade may have been overestimated in the equations.

Notes

1. Undoubtedly some manufactured exports, such as orange juice and packed meat, can be regarded as NRB. However, since they receive the same incentives as the others we decided to treat them as manufactures, which greatly simplified the computations.

2. Because of their depth, three studies are of particular interest: Tyler (1976), Supplicy (1976), and Doellinger et al. (1971). All three models were estimated with quarterly data, though Supplicy also worked with annual data for NRB goods. The Doellinger study covers the period 1963–68, the estimates by Tyler refer to the period 1963–72, and the work by Supplicy is for 1964–1972 II. Supplicy also cites another study by Tyler where he estimates an export supply of manufactures for 1961–70 (Tyler 1971). Generally the estimated price elasticity of the export supply functions turned out positive and significantly different from zero. The estimates yielded elasticities of between 0.9 and 1.4 for manufactures and of about 0.5 for noncoffee NRB exports. For a fuller analysis see Carvalho and Haddad (1978, chap. 4).

3. It is clear that considerations of risk would imply that the importers would be willing to pay a price for diversification of their supply sources.

4. Note that the index of fiscal incentives in the equation is defined by its inverse, which explains the negative sign of the coefficient. This index is in fact $(1 - S)$ where S is the subsidy rate given to manufacturing exports.

5. The risk of not receiving from the local state the ICM credits awarded to exports of manufactures could also explain this low elasticity with respect to the fiscal incentives.

6. The simple correlation coefficient between the logs of the two variables is equal to .99. Therefore collinearity is certainly present in the estimates of the coefficients of the two variables.

7. Significantly different from zero at 10 percent, one tail, in equation (ii).

8. Additional estimates of supply functions are presented in Carvalho and Haddad (1978 chap. 4).

References

Carvalho, José L., and Haddad, Cláudio L. S. 1978. Foreign trade strategies and employment in Brazil. Rio de Janeiro: EPGE/FGV. Mimeographed. A condensed version appears in Volume 1 of this series.

Doellinger, Carlos von; Castro Faria, Hugo Barros de; Carvalho Pereira, José Eduardo; and Horta, Maria Helena T. T. 1971. *Exportações dinâmicas brasileiras*. Rio de Janeiro: IPEA/INPES, Relatório de Pesquisa.

Harberger, Arnold. 1972. Tax policy as a determinant of the level and structure of exports. Paper presented at the Third Inter-American Conference on Taxation, Mexico City, September. Mimeographed.

Supplicy, Eduardo Matarazzo. 1976. *Os efeitos das minidesvalorizações na econômia brasileira*. Rio de Janeiro: Fundação Getúlio Vargas.

Tyler, William G. 1971. Exchange rate flexibility under conditions of endemic inflation: A case study of recent Brazilian experiences. Unpublished paper, U.S. Agency for International Development.

———. 1976. *Manufactured export expansion in Brazil*. Tubingen: J. C. B. Nohr.

4 Country and Sectoral Variations in Manufacturing Elasticities of Substitution between Capital and Labor

Jere R. Behrman

4.1 Introduction

Foreign trade and domestic policy regimes often alter relative primary factor prices. Subsidized credit, differential import taxes that favor capital goods imports, and minimum wages are a few examples. The effect of these policies on the demand for labor and for other primary factors depends critically on the degree of technical substitution among production inputs. A hypothesis frequently maintained (though not always explicitly stated) is that elasticities of substitution between capital and labor are zero. The purpose of this chapter is to test to what extent this and some related hypotheses about the underlying production relations are consistent with empirical realities.

I focus upon estimates of elasticities of substitution between capital and labor for a 1967–73 cross section of seventy countries with up to twenty-seven two-digit manufacturing sectors for each country. The reasons the elasticities of substitution are of interest are well known. (1) As is mentioned above, these elasticities relate to the degree of flexibility in responding to changing domestic and international contexts, whether such changes are due to conscious policies or to other shocks to the system.[1] (2) They also relate to the distribution of income between capital and labor and to changes in this distribution over time, given labor supply and other critical developments, if there are pressures for real payments to such factors to be approximately proportional to their marginal prod-

Jere R. Behrman is associated with the University of Pennsylvania.

I would like to thank the United States Agency for International Development and NBER for support for this study. I also wish to thank the project director, Anne O. Krueger, and anonymous referees for helpful suggestions. I am grateful to E. Goldstein, L. Fronzini, S. Donovan, and particularly L. Ness for research assistance. I alone, of course, am responsible for any errors that remain.

ucts. (3) Their relative magnitudes across sectors enter critically into the determination under neoclassical assumptions of the effects of varying primary factor endowments on the patterns of trade and of relative factor prices. (4) They affect the stability or instability of certain growth paths implied by some aggregate formal models, such as the Harrod-Domar case. (5) In market economies they play a crucial role in determining the extent to which unemployment can occur owing to inappropriate relative factor prices, with one extreme being the well-known Eckaus (1955) case of large unemployment in some developing countries owing to no such substitution possibilities and an incompatible factor mix for given technologies. (6) The appropriateness of many linear planning models, finally, depends on the accuracy of the assumption that such elasticities are close to zero, though this is in part a question of aggregation, since most such models allow substitution among activities, though not within them (see Blitzer, Clark, and Taylor 1975 for a recent review of these models).

Of course there are previous cross-country estimates of these elasticities of substitution that relate to developing countries, as well as a growing number of cross-sectoral and time-series estimates for individual developing countries. Among the former the best known is the study by Arrow, Chenery, Minhas, and Solow (1961), cited hereafter as ACMS. White (1978) reviews many of the latter. He notes that the estimates tend to be concentrated between 0.5 and 1.2, but that they are not as robust as might be desirable to changes in data sets and that a number of them are outside the range indicated above.

As is discussed below, the estimates presented in this paper are subject to many of the same limitations as are previous estimates. Nevertheless, I judge that they make a contribution to our understanding of the underlying substitution possibilities for a number of reasons. (1) The data used pertain to roughly the same period as do the data for most of the other studies in the alternative trade strategies and employment project. Thus they provide a better base for evaluating assumptions about elasticities of substitution in the project than do estimates from much earlier time periods if, as seems plausible, the tremendous changes that have occurred in the past two decades have altered the underlying parameters of production relations. I use data from 1967 to 1973, while those used by ACMS, for example, are from 1950 to 1955. (2) The data used permit the inclusion of many more countries with a richer diversity of experience than has been possible in most, if not all, earlier studies. There are more than three times as many countries in my sample, for example, as in that of ACMS. (3) Using as one observation the average value over several years for a particular sector in a specific country may lessen possible biases due to short-run fluctuations. (4) For the same reason, the maintained hypothesis in the ACMS form (which I also use) regarding the pressures for competitive-like behavior is more palatable. (5) By combining countries and sectors I am able to explore to what extent country-specific or sector-specific characteristics account for the diversity of estimates on which White (1978) and others have commented. (6) Furthermore, I can explore interesting questions regarding the relation of the patterns across countries, either because of specification error or because of differential economic environments, to such characteristics as the level and rate of development, the quality of the labor force, the degree of openness to international trade, the extent of domestic inflation, and the degree of foreign-sector disequilibrium.

4.2 ACMS Model and Assumptions

The most widespread approach for estimating elasticities of substitution between capital and labor is that of ACMS. Because of limitations on the availability of data that are discussed in section 4.4 below, I use the ACMS approach in this paper instead of some more general formulation (e.g., translog production functions).

Assume that there is a well-defined relationship between real value added per unit time (V) and the services per unit time of homogeneous labor (L) and of homogeneous capital (K) that are combined efficiently to produce V. Assume that this relationship has a constant elasticity of substitution (CES, $\sigma = 1/(1+\rho)$) and a constant elasticity of scale (μ). Assume that production behavior approximates profit maximization (or cost minimization) under perfect competition with a given real wage (W). Then relation (1) is the CES production function and relations (2) and (3) are alternative forms of the ACMS relation as derived from the marginal productivity condition in the labor market:[2]

(1) $\qquad V = B[\delta K^{-\rho} + (1-\delta)L^{-\rho}]^{-\mu/\rho}$

(2) $\qquad \ln(V/L) = a + \sigma \ln W + b \ln V,$

where $\qquad a = -\sigma \ln(\mu(1-\delta)B^{-\rho/\mu})$

$\qquad\qquad b = -(1-\sigma)(1-\mu)/\mu.$

(3) $\qquad \ln(V/L) = c + d \ln W + g \ln L,$

where $\qquad c = -\mu/(\mu+\rho)\ln(\mu(1-\delta)B^{-\rho/\mu})$

$\qquad\qquad d = \mu/(\mu+\rho)$

$\qquad\qquad g = -(1-d)(1-\mu).$

Note that relations (2) and (3) both identically collapse to relation (4) if there are constant returns to scale ($\mu = 1$):

(4) $\ln(V/L) = a + \sigma \ln W.$

If there is an additive, independent disturbance term with a zero mean and constant own variance, ordinary least squares (OLS) estimation procedures are appropriate for these relations.

In section 4.4 below I present estimates of a number of variants of the ACMS forms, including ones that allow the parameters to vary systematically across sectors or across countries. One rationale for such varying parameters is casual observation, supported by empirical studies, that productivities and elasticities of substitution indeed do vary at least across sectors. Another reason is possible omitted variables, a topic discussed in section 4.3.

The advantages of estimating elasticities of substitution between capital and labor from the ACMS forms are several. The relations are simple. The data requirements are limited to widely available series (V, L, W). They do not include capital services (K), or the rate of return on capital, both of which are much more rarely available. The elasticity of substitution (σ) enters as a first-order parameter rather than as a second-order parameter as in the original production function of relation (1). Therefore there is more chance of estimating it with some precision from the ACMS form. Finally, conditions often are such that simultaneous bias is not a problem, in contrast to those that are relevant in the direct estimation of the CES function in relation (1).

The disadvantage of the ACMS approach compared with direct estimation of the CES production function is the reliance on the assumption regarding approximate profit maximization under perfect competition. It also shares with the direct estimation of the CES production function a number of other possibly strong assumptions: only capital and labor services enter into the production of real value added, capital and labor are homogeneous, the elasticity of substitution between capital and labor is constant, and capital and labor services are proportional, respectively, to capital and labor stocks. The assumption above about the additive independent disturbance term in the ACMS form in order to use OLS estimates also may be strong, as is discussed in the next section.

4.3   Bias in the Estimation of the ACMS Model

The disturbance term in the ACMS relation may reflect random errors in the variables, omitted variables, and/or specification errors regarding the form of the production function or the existence of behavior approximating profit maximization under perfect competition.[3] Many plausible reasons for including the disturbance term imply that it is not distributed independently of the right-side variables in the ACMS relation. As a result, OLS estimates of the parameters of the ACMS form probably often are biased. I briefly consider three important types of bias in this section.

4.3.1   Random Errors in the Variables

Random errors in the variables may be present for such reasons as random errors in reporting or recording, random fluctuations in capacity utilization and hours of work of employees, cyclical fluctuations in the quality of labor and capital, or random fluctuations in the prices used for deflating reported value added and wage series. The last source is particularly likely for cross-country data that must be translated into a common currency using exchange rates that may fluctuate around equilibrium values.

The simple errors-in-variables model is well known. Consider the true ACMS relation (4) with all variables measured from their means so that the constant can be suppressed, with $y = \ln(V/L)$ and $x = \ln W$ being the true variables, and with an additive disturbance term (e):

$$(5) \qquad y = \sigma x + e.$$

Assume, however, that instead of observing y and x, we measure $Y = y + v$ and $X = x + u$, where v and u are random measurement errors with zero means, constant own variances (var v and var u, respectively), and zero correlations with each other and with the rest of the system. Let $w = e + v - \sigma u$. Then relation (5) can be rewritten in terms of observed variables as:

$$(6) \qquad Y = \sigma X + w.$$

The OLS estimate of σ from relation (6), however, is inconsistent because w and X are correlated so that σ is underestimated:

$$(7) \qquad p\lim \hat{\sigma} = \frac{\sigma}{1 + \text{var } u/\text{var } x}$$

The extent to which the elasticity of substitution is biased toward zero clearly depends on var u/var x. If one knows this ratio a priori, one can adjust for such measurement error.

For the present study there is no a priori information about the degree of random errors in the right-side variable(s).[4] However, for the simplest ACMS form in relation (4) the extent of the measurement error can be explored by reversing the regression (i.e., letting $\ln(V/L)$ be the right-side variable). Ceteris paribus this gives an upper bound estimate for the elasticity of substitution. Thus I can see how narrow or broad a range of estimates is implied by the two OLS estimates.

More generally I attempt to lessen the impact of errors in the annual values of variables by using as much as is possible average values over several years as one observation. To the extent that the sources of such errors are additive random measurement error or random cyclical domestic or foreign-sector fluctuations, this procedure should reduce the importance of random errors in the variables.[5]

Finally, one source of possible random error is the use of different definitions across countries. For example, in the data set for this study, value added is given in factor values for twenty-nine countries, producer values for twenty-six countries, and nonspecified terms for fifteen countries. In forms in which value added is used to define the left-side variable (e.g., relation 4) this does not bias the coefficient estimates (e.g., $\hat{\sigma}$) since var y does not enter into relation (7). In forms in which value added is used as a right-side variable (e.g., the reversed form of relation 4 or relation 2), if such changes in definition are random across countries they cause an error in the variables bias in the coefficient estimate(s). To attempt to lessen such a bias, I include additive dummy variables that are nonzero, respectively, if value added is given in producer values or in nonspecified terms.

4.3.2   Omitted Variables

Probably most important among omitted variables are possible systematic variations in the quality of labor or in product prices. Consider once again the simplest form of the ACMS relation with an additive disturbance term (e) and all variables measured from their means so that the constant can be surpressed. Let P be the appropriate sectoral price deflator, P^* a common deflator that is used across sectors instead of P, and Q a measure of the quality of labor that enters in multiplicatively with the quantity of labor (L) to obtain the total effective labor force. Then the true relation is:

$$(8) \qquad \ln(V/(LQ)) = \sigma\ln(W/Q) + e.$$

However, the estimated relation is:

$$(9) \qquad \ln(VP/(LP^*)) = \sigma\ln(WP/P^*) + e'.$$

Therefore,

$$(10) \qquad e' = (1-\sigma)(\ln Q + \ln(P/P^*)) + e.$$

OLS estimation of relation (9) without including the first right-side term in relation (10) leads to an estimate of σ that is biased toward unity if $\ln(W/P^*)$ is positively correlated with $\ln Q + \ln(P/P^*)$.

$$(11) \qquad \text{plim } \hat{\sigma} = \sigma + (1-\sigma)\left[r_{\ln(W/P^*),\,\ln Q} + r_{\ln(W/P^*),\,\ln(P/P^*)}\right],$$

where the rs refer to the respective regression coefficients in the "auxiliary" regressions of the respective excluded variables on the included variable.

A priori it seems quite probable that in the sample used for this study both of the terms in the right-side bracket of relation (11) are positive.

Both across sectors within countries and across countries there seems to be a direct positive association between real wages and the quality of the labor force. Moreover, sectors within a country with some oligopoly power owing to international trade barriers are likely to have relatively high real wages and relatively high ratios of P/P^*.

In the estimates below I attempt to control for these factors by three means. First, additive sectoral dummy variables are included. They should have significantly nonzero coefficient estimates if there are systematic correlations of high-quality, high-wage labor in certain manufacturing sectors across countries or if there are systematic patterns in differential sectoral protection and associated high sectoral wages across countries. I also include the number of establishments in each sector/country cell as a limited proxy for the degree of domestic oligopolistic power.[6]

Second, important country characteristics are represented by including direct proxy variables that may be related to systematic patterns across countries in the quality of labor and in P/P^*. These variables are discussed in the next section.

Third, the ACMS correction factor for finding the true elasticity of substitution from the estimated value given missing quality of labor data is used. On the basis of a constant elasticity (η) relation between the overall efficiency parameter (B in relation 1) and the real wage, ACMS derive the following:

$$(12) \qquad \sigma = \frac{\hat{\sigma} - \eta}{1 - \eta}.$$

If $\eta < \hat{\sigma} < 1$, relation (12) states that the estimated elasticity of substitution between capital and labor is biased toward 1 because of the association among wages, the overall efficiency parameter, and the quality of labor. ACMS very roughly estimate η to be 0.3.

Before concluding this discussion of my strategy for dealing with possible omitted variables, I note that within this framework it is not possible to distinguish between the situation in which the sectoral and country dummy variables and proxies are controlling for missing variables (such as labor quality) and the one in which they are representing the determinants of different levels of neutral technology or overall productivity (i.e., B in relation 1 that enters into the constants in the ACMS forms). Therefore the results must be interpreted with care.

4.3.3 Simultaneous-Equations Bias

If the real wage is endogenous, even the simplest ACMS form in relation (4) is subject to simultaneous-equations bias. As a result, the elasticity of substitution between capital and labor is underestimated.

If there is such a bias, to deal really adequately with it would require the estimation of a complete multiequation system with some consistent procedure. But the data base for this study is not sufficiently comprehensive for such an approach.

A second best approach that is adopted is to follow the recommendation of Maddala and Kadane (1966) to "reverse" the ACMS relation by estimating the real wage as the dependent variable and the real value added per laborer as the right-side variable. This recommendation is based on their findings in a Monte Carlo study that the estimate of the elasticity of substitution between capital and labor is much more robust under simultaneous-equations problems if estimated in this reversed form than if estimated in the original ACMS form. Note that this procedure also is discussed above in regard to errors in the variables. If the two estimates of the elasticity of substitution differ significantly between the ACMS and the reversed form, with the data set for this study I see no way of identifying the extent to which such a result reflects measurement error versus simultaneous-equations bias. However, the case for real wages being endogenous is not particularly strong. On a priori grounds treating simultaneous-equations bias as a second-order consideration seems satisfactory.

4.4   Data

The basic source for data for this study is a tape, much of which is reproduced in the United Nations (1976). It includes usable data on value added, wages and salaries, the number of employees, and the number of establishments for up to twenty-seven ISIC three-digit manufacturing sectors for seventy countries for up to seven years (1967–73). Table 4.1 indicates the included manufacturing sectors. Table 4.2 gives the countries. By the World Bank (1978) classification, these countries include twelve in the low-income group (1976 GNP per capita under U.S. $250), thirty-five in the middle-income group (developing countries with 1976 GNP per capita over U.S. $250), eighteen industrialized countries, two capital-surplus oil exporters, and three centrally planned economies.

Before these data can be used to estimate the ACMS relations, the value added and wage and salary series must be converted into common real terms. This conversion was made by using official exchange rates to convert to current United States dollars and then deflating by the United States deflator to obtain real values.

As I have mentioned several times, another preliminary step was to average the data over all available years in the period 1967–73. One reason for this averaging is that for various countries data are incomplete in some years. A more basic reason is to lessen the problems of errors in the variables that are discussed above in section 4.3 and thereby obtain better estimates of the fundamental underlying parameters. Such averaging reduces downward biases due to additive random or cyclical fluctuations in reporting and recording the data; in intensity of use and quality of capital and labor (i.e., shutting down old equipment or laying off less productive workers in periods of lessened demand); and in prices, wages, and exchange rates. A third reason for such averaging is that it allows one to work out adjustment processes of a physical sort and in regard to price expectations. A final reason is that the maintained hypothesis of approximate profit maximization under perfect competition is more palatable over longer periods because, in comparison with annual units of observation, there is more time for information to become widespread and for substitutes to develop or be imported.

In addition to the basic data, sectoral dummy variables and proxies for country characteristics are used to attempt to control for missing variables (see section 4.3) and to explore hypotheses regarding systematic variations in the parameters of the underlying production relations. The country characteristics include: real GDP per capita and life expectancy at birth to represent the level of development and the quality of labor; exports plus imports relative to GNP to represent the degree of openness to the foreign sector; the rate of inflation to represent internal price stability; the ratio of the black market to the official exchange rate to represent disequilibrium in the foreign sector;[7] wages as a proportion of national income to represent the factoral distribution of income; and the rate of growth in per capita real product to represent dynamism (see the Appendix for data sources). This set of variables includes only a limited number of imperfect measures of possible relevant country characteristics. Nevertheless, the results obtained by using them should be suggestive regarding omitted variable biases or the degree of homogeneity of parameters of the production relations.

For some of these country variables, as well as for the number of establishments in each sector, data are not available for all observations. Under the assumption that such missing values are random,[8] the Monte Carlo studies of Hester (1976) and of Behrman, Flesher, and Wolfe (1979) suggest that the Glasser (1964) method of moments is relatively robust. In this method each bivariate moment is calculated on the base of all overlapping observations on the relevant two variables. This method is used here.

Of course there are several important limitations of the data set. Most of these are shared with many data sets that are used for estimating parameters of production relations. First, the basic data are sector averages, not observations for individual plants or firms. I am assuming that the relations that are estimated on the basis of these average data also hold on a more micro level. However, they presumably incorporate not only technical substitution in the purest production function sense, but also changes in composition of production and processes within the three-digit sectors.[9] As such they probably incorporate other dimensions

Table 4.1   ISIC Industrial Sectors Included in Study and Estimated Sectoral Effects

ISIC Number	Industrial Sector	Number of Countries	Estimates of Coefficients of Additive Sectoral Dummy Variables from Regression				Estimated Sectoral Increments to σ from Regression 6-1
			3–4	3–6	3–7	3–14	
312	Food products	68	.42[a]	–.11	.28[a]	.15	.05[a]
313	Beverages	67	.81[a]	.52[a]	.83[a]	.63[a]	.11[a]
314	Tobacco	62	1.08[a]	.96[a]	.97[a]	1.06[a]	.14[a]
321	Textiles	70	.18[b]	–.23[a]	–.04	–.01	.02[b]
322	Wearing apparel	68	.10	–.34[a]	–.21[a]	–.08	.01
323	Leather and products	64	.12	–.09[a]	–.20[a]	.09	.01
324	Footwear	61	.04	–.22[a]	–.18[b]	–.07	.00
331	Wood products	68	.17[b]	–.24[a]	–.11	.01	.02
332	Furniture and fixtures	64	.04	–.35[a]	–.10	–.16[b]	.00
341	Paper and products	66	.36[a]	.09	.22[a]	.27[a]	.05[a]
342	Printing and publishing	65	.04	–.33[a]	.11	–.18[b]	.01
351	Industrial chemicals	69	.57[a]	.33[a]	.61[a]	.42[a]	.08[a]
352	Other chemical products	57	.60[a]	.27[a]	.66[a]	.40[a]	.08[a]

353	Petroleum refineries	1.00ª	1.07ª	1.29ª	.95ª	.13ª
354	Petroleum, coal products	.35ª	.48ª	.29ª	.43ª	.03ª
355	Rubber products	.40ª	.15ᵇ	.31ª	.28ª	.05ª
356	Plastic products, n.e.c.	.33ª	.09	.09	.28ª	.04ª
361	Pottery, china, etc.	.07	-.02	.05	.04	.01
362	Glass and products	.12	-.01	.06	.05	.02
369	Nonmetal products, n.e.c.	.35ª	-.04	.20ª	.18ᵇ	.05ª
371	Iron and steel	.33ª	.25ª	.32ª	.28ª	.03ª
372	Nonferrous metals	.23ª	.29ª	.33ª	.24ª	.03ª
381	Metal products	.23ª	-.19ª	.21ª	-.00	.03ª
382	Machinery, n.e.c.	.06	-.24ª	.06	-.11	.00
383	Electrical machinery	.24ª	-.06	.24ª	.06	.03ª
384	Transport equipment	.08	-.24ª	.06	-.11	.01
385	Professional goods					

NOTE: The data source is given in Section 4.4. Data are not available for all countries for all sectors because some countries report no production in some sectors. The regressions referred to in the last five column heads are given below in tables 4.3 and 4.6.

ªSignificantly nonzero at 5 percent level.

ᵇSignificantly nonzero at 10 percent level.

of the adjustment process that are of interest in regard to the question of the degree of macro response to trade regimes and development policies additional to pure technical substitution. Second, the diversity of included countries makes suspect the assumption that the sectors and variables are homogeneous. As I noted in the previous section, this can

Table 4.2   Countries Included in Study Classified into World Bank Categories

Low-income countries	Middle-income countries (cont.)
1. Ethiopia	38. Iraq
2. Bangladesh	39. Cyprus
3. Somalia	40. Barbados
4. Zaire	41. Yugoslavia
5. India	42. Portugal
6. Mozambique	43. Malta
7. Pakistan	44. Greece
8. Tanzania	45. Singapore
9. Madagascar	46. Spain
10. Indonesia	47. Israel
11. Kenya	
12. Uganda	*Industrialized countries*
	48. South Africa
Middle-income countries	49. Ireland
13. Egypt	50. Italy
14. Mauritania	51. United Kingdom
15. Nigeria	52. New Zealand
16. Bolivia	53. Japan
17. Philippines	54. Austria
18. Zambia	55. Finland
19. Papua New Guinea	56. Australia
20. Rhodesia	57. Netherlands
21. Ghana	58. Luxembourg
22. Jordan	59. Belgium
23. Colombia	60. Federal Republic of Germany
24. Guatemala	61. Norway
25. Ecuador	62. Denmark
26. Republic of Korea	63. Canada
27. Dominican Republic	64. United States
28. Peru	65. Sweden
29. Tunisia	
30. Malaysia	*Capital surplus oil exporters*
31. Turkey	66. Libya
32. Chile	67. Kuwait
33. Jamaica	
34. Mexico	*Centrally planned economies*
35. Brazil	68. Hungary
36. Fiji	69. Poland
37. Panama	70. Czechoslovakia

Note: Based on World Bank (1978). Within categories countries are ranked in ascending order of 1976 GNP per capita.

lead to errors in the variables and to omitted-variable biases. I attempt to control for heterogeneity by using the sectoral and country dummy variables and characteristics discussed above, but undoubtedly such controls are imperfect. Third, the basic data set does not include some variables that would be useful. Examples include capital stocks, rates of return on capital, measures of the quality of labor, and better concentration indexes. Therefore I am limited in the range of hypotheses that can be explored in regard to functional forms, market behavior, and missing variables. Fourth, the data are cross sectional, but for many purposes elasticities of substitution between capital and labor are of interest for questions regarding what happens with changes over time. For my results to have relevance for such issues, I must assume that differences across countries are related to dynamic changes over time in one country.

These disadvantages are significant. But the advantages are also substantial, and in my judgment they are more than sufficient to warrant the empirical explorations of this study. By combining across sectors and across countries it is possible to have a large number of observations (1,723) to estimate the parameters of interest, as well as sectoral or country-specific deviations from them.[10] The range of country experiences includes a number of developing countries for which the results are of particular interest for the project on alternative trade strategies and employment. The range of countries also makes more probable the identification of parameters in the underlying production relations because of great variations in fixed capital stocks and in relative prices. The sector and country dummy variables and characteristics permit some, albeit imperfect, control for missing variables. Finally, the possibility of using average data over several years may lessen considerably the errors-in-variables problems discussed above, it allows the estimation of longer-run, more fundamental underlying parameters, and it makes the maintained hypothesis of approximate profit maximization under perfect competition more palatable.

4.5   Estimates of the Variants of the ACMS Relation from a Cross-Sector, Cross-Country Sample

Based on the considerations discussed in sections 4.2 and 4.3 and the data described in section 4.4, I have estimated a number of variants of the ACMS relation. Table 4.3 summarizes some of the more interesting estimates of the basic model and extensions thereof that involve additive terms. Table 4.4 gives some of the more interesting estimates of the "reversed" model with $\ln W$ instead of $\ln(V/L)$ as the dependent variable. Table 4.5 gives a grouping of the industrial sectors on the basis of the estimates. Table 4.6 includes some estimates of the basic model with multiplicative terms. The convention is adopted of referring to the var-

Table 4.3   **Estimates of ACMS Relation with ln (V/L) as Dependent Variable and with Additive Sectoral and Country Variables**

Regression Number	Constant	ln W	ln V	ln L	Sector Dummies[a]	ln Number of Establishments	GDP per Capita	Life Expectancy	Trade/GNP	Infla-tion[b]	Black Market/Official Exchange Rate	Wages/National Income	Growth in Product per Capita[b]	$\bar{R}^2$/SE
												In of Country Characteristics		
3-1	1.22 (9.9)	.94 (57.7)												.66 .65
3-2	2.09 (17.5)	.79 (48.0)	.092 (20.0)											.73 .59
3-3	1.43 (11.8)	.91 (55.6)		.056 (10.3)										.68 .63
3-4	1.20 (8.8)	.91 (59.4)			Yes Table 4.1									.72 .59
3-5	1.23 (10.3)	.91 (57.1)				.055 (12.1)								.69 .63
3-6	1.59 (12.8)	.83 (58.4)			Yes Table 4.1	.092 (19.8)								.78 .54
3-7	1.10 (9.2)	.35 (12.0)			Yes Table 4.1		.63 (21.9)							.78 .53
3-8	−.030 (0.1)	.87 (51.1)			Yes			.36 (4.2)						.72 .59

Eq.	(1)	(2)	Dummies										R^2	SE
3-9	1.05 (7.7)	.91 (60.4)	Yes					−.18 (7.1)					.73	.59
3-10	1.22 (9.0)	.90 (59.4)	Yes						.16[c] (4.7)				.72	.59
3-11	1.14 (8.2)	.91 (59.4)	Yes							.12 (3.0)			.72	.59
3-12	1.23 (9.0)	.87 (67.4)	Yes								.041 (3.8)		.72	.60
3-13	1.14 (8.5)	.89 (58.7)	Yes									.045 (6.8)	.73	.59
3-14	−2.56 (9.8)	1.00 (68.7)	Yes	Table 4.1	.044 (9.9)	−.24 (17.8)	1.18 (20.0)	−.10 (3.6)	.00[c] (0.2)			−.081 (25.6)	.73	.58
3-15	1.78 (5.2)	.84 (54.6)	Yes		.089 (16.9)	−.10 (1.2)		−.51[c] (0.2)	.10[c] (2.8)	.18 (4.3)		.040 (6.0)	.78	.53
3-16	2.04 (6.4)	.84 (57.0)	Yes		.089 (16.8)	−.14 (1.7)		.87[c] (0.3)	.18[c] (5.9)		−.68[c] (0.9)	.032 (5.3)	.78	.53

Note: All regressions are ordinary least squares using Glasser's (1964) method of moments for any missing observations. The data are described in section 4.4 and the Appendix. R^2 is the coefficient of determination corrected for degrees of freedom. SE is the standard error of the estimate. Absolute values of t statistics are given beneath point estimates. The sample includes 1,723 observations from the twenty-seven industrial sectors in Table 4.1 and the seventy countries in table 4.2. Dummy variables for definitional changes for value added were included in all estimates and have significantly nonnegative coefficient estimates that are not reported in this table.

[a]"Yes" implies that twenty-six sectoral dummy variables were included. "Table 4.1" implies that the coefficient estimates are given in table 4.1.

[b]Not in ln form.

[c]Multiplied by 10^{-2}.

Table 4.4   Estimates of "Reversed" ACMS Relation with lnW as Dependent Variable

| | | | | | In of Country Characteristics | | | | | | |
Regression Number	Constant	ln (V/L)	Sector Dummies[a]	ln Number of Establishments	GDP per Capita	Life Expectancy	Trade/GDP	Inflation[b]	Black Market/Official Exchange Rate	Wages/National Income	Growth in Product per Capita	$\bar{R}^2$/SE
4-1	1.69 (16.7)	.70 (57.7)										.67 .56
4-2	-1.61 (7.1)	.74 (68.7)	Yes	-.048 (10.1)	.024 (2.3)	.78 (14.5)	.28[c] (0.1)	-.087[c] (3.0)			-.020 (6.2)	.73 .50
4-3	-1.74 (5.4)	.76 (5.46)	Yes	-.054 (10.2)		.83 (10.3)	.34[c] (0.1)	-.021[c] (0.6)	-.20 (4.9)		-.038 (6.0)	.73 .51
4-4	-2.81 (9.2)	.79 (57.0)	Yes	-.059 (11.0)		1.12 (14.9)	.020 (0.8)	-.10[c] (3.1)		-.053 (6.8)	-.048 (8.2)	.73 .51

NOTE: See note to table 4.3.

[a]"Yes" means that twenty-six sectoral dummy variables were included, but their coefficient estimates are not reported here.

[b]Not in ln form.

[c]Multiplied by 10^{-2}.

ious estimates by the table number and the row number (i.e., regression 3-1 refers to the first regression in table 4.3).

4.5.1 Basic ACMS Model

Regressions 3-1 and 4-1 are estimates of the basic ACMS model and its reversed form under the maintained hypothesis of constant returns to scale in relation (4). Both are consistent with about two-thirds of the variance in the respective dependent variables. The former gives an estimated elasticity of substitution of 0.94, the latter implies 1.43. Under the assumption of random error in the variables, the former is biased downward and the latter is biased upward. If the wage rate is simultaneously determined, the Maddala and Kadane (1966) Monte Carlo experiments imply that the latter is less likely to be contaminated by simultaneous-equations bias. Thus these estimates suggest an elasticity of substitution between capital and labor of about the Cobb-Douglas value of 1 or perhaps somewhat higher.

Because I do not think there is a simultaneous-equations problem, I do not focus below on the reversed estimates. To keep the presentation manageable, in fact, I emphasize the estimates from the direct ACMS form with only occasional reference to the reversed form. The reader should keep in mind, however, that if there is random measurement error in the real wage series (the effect of which is not offset by any other measurement error in right-side variables), then the estimate of the elasticity of substitution from the direct ACMS form is biased downward.

If there is random measurement error in the $\ln(V/L)$ series, it does not bias the estimate of the elasticity of substitution from the direct ACMS form (see relation 7 above). However, it biases downward the estimate of the inverse of this elasticity in the reversed form. As is discussed in section 4.3 above, one possible source of such random error is the alternative definitions that are used across countries for value added. The dummy variables that are mentioned in section 4.3 to represent these changes indeed do have significantly nonzero coefficients when they are included in the regressions. However, whether they are included or not does not alter the estimate of the elasticity of substitution from the reversed ACMS form by as much as 1 percent. Therefore these estimates do not indicate that this source of random measurement error is very important.

4.5.2 Returns to Scale

If the returns to scale are not constant (i.e., if $\mu \neq 1$), the basic direct ACMS form can be written as in relations (2) and (3). Regressions 3-2 and 3-3 are estimates of these relations. In both cases the additional variables have coefficient estimates that are significantly nonzero at standard significance levels, and the extent of overall consistency with the variation in the dependent variable increases slightly. In both cases the estimate of the elasticity of substitution drops somewhat—to 0.79 and 0.86, respectively. Thus the additional variables ($\ln V$ and $\ln L$, respectively) seem to be representing some systematic variable(s) whose exclusion leads to a small upward bias ceteris paribus in the estimated elasticity of substitution from the simplest ACMS form.

However, the magnitude of the estimates suggests that the additional variables are not representing returns to scale alone. They imply values of μ of 1.80 and 1.58, respectively! Such high returns to scale are not credible.

Although I am comfortable with the assumption that there is not a significant simultaneity problem in estimating the ACMS relation with $\mu = 1$ as a maintained hypothesis, if $\mu \neq 1$ so that $\ln V$ or $\ln L$ enter in as right-side variables, simultaneity may be a problem. In addition to the ACMS relation, there is the production function in relation (1) that determines simultaneously $\ln V$ and $\ln L$. Could such simultaneity bias be the explanation for the very high estimates of μ? No. Griliches and Ringstad (1971) demonstrate that the simultaneity bias in this system leads to a downward bias in the estimate of μ, not an upward one.[11]

Another possibility is that the $\ln V$ and $\ln L$ are representing sectoral or country characteristics that have a significant role in an extended ACMS model because of omitted variables or because the coefficients vary systematically across countries or sectors or both. The estimates are consistent with such a hypothesis in that the implied values of μ change dramatically depending on what sector and country variables are included. Apparently there is considerable multicollinearity between $\ln L$ and $\ln V$ and various linear combinations of the sector and country variables. The implied μs range from -2.38 to 1.80, with almost no a priori plausible values.[12]

Therefore I have adopted the maintained hypothesis that the returns to scale are constant for the remaining estimates. To the extent that there really are returns to scale, the maintained hypothesis of constant returns to scale may bias somewhat the coefficient estimates for correlated sector and country variables. The impact of including or not including $\ln V$ and $\ln L$ on the estimates of the elasticity of substitution, however, is never larger than 0.05 once sectoral dummy variables and some country characteristics are included. Thus maintaining the hypothesis of constant returns to scale apparently does not substantially alter any conclusions about the magnitude of the elasticity of substitution between capital and labor.

4.5.3   Additive Sectoral Characteristics

In section 4.4 the possibility is discussed that there may be systematic sectoral differences in the quality of labor or in the ratio of the true to the common price deflator that is used. The right-side term in relation (11) gives the bias that may result from such sectoral differences. A priori it seems that the bias probably is toward a value of 1 for the estimate of the elasticity of substitution.

I explore the possibility of controlling for these, or other, systematic additive sectoral differences by including sectoral additive dummy variables. Regressions 3-4 and the associated column in table 4.1 are the result of adding these dummy variables to the basic ACMS relation with constant returns to scale. The estimated elasticity of substitution drops from 0.94 to 0.91, which suggests that the effect of such sectoral patterns on the elasticity of substitution, if any, is small.

Of course the significantly nonzero sectoral dummy variable coefficient estimates in fact may not be representing systematic sectoral differences that could bias the estimates of the elasticity of substitution. Instead they may be representing sectoral differences in the parameters that make up the constant term. Assume, for example, that all parameters of the production relation are identical across sectors except for the multiplicative neutral technology term, B in relation (1). Then the solution of the definition of the constant term in relation (2) (still with $\mu = 1$) gives the following ratio of neutral technology terms for the ith and jth sectors:

$$(13) \qquad \frac{B_i}{B_j} = e^{(a_i - a_j)/\rho\sigma}.$$

On the basis of these assumptions and the estimates in regression 3-4, to provide a specific illustration, B_{351}/B_{354} equals 11.5. Under these assumptions, thus, the estimated coefficient of the sectoral dummy variables may be representing rather large differences in the sectoral neutral technology parameters. With the present data set, unfortunately, I see no way to identify the extent to which these significantly nonzero coefficient estimates of the sectoral dummy variables are due to an omitted variable problem or to systematic sectoral differences in the components of the constant term.

I also explore the possibility of controlling for sectoral differences by including the number of establishments per sector. This variable might be related to the degree of domestic oligopoly power. The fewer the number, ceteris paribus, the greater such power and the more there is a bias in using a common deflator across sectors—but also the greater may be the multiplicative neutral technology parameter (albeit for price, not technological, reasons). On the other hand, the larger the number of firms, the greater is the competitive pressure to operate efficiently with current-practice technology and thus to have a higher multiplicative neutral technology factor. Thus the sign of this variable is not obvious a priori. However, the rationale for its use does suggest that it might interact with the degree of openness of the economy, since foreign competition substitutes for domestic competition in open economies.

Regression 3.5 includes the ln of the number of establishments in the basic ACMS relation. Its inclusion by itself causes the estimate of the elasticity of substitution to drop from 0.94 to 0.91, which is not a substantial amount. The identification problem remains: the number of firms in each sector may be representing omitted variables (e.g., differential sectoral prices) or it may be due to the dependence of some components in the constant term on the number of firms in the industry. To the extent that the latter possibility is the true one and only B varies across sectors, the positive sign may imply that more establishments lead to higher neutral technology terms through greater pressure for efficiency and adoption of best-practice technology. Alternatively, if δ varies across sectors the positive sign may suggest that more firms lead to larger capital shares, ceteris paribus.

A comparison of regressions 3-15 and 3-16 reveals no evidence to support the conjecture of a significant interaction between the number of establishments and variables pertaining to the openness or degree of disequilibrium in the foreign sector. However, consideration of regressions 3-5, 3-6, 3-7, and 3-14 suggests that there is some interaction among this variable, the sectoral dummy variables, and the ln of real per capita income. Despite such interactions, tables 4.3 and 4.4 suggest that an estimate of a positive coefficient for the number of establishments in the direct ACMS form (and therefore negative in the reversed form) is quite robust.

The association between the ln of the number of establishments and the sectoral dummy variables is not surprising. It may reflect similarities across countries in patterns of sectoral demands and domestic production and in choices of technology. When both the number of establishments and the sectoral dummy variables are included, the estimated elasticity of substitution drops to 0.83, the coefficient estimate of the ln of the number of establishments almost doubles, and some of the coefficient estimates for the dummy variables change significantly (regression 3-6).

The association between the ln of the number of establishments and the ln of per capita GDP also is not surprising. Higher per capita income countries tend to have a greater B, more total economic activity, and more establishments in the industrial sectors.

The implications of these associations for the pattern of sectoral dummy variable coefficient estimates are clear in tables 4.1 and 4.5. No matter what other variables are included in the regressions, four patterns emerge: one if neither the number of establishments nor the per capita GDP is included (e.g., regression 3-4), one if only the number of establishments is included (e.g., regression 3-6), one if only per capita GDP is included (e.g., regression 3-7), and one if both are included (e.g., regression 3-14). For some sectors the coefficient estimates do not vary much across these four possibilities. For others interaction is much more important, so the estimates differ much more across these possibilities.

Table 4.5   **Grouping of ISIC Industrial Sectors by Signs of Significantly Nonzero Additive Dummy Variable Coefficient Estimates in Table 4.1**

1. *Not significantly nonzero*
   361 Pottery, china, etc.
   362 Glass and products
   385 Professional goods

2. *Significantly positive*
   314 Tobacco
   353 Petroleum refineries
   313 Beverages
   352 Other chemical products
   351 Industrial chemicals
   371 Iron and steel
   354 Petroleum, coal products
   355 Rubber products
   372 Nonferrous metals

3. *Significantly less than group 1 if control for number of establishments, otherwise not*
   321 Textiles
   322 Wearing apparel
   323 Leather and products
   324 Footwear
   331 Wood products
   332 Furniture and fixtures
   342 Printing and publishing
   382 Machinery, n.e.c.
   384 Transport equipment

4. *Significantly greater than group 1 if no control for number of establishments, otherwise not*
   312 Food products
   341 Paper and products
   356 Plastic products, n.e.c.
   383 Electrical machinery

5. *Significantly greater than group 1 if no control for number of establishments, but significantly less if control*
   381 Metal products

Table 4.5 groups the twenty-seven ISIC industrial sectors according to the estimates obtained in these four possibilities. The first group is the reference group. The three included sectors remain the same under all four specifications.

The second group has significantly positive estimates that are robust under alternative specifications. The sectors are roughly in descending order of these estimates. In some cases the sectors seem to be high-technology and capital-intensive (e.g., petroleum refineries, industrial and other chemicals), which may imply relatively high values of the multiplicative neutral technology factor. In other cases, such as for tobacco and beverages, the high values may reflect the relatively great protection often granted by foreign trade regimes.

The third group has significantly negative estimates if the ln of the number of establishments is included (though not always if also the ln of GDP per capita is added), but nonsignificant ones otherwise. It seems to be composed of relatively low-technology, labor-intensive industries.

The fourth group is not significantly different from the reference group if the ln of the number of establishments is included, but otherwise it has significantly positive estimates. It seems to be composed of industries that are intermediate between groups 2 and 3 in technology and capital intensity.

The fifth group is composed of only one sector—metal products—and combines the significantly nonzero features of groups 3 and 4.

4.5.4 Additive Country Variables

I include additive country variables in the ACMS form for reasons similar to the reasons I include additive sectoral dummies: (1) They may lessen the bias due to omitted variables (section 4.3). (2) The production parameters in the constant term may vary systematically across countries. As with the sectoral variables, I generally am unable to identify the relative importance of these two reasons in explaining the significance of these variables.

Regressions 3-7 through 3-13 each include one of the seven country characteristics discussed in section 4.4 in addition to the sectoral dummy variables in the direct ACMS form. Regressions 3-14 through 3-16 include groups of four country variables in addition to the ln of the number of establishments and the sectoral dummy variables in the direct ACMS form. Only four country variables are included in each regression because of high multicollinearity among some combinations of these variables. Regressions 4-2 through 4-3 are identical to regressions 3-14 through 3-16 except that the reversed ACMS form is used. The coefficients of the country variables in the reversed form are the coefficients in the direct form multiplied by $-1/\sigma$.

I now consider the country variables seriatim as they are discussed in section 4.4 and as their coefficient estimates are presented in tables 4.3 and 4.4.

1. *Real GDP per capita and life expectancy at birth* are included to represent the level of development and the quality of labor. Included alone without any other country variables, both have positive significantly nonzero coefficients, and both are associated with lower estimates of the elasticity of substitution. Their addition causes a drop of the estimate of that elasticity from 0.91 in regression 3-4 to 0.35 in regression 3-7 and to 0.87 in regression 3-8. Prima facie these declines might suggest that the failure to correct for labor quality in other regressions causes a significant and perhaps substantial bias toward one in the estimated value of the elasticity of substitution between capital and labor.

If, alternatively, the significant coefficient estimates for these variables represents entirely differential multiplicative neutral technology terms (i.e., Bs in relation 1) across countries, then their impact is substantial. Under assumptions analogous to those that are discussed above in regard to relation (13), but with the subscripts referring to the ith and jth countries now, a difference of one standard deviation in GDP per capita across countries and the estimates in regression 3-7 imply B_i/B_j equals 3.2, and a difference of one standard deviation in life expectancy at birth across countries and the estimates in regression 3-8 imply B_i/B_j equals 1.7.

However, I am wary of placing too much weight on these estimates because they are not very robust and because these variables, particularly the GDP per capita, cause some perplexing patterns in other coefficients. For example, if both of these variables (and no other country variables) are included, ln GDP per capita has a coefficient estimate of -16.1, ln life expectancy at birth has a coefficient estimate of 43.4, and the estimate of the elasticity of substitution is 11.2! If both are included with other country variables, as in regression 3-14, the coefficient estimates become more moderate and the estimated elasticity of substitution is 1.00.

Other examples could be given but would serve little purpose. The basic point is that the coefficient estimates of these two variables do not seem very robust, and the impact of including the ln real GDP per capita variable in particular on the estimate of the elasticity of substitution often is substantial, though under changes in other specifications this elasticity estimate is quite robust. Because of the lack of robustness that is associated with the ln GDP per capita and ln life expectancy at birth variables, no very confident positive conclusions can be reached concerning their possible importance.

As an alternative to using country variables to attempt to control for cross-country labor quality differentials, the ACMS adjustment in relation (12) is mentioned above. For an estimated elasticity of substitution of 0.91 (the modal value in table 4.3), this adjustment gives a corrected value of 0.87.

2. *Exports plus imports relative to GNP* is included to represent the degree of openness to the foreign sector. When this is the only country variable included it has a significantly negative coefficient but does not affect the estimate of the elasticity of substitution (regression 3-9). Given these estimates and assumptions analogous to those made in regard to relation (13) above, a difference of one standard deviation across countries in this variable implies B_i/B_j equals 0.32. Prima facie one possible interpretation is that this variable is serving as an inverse proxy for the state of development. Ceteris paribus, the higher the level of development, the greater the multiplicative technology term (i.e., B) and the less the dependence on international trade.

However, the other regressions do not seem to support such an interpretation. When this variable is included with the measures of the level of development, as in regression 3-14, it continues to have a significantly negative coefficient estimate (albeit of smaller absolute magnitude). With many other specifications (e.g., regressions 3-15, 3-16, 4-2, 4-3, 4-4), it does not have a significantly nonzero coefficient. Therefore these regressions do not give much support for a strong role for the openness of the economy to foreign trade as measured by this ratio.

3. *The rate of inflation* is included to represent internal price stability. When it is the only country variable included, it has a significantly positive coefficient estimate, but it does not seem to alter substantially the estimate of the elasticity of substitution (regression 3-9). Given these estimates and assumptions analogous to those underlying relation (13) above, once again, a difference of one standard deviation in the rate of inflation across countries implies B_i/B_j equals 1.97. When other country variables are added to the specification, the sign (if not the magnitude) of the coefficient estimate for this variable remains fairly robust, though not always significantly nonzero.

A priori this variable is included for two reasons. (1) Inflation might have some effect on the estimated elasticity of substitution by representing systematic variation across countries in P/P^* in relation (11). A comparison of regressions 3-4 and 3-9 does not support this alternative. (2) Internal price disequilibrium might lower internal production efficiency and thus B. However, the significantly positive coefficient is consistent with the opposite interpretation.[13]

4. *The ratio of the black market to the official exchange rate* is included to represent foreign sector disequilibrium. The coefficient estimates for this variable are positive in the ACMS form and negative in the reversed form. The point estimates in regression 3-11 and relation (13) imply that a difference of one standard deviation in this ratio across countries gives B_i/B_j equal to 1.66.

A comparison of regressions 3-4 and 3-10 suggests that this ratio is not controlling for a systematic pattern in P/P^* in relation (11) that a priori might seem to cause a bias in the estimated elasticity of substitution. However, the positive sign of the estimate is somewhat puzzling. It does not support the hypothesis that greater foreign sector disequilibrium is associated across countries with lower neutral productivities (i.e., value of B in relation 1). What is important to this study, however, is that the estimate of the elasticity of substitution is quite robust when this variable is included.

5. *The ratio of wages to national income* is included to represent the factoral income distribution. When it is the only country variable included in regression 3-12, it has a significantly positive coefficient that implies (under the necessary assumptions) B_i/B_j equals 1.18 for a differ-

ence of one standard deviation across countries. Its inclusion also results in a drop in the estimated elasticity of substitution from 0.91 to 0.87. Consideration of what happens under specification change in other regressions in tables 4.3 and 4.4 and in ones not reported here, however, leads me to conclude that this variable probably is serving as a proxy for the quality of labor. The drop in the estimated elasticity of substitution (that incidentally is the same as is obtained from the ACMS adjustment for the quality of labor) or the increase in B, or both, reflects the tendency for the wage share to be positively associated across countries with the quality of labor.

6. *The rate of growth of per capita product* is included to represent the relative degree of dynamism across countries. When it is the only country variable included in regression 3-13, its inclusion lowers slightly (probably not significantly) the estimated elasticity of substitution from 0.91 to 0.89. The magnitude of the significantly positive coefficient estimate implies that B_i/B_j equals 2.45 under the assumptions given above for a difference of one standard deviation across countries. Except when this variable is included with indicators of the level of development as in regressions 3-14 and 4-2, the sign and the approximate magnitude of its coefficient estimates are robust under specification changes. There seems to be reasonable support for there being an association between economic growth and the levels of the multiplicative technology terms.

4.5.5 Multiplicative Sectoral and Country Variables

As is discussed above, I explore the effect of including additive country variables to attempt to control for missing variable bias and to see if there is evidence that the parameters of the production relation that enter into the constant term are related to sectoral or country characteristics. Of course the elasticity of substitution itself may be related to sectoral or country characteristics. The results of a limited exploration of such a possibility are now considered. The exploration is limited because of the greater computational difficulties and lesser robustness encountered with the estimates of these multiplicative forms.[14] Table 4.6 includes some relevant estimates.

Regression 6-1 posits that the elasticity of substitution in the direct ACMS relation is a function of sectoral dummy variables only. The estimates imply that the elasticities vary across sectors from 0.86 to 1.00, with the increment above 0.86 given in the last column in table 4.1. The mean value of 0.90 is almost identical to the value estimated in regression 3.4 with additive sectoral dummies. Across sectors there seems to be a definite relation between the estimated additive and multiplicative estimates. All of the group 2 sectors in table 4.2, for example, have estimated significant positive incremental elasticities of substitution—including the five highest values. Thus the additive and the multiplicative sectoral

Table 4.6   Estimates of ACMS Relation with Elasticity of Substitution Dependent on Sectoral and Country Characteristics

Regression Number	Constant	lnW	lnW × Sector Dummies	lnW × ln Number of Establishments	lnW × ln of Country Characteristics							Implied Mean σ	$\bar{R}^2$/SE
					GDP per Capita	Life Expectancy	Trade/GDP	Inflation	Black Market/Official Exchange Rate	Wages/National Income	Growth in Product per Capita[b]		
6-1	1.52 (13.1)	.86 (47.7)	Yes Table 4.1									.90	.72 .59
6-2	.93 (7.5)	.70 (11.5)		.44[c] (6.2)	−.018 (10.3)	.095 (11.7)	−.021 (5.3)	.79[d] (1.6)			−.49[c] (9.9)	.98	.67 .64
6-3	1.40 (10.9)	.90 (13.8)		.64[c] (9.1)		−.011 (0.8)	−.014 (3.5)	.98[d] (1.7)	.028 (4.0)		.56[c] (5.3)	.91	.70 .62
6-4	1.44 (11.3)	.97 (15.3)		.64[c] (9.1)		−.029 (2.2)	−.012 (3.0)	2.28[d] (4.7)		.088 (0.8)	.53[c] (5.4)	.91	.69 .62

NOTE: See note to table 4.3.

[a]See note a to table 4.3.

[b]Not in ln form.

[c]Multiplied by 10^{-2}.

[d]Multiplied by 10^{-4}.

dummy variables may be representing partially the same phenomenon. In any case, even if all the variation in the sectoral multiplicative estimates is allocated to sectoral differences in the elasticities of substitution, such variations are not very large.

The remaining regressions in table 4.6 posit elasticities of substitution that depend on the ln of the number of establishments and on different groups of five country variables. The implied mean elasticities of substitution are 0.98, 0.91, and 0.91, respectively. All three of these estimates are close to those in table 4.3. Table 4.7 summarizes the implications for the elasticity of substitution of these estimates and increases of one standard deviation in the included multiplicative variables.

The estimates imply that the number of establishments has a greater effect on the elasticity of substitution than do any of the country variables for variations of the types experienced in the sample. An increase of one standard deviation in the number of establishments in a sector is associated with an increase of 0.03 to 0.04 in the elasticity of substitution (table 4.7). This may reflect that more establishments in a sector increase the pressure for efficient behavior and for exploring substitution possibilities. Alternatively, more establishments may be associated with greater heterogeneity of products and of underlying product technologies. In any case, the estimated effect is not large.

The estimated effect on the elasticity of substitution of variations in the country variables of magnitudes observed in the data set is even smaller. Moreover, interpretation is difficult because of interactions among the linear combinations of the variables similar to those discussed above in regard to the additive country variables. Taken at their face value, however, the estimates imply a few interesting observations.

The level of per capita GNP is negatively associated with the elasticity of substitution, which is consistent with casual observations about there

| Table 4.7 | | Implied Changes in Elasticity of Substitution Owing to Increases of One Standard Deviation in Sectoral and Country Variables | | | | | | |

		In of country characteristics						
Regression Number	ln Number of Establishments	GDP per Capita	Life Expectancy	Trade/ GDP	Inflation[a]	Black Market/ Official Exchange Rate	Wages/ National Income	Growth in Product per Capita[a]
6-2	.03	−0.2	.02	− .01	.00			− .01
6-3	.04		− .00	− .01	.00	.01		.01
6-4	.04		− .01	− .01	.01		.00	.01

NOTE: Coefficient estimates in table 4.6 multiplied by one standard deviation of underlying data series.

[a]Not in ln form.

being fewer substitution possibilities with more advanced technology. The negative coefficient estimates of life expectancy (when GDP per capita is not included) may reflect a similar phenomenon of less substitution when labor is of higher quality and more specialized. The negative coefficient estimates of the degree of openness and the positive one for the foreign sector disequilibrium, finally, may both reflect the lesser heterogeneity of production techniques and of subsectoral products when a country specializes more in its areas of comparative advantage and trades more internationally.

4.6   Conclusion

I have presented new estimates of the elasticity of substitution between capital and labor based on 1,723 observations from twenty-seven three-digit ISIC industrial sectors for seventy countries for the period 1967–73. This is a much more extensive data set with a richer diversity of countries than has heretofore been used. Moreover, by using average data for 1967–73 for each observation I am able to lessen downward biases due to additive recording errors and cyclical fluctuations and make the maintained hypothesis of approximate profit maximization under perfect competition more palatable. Furthermore, I am able to explore the effect of sectoral and country characteristics on the estimated parameters.

I carefully consider various sources of biases and attempt to control for them in my estimations. Measurement error may mean the true elasticity is somewhat higher than I estimate; omitted variable bias may mean it is somewhat lower. The estimated values are slightly higher for sectors with more establishments (and therefore more domestic competition?) and for those with more advanced and more capital-intensive technology (group 3 in table 4.5). They are affected even less by country than by sectoral characteristics.

I conclude that under the maintained hypotheses my estimates provide strong support for an elasticity of substitution between capital and labor across industrial sectors and across countries near the Cobb-Douglas value of 1.0. This result is quite robust under the alternative specifications that I consider, with a single caveat about the puzzling role of real per capita GDP. Sectoral and country variations appear to primarily affect not the elasticity of substitution, but the multiplicative neutral technology or overall productivity term (B in relation 1).

This elasticity estimate probably incorporates three phenomena: (1) underlying technical substitution possibilities on a more micro level; (2) variations in optimal factor service flows per unit of factor stocks on a more micro level; and (3) changes in product composition in the components of the three-digit sectors. Although I can not decompose my estimates into the contributions of these three phenomena, from the point of view of aggregate trade and more general development policy it is this composite response that is important—and this study suggests that it is substantial.

Such a value for the elasticity of substitution between capital and labor has several important implications. First, it brings into question the frequent specification of planning models and of other analyses that capital/labor coefficients are fixed. This maintained hypothesis seems to overstate the technological rigidities and may lead to inappropriate conclusions.

Second, under neoclassical assumptions regarding factor payments, elasticities of substitution near one imply that the long-run factoral distribution of income between capital and labor is not altered much by differential growth rates of the two factors. If labor grows relatively slowly, the equilibrium wage increases to compensate so that the wage share remains about the same proportion of national income.

Third, the limited variation across three-digit industrial sectors suggests that aggregation to the overall manufacturing level may not be misleading for some analysis.[15] Of course the implications of aggregation generally also depend on other parameters that may or may not be homogeneous across industrial subsectors.

Fourth, and perhaps most important, an elasticity of substitution between capital and labor near the Cobb-Douglas value suggests considerable flexibility in responding to trade and domestic-sector policies that alter the relative costs of capital and labor services. Examples of such policies are legion. Capital subsidies through favorable import and credit treatment and minimum wages are illustrations of frequently used policies that increase the cost of labor relative to that of capital. The estimated value of the elasticity of substitution between capital and labor implies that manufacturing enterprises can respond to such incentives and use relatively more capital and less labor. In many contexts such responses may exacerbate employment problems.

Appendix: Sources of Data for Country Characteristics

Real GDP per capita is for 1970 as estimated from detailed price comparisons and purchasing power calculations by the method given in Kravis, Kenessey, Heston, and Summers (1975) and Kravis, Heston, and Summers (1978). Data are not available for seven countries: Czechoslovakia, Luxembourg, Mauritius, Mozambique, Poland, Rhodesia, and Yugoslavia.

Life expectancy in years at birth in 1970 is from World Bank (1976) and Hansen (1976).

Exports plus imports relative to GNP are calculated from data in World Bank (1976) and United Nations (1975). Data are not available for four countries: Mozambique, Poland, Rhodesia, and Singapore.

The average annual rates of inflation for 1967–73 are calculated from data in International Monetary Fund (1976). Data are not available for three countries: Kuwait, Papua New Guinea, and Uganda.

The average ratios of the black market exchange rate to the official exchange rate for 1967–73 are calculated from data in Pick's (1975, 1976), International Labor Organization (1977), and United Nations (1977). Data are not available for eleven countries: Barbados, Fiji, Guatemala, Jamaica, Luxembourg, Madagascar, Malta, Mauritius, Mozambique, Papua New Guinea, and Somalia.

The average wage shares in national income for 1967–73 are calculated from data in International Labor Organization (1977). Data are missing for twenty-two countries: Bangladesh, Barbados, Brazil, Cyprus, Czechoslovakia, Dominican Republic, Ethiopia, Ghana, Guatemala, Hungary, Indonesia, Mozambique, Nigeria, Pakistan, Philippines, Poland, Rhodesia, Singapore, Sweden, Tunisia, Turkey, and Yugoslavia.

The growth rates of real GNP per capita for 1967–73 are given in World Bank (1975). Data are not available for nine countries: Barbados, Chile, Cyprus, Fiji, Kuwait, Luxembourg, Madagascar, Malta, and Mauritius.

Notes

1. While reasonably large elasticities of substitution between capital and labor promote flexibility, they do not guarantee it. Other constraints, including those of a macro nature, may severely restrict the possibilities of response. For an empirical example, see Behrman (1972b, 1977).

2. If a wider class of production functions is allowed, it may not be possible to identify whether the returns from scale are not constant or whether the production function is not homothetic. For example, the Mukerji (1963) production function below leads to the subsequent marginal productivity relation, and the latter is statistically indistinguishable from relation (4):

$$V = \left[B \, \delta K^{-\rho_1} + (1 - \delta)L^{-\rho_2} \right]^{-1/\rho_o}$$
$$\ln (V/L) = a' + b' \ln W + c' \ln L,$$
$$\text{where } b' = 1/(1 + \rho_o)$$
$$c' = b' \, (\rho_2 - \rho_o).$$

3. In writing this section I have benefited from reading Nerlove (1967) and Griliches and Ringstad (1971), to which the interested reader is referred for more extensive discussions of these issues.

4. If there is more than one right-side variable, but only one has measurement error, its coefficient estimate is unambiguously biased toward zero, but the coefficient estimates of the other variables may be biased in either way (but the bias can be calculated). However, if more than one right-side variable is measured with error, the expressions for correcting for

measurement error become much more complex, and all coefficients may be under- or overestimated. See Levi (1973) and Theil (1961) for further discussion.

5. Behrman (1972a), Ferguson (1965), Oi (1962), and Okun (1962) further consider errors in the variables owing to cyclical fluctuations.

6. A more satisfactory measure, such as the market share of the largest three of four firms or the Herfindahl-Hirschman index of concentration, cannot be calculated with the available data.

7. If there are no restrictions on foreign exchange movements, the free or black market exchange rate basically is identical to the official rate, and this ratio is one. If there are restrictions on foreign exchange movements owing to a disequilibrium situation in which the domestic currency is overvalued, the free or black market exchange rate exceeds the official exchange rate, and this ratio exceeds one. For further discussion of this variable, see Behrman (1976, 1977).

8. In principle it would be possible to test the maintained hypothesis that such missing observations are random (e.g., Behrman and Wolfe 1980; Behrman, Wolfe, and Tunali 1980; Heckman 1974; or Maddala 1978), but to do so would be beyond the scope of this study.

9. They also may reflect micro adjustments in the optimal factor service flows per unit of factor stock. See Winston (1974).

10. The total number of observations is less than the product of twenty-seven sectors and seventy countries (i.e., 1,890) because some countries do not produce items in some sectors. Table 4.1 indicates the number of countries for which data for each sector are available.

11. Their derivation is for the Cobb-Douglas case, but my estimates suggest that for my data the Cobb-Douglas assumption of an elasticity of substitution equal to one is approximately satisfied.

12. Such a calculation is meant to merely be suggestive. If in fact all of the other parameters were constant across sectors and all production factors were homogeneous, all factors would be used most productively in the sector with the highest B, which would tend to cause offsetting changes in relative sectoral product prices under most forms of market organization. Because of international trade barriers, in fact, comparisons of Bs across countries (as are presented below) under these assumptions probably are more realistic than are comparisons across sectors.

13. Consideration of regression 3-14 alone might suggest that the rate of inflation is highly associated with the level of development and merely representing it. However regression 4-2 does not seem to support such an interpretation.

14. For the same reasons, I do not present estimates that include both additive and multiplicative sectoral or country variables.

15. Of course the analysis of this study is conditional upon aggregation to the three-digit level being satisfactory.

References

Arrow, K. J.; Chenery, H. B.; Minhas, B. S.; and Solow, R. M. (ACMS). 1961. Capital-labor substitution and economic efficiency. *Review of Economics and Statistics* 43:225–50.

Behrman, J. R. 1972a. Sectoral elasticities of substitution between capital and labor in a developing economy: Time series analysis in the case of postwar Chile. *Econometrica* 40:311–28.

———. 1972b. Short-run flexibility in a developing economy. *Journal of Political Economy* 80:292–313.

————. 1976. *Foreign trade regimes and economic development: Chile*. A Special Conference Series on Foreign Trade Regimes and Economic Development, vol. 8, National Bureau of Economic Research. New York: Columbia University Press.

————. 1977. *Macroeconomic policy in a developing country: The Chilean experience*. Contributions to Economic Analysis, no. 109. Amsterdam: North-Holland.

Behrman, J. R., and Wolfe, B. L. 1980. Human capital investments on women and fertility in a developing country: Extensions to include health and nutrition and to deal with incomplete data problems. Madison: University of Wisconsin. Mimeographed.

Behrman, J. R.; Wolfe, B. L.; and Flesher, J. 1979. Some Monte Carlo experiments for dealing with randomly missing observations in social science data. Philadelphia: University of Pennsylvania. Mimeographed.

Behrman, J. R.; Wolfe, B. L.; and Tunali, I. 1980. Determinants of women's earnings in a developing country: A double selectivity, extended human capital approach. Philadelphia: University of Pennsylvania. Mimeographed.

Blitzer, C. R.; Clark, P. B.; and Taylor, L., eds. 1975. *Economy-wide models and development planning*. London: Oxford University Press.

Eckaus, R. S. 1955. The factor proportions problem in underdeveloped countries. *American Economic Review* 45:539–65.

Ferguson, C. E. 1965. Substitution, technical progress, and returns to scale. *American Economic Review* 55:296–305.

Glasser, M. 1964. Linear regression analysis with missing observations among the independent variables. *Journal of the Americal Statistical Association* 59:834–44.

Griliches, Z., and Ringstad, V. 1971. *Economies of scale and the form of the production function: An econometric study of Norwegian manufacturing establishment data*. Contributions to Economic Analysis, no. 72. Amsterdam: North-Holland.

Hansen, R. D. 1976. *The U.S. and world development: Agenda for action*. New York: Praeger.

Heckman, J. 1974. Shadow-prices, market wages, and labor supply. *Econometrica* 42:679–94.

Hester, D. D. 1976. Estimation from incomplete samples. Madison: University of Wisconsin. Mimeographed.

International Labor Organization. 1977. *Yearbook of labor statistics*. Geneva: International Labor Organization.

International Monetary Fund. 1976. *International financial statistics*. Washington, D.C.: International Monetary Fund.

Kravis, I. B.; Heston, A.; and Summers, R. 1978. *International compari-*

sons of real product and purchasing power. United Nations International Comparison Project, phase 2. Baltimore: Johns Hopkins University Press.

Kravis, I. B.; Kenessey, Z.; Heston, A.; and Summers, R. 1975. *A system of international comparisons of gross product and purchasing power.* United Nations International Comparison Project, phase 1. Baltimore: Johns Hopkins University Press.

Krueger, A. O. 1978. Alternative trade strategies and employment in LDC's. *American Economic Review* 68:270–74.

Levi, M. D. 1973. Errors in the variables bias in the presence of correctly measured variables. *Econometrica* 41:985–86.

Maddala, G. S. 1978. Selectivity problems in longitudinal data. *Annals de l'insée,* 423–50.

Maddala, G. S., and Kadane, J. B. 1966. Some notes on the estimation of the CES production function. *Review of Economics and Statistics* 48:340–44.

Mukerji, V. 1963. Generalized SMAC function with constant ratios of elasticities of substitution. *Review of Economic Studies* 30:233–36.

Nerlove, M. 1967. Recent empirical studies of the CES and related production functions. In *The theory and empirical analysis of production,* ed. M. Brown. Studies in Income and Wealth, no. 31. New York: National Bureau of Economic Research.

Oi, W. Y. 1962. Labor as a quasi-fixed factor. *Journal of Political Economy* 70:538–53.

Okun, A. M. 1962. Potential GNP: Its measurement and significance. *Proceedings of the Business and Economics Statistics Section of the American Statistical Association,* pp. 98–104.

Pick's. 1975, 1976. *Pick's currency yearbook.* New York: Pick's.

Sewell, J. W. 1977. *The United States and world development: Agenda 1977.* New York: Praeger.

Theil, H. 1961. *Economic forecasts and policy.* 2d rev. ed. Amsterdam: North-Holland.

United Nations. 1975. *United Nations national income accounts.* New York: United Nations.

———. 1976. *Yearbook of industrial statistics, 1974 edition.* Vol. 1. *General industrial statistics.* New York: United Nations.

———. 1977. *Monthly Bulletin of Statistics.*

White, L. 1978. The evidence on appropriate factor proportions for manufacturing in less developed countries: A survey. *Economic Development and Cultural Change* 27:27–60.

Winston, Gordon C. 1974. Factor substitution, ex ante and ex post. *Journal of Development Economics* 1:145–63.

World Bank. 1975. *World Bank Atlas.* Washington, D. C.: World Bank.

————. 1976. *World Tables 1976*. Baltimore: Johns Hopkins University Press.

————. 1978. *World Development Report, 1978*. Oxford: Oxford University Press.

5   The Substitution of Labor, Skill, and Capital: Its Implications for Trade and Employment

Vittorio Corbo and Patricio Meller

5.1 Introduction

One of the important questions that arise when we consider the implications of alternative trade strategies for employment is the relation of the skill composition of the labor force to the determinants of comparative advantage. Leontief originally conjectured that it was the skills of the American labor force that gave the United States its relatively high labor (in efficiency units) to capital endowment. Since that time, the importance of skills as an explanatory variable in trade flows has repeatedly been found (e.g., Keesing 1966 and Baldwin 1971).

Despite these empirical findings, questions remain as to the appropriate way to model human capital. Trade theory has long been centered upon a two-factor model of the factor proportions explanation of trade. Trade theorists have tended to maintain this framework by attempting to aggregate two of the three factors of production, generally human and physical capital (Kenen 1965). In this regard, questions arise about the appropriate aggregation: Is human capital a close or perfect substitute for physical capital, or is human capital appropriately regarded as labor-augmenting, increasing a country's endowment of efficiency units of labor?

Vittorio Corbo is associated with Instituto de Economia, Pontificia Universidad Católica, Santiago, Chile; Patricio Meller is associated with Corporación de Investigaciónes Económicas para Latinamerica (CIEPLAN), Universidad de Chile, Santiago.

We are grateful for the comments of Jere R. Behrman, Ernest R. Berndt, Franklin M. Fisher, Anne O. Krueger, and a special referee on previous drafts of this chapter. We are indebted to Terry Echaniz, Lisa Horowitz, and José Vrljicak for very efficient research assistance and programming. We are also thankful to NBER and the Canada Council General Research Fund from the Sir George Williams Faculty of Arts of Concordia University for financial support. At the time this research was being carried out, Patricio Meller was a Rockefeller Foundation Research fellow at NBER.

In this chapter we attempt to investigate this question by applying modern production-function estimation to Chilean data for forty-four manufacturing four-digit industries. Whereas, traditionally, econometricians estimated production functions after aggregating unskilled labor and human capital to form one labor factor (Hildebrand and Liu 1965; Griliches and Ringstad 1971), the modern approach is to test for the appropriate aggregation. Aggregation is studied as a problem of forming a "jelly" of factors. The aggregator function need not be linear in the variables. Testing has usually been done within the context of a maintained hypothesis about the form of the production function.

The translog production function has been the most widely used hypothesis with respect to the technology. For this case, Berndt and Christensen (1973a) have shown that, except in cases of fixed proportions or perfect substitution, one consistent aggregate of different productive inputs exists if and only if "some" elasticities of substitution between pairs of factors are equal. For example, in the case of the three factors, unskilled labor (L), skill or human capital (S), and physical capital (K), combining unskilled labor and skill into one aggregate—labor—is valid if $\sigma_{LK} = \sigma_{SK}$. On the other hand, combining human and physical capital is appropriate if $\sigma_{SL} = \sigma_{KL}$. There already exists a considerable empirical literature oriented toward examining which are the consistent aggregates of the different productive inputs (Berndt and Christensen 1973b, 1974, Humphrey and Moroney 1975; Stern 1976; Corbo and Meller 1979a). This is the approach followed in this paper.

In addition to the question of appropriate aggregation, it is also important to ascertain the degree of complementarity or substitutability between different pairs of factors, and to determine whether there exists some difference in the substitutability between pairs of inputs among tradable manufacturing sectors (i.e., manufacturing industries that produce exportables or import-competing goods).[1] For instance, is there greater complementarity between physical capital and skill for the exportable manufacturing industries than for the import-competing ones? For classification of industries according to their trade category, we have used the same criteria and information used in our previous study, Corbo and Meller (1981).

In section 5.2 we describe the properties and characteristics of the translogarithmic production function; we also discuss the notions of separability and aggregation and explain the logic and sequence of tests on the translogarithmic function to be able to verify the different hypotheses of input aggregation. In section 5.3 we present the information related to the data and the econometric and statistical results of the different tests. In section 5.4 we present the conclusions based on the empirical results.

5.2 Translog Production Function Characteristics

The properties of the translogarithmic production function are briefly the following (see Berndt and Christensen 1973a):

1. A general translog is not a homothetic function; therefore the level of production affects the technological characteristics.

2. A priori assumptions are not required in relation to the elasticities of output with respect to factor input. Therefore the monotonicity property of estimated functions has to be verified.

3. A priori assumptions are not required in relation to the convexity of the isoquants. That is, the elasticities of substitution between factors are not restricted a priori to be nonnegative, so that the convexity condition has to be checked.

4. Given the nonhomotheticity property, the monotonicity and convexity conditions have to be checked at each point of the isoquant map to be able to have a well-behaved production function. In other words, the elasticities of output with respect to factor inputs and the elasticities of substitution between factors are not necessarily constant and may vary along each isoquant. Moreover, they depend on the production level.

5. The Cobb-Douglas is a special case of the translog function.

6. The translog function is linear in the parameters, so that it is possible to use linear regression techniques for estimation.

7. Finally, the most important property for this study is that the translog does not impose a priori assumptions related to the separability between the inputs; separability between the inputs can be tested. This property permits determination of whether the conditions for a consistent aggregate of the different pairs of productive factors are met.

The translog function with symmetry imposed ($\gamma_{sk} = \gamma_{ks}$) can be written as:

$$(1) \quad \ln Y_{ij} = \alpha_0^i + \alpha_1^i \ln L_{ij} + \alpha_2^i \ln S_{ij} + \alpha_3^i \ln K_{ij}$$

$$+ \tfrac{1}{2}\gamma_{11}^i (\ln L_{ij})^2 + \gamma_{12}^i (\ln L_{ij})(\ln S_{ij})$$

$$+ \gamma_{13}^i (\ln L_{ij})(\ln K_{ij}) + \tfrac{1}{2}\gamma_{22}^i (\ln S_{ij})^2$$

$$+ \gamma_{23}^i (\ln S_{ij})(\ln K_{ij}) + \tfrac{1}{2}\gamma_{33}^i (\ln K_{ij})^2,$$

where γ is value added, L is labor, S is skill, K is capital, i is an index of a four-digit ISIC industry, and j is an index of a firm within the ith industry.

The hypothesis of constant returns to scale can be tested directly from (1). Constant returns to scale implies a set of restrictions on the parameters of the function (see Berndt and Christensen 1973b, p. 84). A production function is considered well-behaved if it has positive marginal products for each input (i.e., positive monotonocity) and if it is quasi-concave.

The translog function is strictly quasi-concave (strictly convex isoquants) if the bordered Hessian matrix is negative definite. In the case of three inputs, this requires the bordered principal minors of the Hessian matrix to be positive and negative respectively. The translog function does not satisfy these restrictions globally. Still, if we can find wide enough regions in input space (including the observed output and input levels) where these restrictions are satisfied, then the translog function is considered well behaved. To do this, monotonicity and quasi-concavity of the estimated translog function must be checked at every data point in the sample.

Now let us examine the concepts of aggregation and separability of inputs. To this effect, we follow closely Green (1964) and Berndt and Christensen (1973a).

Intuitively, one would think that aggregating two production inputs would require perfect substitutability between them in the production process. But it is very rare to find two productive factors having perfect substitution between them. In economic theory, aggregation has a less restrictive meaning.

We say that aggregation is consistent when using more detailed information than contained in the aggregate results in no difference in the analysis of the problem. The conditions for aggregating two inputs, X_1, and X_2, and obtaining a consistent aggregate input X, require forming an index of consistent quantity Q for the aggregate of the inputs X_1 and X_2, such that when multiplying by an aggregate price index P, of components P_1 and P_2 associated with X_1 and X_2, it should give us the total cost of the inputs (Green 1964).[2] This concept of consistent aggregation is closely related to the concept of functional separability developed by Leontief.

It is said that two variables X_1 and X_2 are functionally separable from a third variable Z if and only if $F(X_1, X_2, Z) = G(H[X_1, X_2], Z)$. The mathematical condition for the variables X_1 and X_2 to be functionally separable from Z is that:

$$\frac{\partial}{\partial Z}\left(\frac{\partial F/\partial X_1}{\partial F/\partial X_2}\right) = 0.$$

Assuming that X_1, X_2, and Z are inputs in a productive process, the condition of functional separability implies that the marginal rate of technical substitution between the inputs X_1 and X_2 is independent of the third input Z. In other words, if we keep the inputs X_1 and X_2 constant and increase the input Z, the increase in Z would affect in equal proportion the marginal productivities of X_1 and X_2; the effect of Z is similar to that of the neutral technical progress described by Hicks (Humphrey and Moroney 1975).

That two variables $(X_1$ and $X_2)$ are functionally separable from a third one (Z) implies that those two variables $(X_1$ and $X_2)$ can be aggregated; in other words, it is possible to find an index of consistent quantity and an aggregated price index that would permit a consistent aggregation (see Green 1964).

Berndt and Christensen (1973a) have shown that, in general, conditions of functional separability of two variables are equivalent to certain equality conditions between the elasticities of substitution between factor inputs. In other words, that the inputs X_1 and X_2 are functionally separable from the input Z implies (as a necessary and sufficient condition) that $\sigma_{1Z} = \sigma_{2Z}$ (the elasticity of substitution between X_1 and Z is equal to the elasticity of substitution between X_2 and Z).

Therefore, in the case of a productive process with three inputs, the problem of aggregation of two inputs can be transformed into the problem of examining the equality of the elasticities of substitution between those two inputs with respect to the third factor.

Introducing the condition of equality of the elasticities of substitution between inputs implies certain restrictions on the parameters of the function; these restrictions can be tested econometrically. In the case of the translog function of equation (1), three types of pairwise weak separability may exist: the weak separability of L and S from K, L and K from S, and S and K from L. Furthermore, for the translog function, these separability conditions are fulfilled globally if and only if some specific set of restrictions on the parameters of the function is fulfilled.[3] Global separability imposes more restrictive conditions on the parameters of the translog function; that is, it requires all $\gamma_{ij} = 0$ for $i \neq j$.[4]

5.3   Data and Statistical Results

5.3.1   Data

For our data, the basic unit of information is the establishment as defined in the 1967 Chilean census of manufactures. There are 11,468 establishments, grouped into eighty-five industries according to the four-digit International Standard Industrial Classification (ISIC). From these eighty-five industries we selected a subset of forty-four that allow at least ten degrees of freedom for the estimation of equation (1). Within each industry we selected a subset of establishments that satisfied each of the following restrictions.

1. Number of days worked by the establishment ≥ 50
2. Wage bill of blue-collar workers > 0
3. Book value of machinery > 0
4. Gross value added > 0
5. Nonwage gross value added > 0
6. Number of persons employed ≥ 10
7. Number of white-collar workers > 0

8. Number of blue-collar workers > 0
9. (Book value of machinery/gross value added)$_{ij}$ $>1/10$ (Book value of machinery/gross value added)$_i$

All these restrictions are self-explanatory with perhaps the exception of restriction 9. That was used to eliminate establishments that satisfied restriction 3 but had a very small value for the book value of machinery. When the ratio of book value to value added for a particular establishment was less than one-tenth that of the remainder of the industry, the firm was eliminated from the sample.

The definitions of the variables used in our estimate are as follows:

L = Average annual number of man-days. It is measured as the sum of production workers, blue-collar workers in auxiliary activities, white-collar workers, and entrepreneurs times the number of days worked by the establishment.[5] The units of L are defined in such a way that for a given industry i, the mean of L equals one.

S = Skill-days units, average annual number of equivalent blue-collar-days minus L.[6] The equivalent number of blue-collar-days is measured as the ratio of the total wage payments, plus an imputation for entrepreneurs, to the minimum wage rate of the whole industrial sector.[7] The units of S are defined in such a way that for a given industry i, the mean of S equals one.

K = Book value of machinery at 1967 prices less accumulated depreciation.[8] The units of K are defined in such a way that for a given industry i, the mean of K equals one.

Y = Gross value added at 1967 prices.[9] The units of Y are defined in such a way that for a given industry i, the mean of Y equals one.

5.3.2   Statistical Results

In all our estimates, the ordinary least squares (OLSQ) estimating procedure was used. A difficulty with the use of OLSQ is that the regressors (the factor quantities) are firms' decision variables as much as the production level. Failure to take account of this problem introduces contemporaneous correlation between the regressors and the random error of the regression (the simultaneity problem). In such a case, the OLSQ estimates of equation (1) are biased and inconsistent. Consistent estimates could be obtained by using an instrumental variable (IV) estimator; however, in cross-sectional analysis, the usual instruments—lagged values of the explanatory variables—are usually so highly correlated with the variables for which they are serving as instruments that the

OLSQ and IV results are not very different (Griliches 1967, p. 277). In our case, only one cross section was available, and consequently there was no variable that could be used as an instrument. Therefore we have estimated our model using OLSQ, and thus our results may be subject to some simultaneous-equation bias.

It could be argued that more efficient estimates might be obtained by using the set of equations derived from profit maximization in perfectly competitive product and factor markets, assuming further that the translog function is locally concave around the equilibrium. This is the procedure used in almost all estimates of translog functions. As with any other full-information method, we can be confident of obtaining more efficient estimates only so long as the assumptions used to derive the system of equations are true. If they are not, a specification error is introduced that will have unknown consequences for the properties of our estimates. In the case of Chilean manufacturing there is the strong danger of specification error owing to the presence of noncompetitive elements.[10] For this reason, we estimated the production function directly.

The problem of heteroskedasticity is minimized in our estimation procedure because we work with all the variables scaled in such a way that their means are equal to one. In this way, values of the variables are of similar magnitude.

Turning to the results of the direct estimation of the translog function, in table 5.1 we present estimates of the unconstrained translog function for the forty-four industries. These are the industries for which we have ten or more degrees of freedom. As can be seen, the number of firms was very large for some industries, ranging as high as 293 for sector 3117 (bakery products). The R^2s are extremely high for cross-section regressions. The lowest one is 0.649 for sector 3132 (wine industry), and all but five are above 0.8.

The first test performed for the general translog model was for constant returns to scale (CRTS). In only three cases out of forty-four is CRTS rejected at the 1 percent level.[11] These are bakery products (ISIC 3117), wearing apparel except footwear (ISIC 3220), and cement for construction (ISIC 3693).

For the forty-one CRTS sectors, we tested further for a Cobb-Douglas technology. For thirty-five out of the forty-one sectors the Cobb-Douglas technology could not be rejected (see table 5.2). There are six CRTS sectors for which the Cobb-Douglas technology was rejected: spinning, weaving, and finishing textiles (3211); sawmills, planing, and other wood mills (3311); printing, publishing, and allied industries (3420); furniture and fixtures primarily of metal (3812); special industrial machinery (3824); and machinery and equipment not elsewhere classified (3829). For these six sectors we proceeded further to test for pairwise linear and nonlinear separability.

Table 5.1   Unconstrained Translog Function

$$\ln y = \alpha_0 + \alpha_1 \ln LM + \alpha_2 \ln LS + \alpha_3 \ln K + \tfrac{1}{2}\gamma_{11} (\ln LM)^2 + \tfrac{1}{2}\gamma_{22} (\ln LS)^2 + \tfrac{1}{2}\gamma_{33} (\ln K)^2 + \gamma_{12} (\ln LM)(\ln LS) + \gamma_{13} (\ln LM)(\ln K) + \gamma_{23} (\ln LS)(\ln K)$$

ISIC Code	Number of Observations	α_0	α_1	α_2	α_3	γ_{11}	γ_{22}	γ_{33}	γ_{12}	γ_{13}	γ_{23}	R^2	SSR
3111	100	-.0969 (-.951)	.6357 (4.369)	.4484 (3.713)	.1486 (1.683)	.0561 (.222)	.1278 (1.872)	-.0657 (-.868)	-.1966 (-2.002)	.1907 (2.173)	-.0519 (-.745)	.7909	37.011
3112	46	.0258 (.160)	.2066 (.658)	.3159 (1.296)	.4424 (2.252)	.4330 (.683)	.1070 (1.475)	.2475 (1.077)	-.2462 (-.865)	-.2865 (-1.038)	-.0014 (-.008)	.8753	15.751
3113	32	-.0949 (-.470)	.4555 (.828)	.3746 (1.576)	.3852 (1.012)	.2912 (.330)	.0124 (.141)	.2608 (.616)	.2610 (.723)	-.2727 (-.491)	-.0801 (-.509)	.8405	7.884
3114	37	.2072 (1.645)	.2896 (1.012)	.2618 (1.468)	.2779 (1.663)	.1795 (.669)	.0056 (.140)	.0117 (.071)	-.2531 (-1.248)	-.0026 (-.134)	.0965 (.769)	.8795	5.374
3115	34	.1007 (.656)	.5486 (2.159)	.6210 (2.401)	.4300 (2.253)	-.7311 (-2.152)	.1258 (.316)	-.4432 (-1.846)	.3926 (1.525)	.1704 (.826)	.0105 (.041)	.8386	6.674
3117	293	-.1798 (-3.364)	.6429 (9.618)	.3099 (8.074)	.1947 (4.334)	.0176 (.133)	.0508 (6.298)	-.0157 (-.419)	-.0247 (-1.451)	.0105 (.184)	.0186 (1.763)	.7891	54.246
3119	26	.0346 (.213)	.0499 (.224)	.3450 (1.856)	.5376 (3.126)	.6473 (1.070)	-.1198 (-.361)	-.0432 (-.370)	-.3063 (-1.554)	-.1509 (-.405)	.2314 (1.353)	.9722	2.032
3121	39	-.9560 (-4.973)	.5394 (1.537)	.7454 (2.571)	.0411 (.187)	-.0076 (-.007)	.1891 (2.273)	-.3394 (-1.370)	-.4169 (-.922)	.3795 (.913)	.1794 (.968)	.8747	10.589
3131	25	-.0454 (-.159)	-.2487 (-.663)	.9613 (3.760)	.1758 (.830)	.7664 (.724)	.6798 (2.222)	-.1462 (-.588)	-.7801 (-1.638)	-.2237 (-.786)	.1166 (.480)	.8530	5.737
3132	70	-.2464 (-1.676)	.9611 (5.338)	-.0270 (-.255)	.1246 (.809)	.4401 (1.570)	-.0116 (-.495)	-.2697 (-1.277)	.0522 (1.194)	.0826 (.441)	-.0298 (-.640)	.6490	26.827

3211	232	.0852 (1.417)	.5868 (6.987)	.3312 (5.526)	.0491 (.840)	−.0984 (−.828)	.0399 (2.569)	−.1285 (−2.798)	−.0028 (−.064)	.1065 (1.889)	−.0088 (−.238)	.8872	48.005
3212	22	.2000 (1.631)	.6872 (3.083)	−.0094 (−.048)	.2559 (1.568)	.2532 (.386)	−.8880 (−2.042)	−.1742 (−.395)	.6950 (1.479)	−.4157 (−.690)	.2281 (.989)	.9154	1.321
3213	145	−.1369 (−2.127)	.7275 (5.568)	.2034 (2.395)	.1910 (2.476)	−.0781 (−.281)	.0062 (.384)	.0496 (.669)	.0960 (.954)	−.0530 (−.459)	−.0354 (−.591)	.8996	23.278
3220	239	−.1254 (−2.439)	.7577 (8.059)	.2678 (4.491)	.1562 (2.614)	−.1419 (−.791)	.0278 (2.004)	.0704 (.979)	.6999 (1.421)	−.0665 (−.774)	−.0434 (−1.046)	.8643	48.143
3231	57	−.0689 (−.554)	.9764 (3.610)	.1041 (.473)	.0799 (.614)	−.6704 (−.897)	−.1552 (−.753)	−.0126 (−.081)	.2915 (1.314)	.2156 (.719)	−.1183 (−.663)	.8507	12.469
3233	30	.0992 (.606)	.0859 (.224)	.5592 (2.900)	.4361 (2.120)	.3751 (.300)	.1526 (.852)	.3786 (1.696)	−.2934 (−.626)	−.4114 (−.913)	.0132 (.098)	.8408	3.907
3240	138	−.1239 (−1.915)	.3517 (3.046)	.3896 (4.768)	.3604 (5.326)	.0924 (.376)	.0118 (.211)	.1992 (2.504)	.0613 (.633)	−.2323 (−2.202)	.0054 (.097)	.9195	21.566
3311	252	.1255 (2.260)	.4704 (7.824)	.3197 (7.410)	.1448 (3.311)	.0542 (.723)	.0542 (5.804)	−.9920 (−2.479)	−.0496 (−2.235)	.0202 (.441)	.0059 (.419)	.7956	65.886
3312	27	−.0376 (−.241)	.2378 (.991)	.1928 (1.949)	.3681 (3.626)	−.5919 (−.906)	.0202 (.708)	.2552 (1.642)	−.1667 (−1.778)	.0750 (.275)	.0069 (.165)	.8176	2.478
3320	132	−.0998 (−1.279)	.5238 (4.813)	.2539 (3.698)	.2824 (3.657)	−.0079 (−.029)	.0307 (1.938)	.0278 (.338)	−.0337 (−.471)	−.0175 (−.146)	.0358 (.873)	.8194	26.851
3411	19	.0101 (.048)	.4048 (.575)	.2956 (.410)	.2517 (1.512)	−2.2174 (−1.041)	1.9648 (1.503)	.3246 (1.587)	.2409 (.311)	.8514 (1.326)	−1.2373 (−1.609)	.9868	1.011
3420	149	.0632 (1.057)	.1452 (1.738)	.6026 (8.825)	.2452 (4.411)	.2193 (1.594)	.0794 (6.449)	−.0173 (−.385)	−.1518 (−2.014)	−.0570 (−.868)	.0546 (2.884)	.9091	23.040
3511	32	.1717 (.522)	.5276 (1.417)	.7685 (1.834)	−.4997 (−1.732)	1.2334 (1.462)	−.2198 (−.554)	−.6203 (−2.758)	−.5226 (−1.238)	.1866 (.651)	.2736 (1.046)	.7520	10.512

Table 5.1 (continued)

ISIC Code	Number of Observations	α_0	α_1	α_2	α_3	γ_{11}	γ_{22}	γ_{33}	γ_{12}	γ_{13}	γ_{23}	R^2	SSR
3521	25	-.1717 (-.870)	.6832 (1.527)	-.0326 (-.075)	.5779 (2.471)	1.9223 (1.153)	.2698 (.603)	.6510 (.690)	-.7128 (-1.001)	-.0654 (-.063)	-.5540 (-1.417)	.9259	2.362
3522	45	.1518 (1.753)	.3642 (1.668)	.2531 (1.330)	.2847 (2.065)	-.0685 (-.081)	-.4998 (-2.123)	-.3249 (-1.776)	.1172 (.359)	-.1271 (-.357)	.3850 (1.295)	.9267	5.148
3523	52	.0928 (.620)	.6236 (1.503)	.3625 (1.251)	.2749 (1.581)	-.4711 (-.422)	.3221 (1.164)	.1360 (.939)	-.0827 (-.174)	.1991 (.644)	-.2571 (-1.687)	.9054	11.740
3529	37	.0857 (.425)	.0978 (.464)	.4629 (1.254)	.3359 (1.058)	.0322 (.076)	-.0171 (-.074)	-.3226 (-1.614)	-.2956 (-1.020)	.1499 (.653)	.2963 (1.151)	.8459	8.774
3559	24	.4050 (1.832)	.2203 (.393)	.5989 (1.646)	.2153 (.839)	-.1486 (-.278)	-.1439 (-.494)	-.1302 (-.3021)	-.1194 (-.383)	-.0417 (-.109)	.2631 (.935)	.9441	2.296
3560	77	-.0313 (-.315)	.2301 (1.816)	.5860 (5.642)	.2402 (2.751)	-.0234 (-.073)	.0910 (2.414)	-.2111 (-2.008)	-.2297 (-1.606)	.1478 (.994)	.1633 (1.512)	.8565	16.666
3620	32	-.0412 (-.316)	.0190 (.095)	.6888 (2.923)	.1808 (1.175)	-.0205 (-.055)	-.3357 (-.711)	-.0137 (-.101)	.2631 (.730)	-.3814 (-2.183)	.3024 (1.488)	.9480	3.830
3693	39	.0102 (.090)	.3179 (1.685)	.4565 (4.293)	.1966 (2.544)	.5817 (1.950)	.0551 (2.683)	.0497 (.529)	.0421 (.864)	-.4759 (-3.270)	.1008 (1.473)	.9178	3.818
3710	42	.0324 (.208)	.1465 (.731)	.5536 (2.749)	.1791 (1.365)	.2204 (.651)	.1878 (.523)	-.0360 (-.278)	-.1708 (-.625)	-.0265 (-.136)	-.0274 (-.150)	.8996	9.126
3811	26	-.0991 (-.473)	.4356 (1.105)	.5703 (1.550)	.0732 (.264)	.6465 (.592)	.1235 (.237)	-.1083 (-.313)	-.3929 (-.667)	-.0828 (-.278)	.1734 (.394)	.8977	4.266

	n											R^2	F
3812	47	-.0973 (-.821)	.3576 (1.625)	.5318 (3.260)	.2389 (2.023)	1.1467 (1.555)	.1032 (.882)	.0701 (.686)	-.5705 (-3.262)	-.1552 (-.627)	.1122 (1.127)	.9161	6.134
3813	76	.0350 (.292)	.5016 (3.659)	.3285 (2.870)	.3630 (4.166)	-.1609 (-.615)	.0513 (2.264)	.1348 (1.764)	-.0454 (-.419)	-.0547 (-.586)	-.0362 (-.538)	.8736	15.811
3814	56	.0826 (.837)	.1063 (.708)	.4646 (3.380)	.3759 (3.852)	.1110 (.425)	.0682 (1.958)	.0627 (.682)	-.0075 (-.061)	0.0833 (-.939)	-.0203 (-.274)	.9193	8.170
3815	31	-.0128 (-.077)	.3888 (1.514)	.5902 (2.120)	.2002 (1.087)	-.3193 (-.534)	.3796 (1.267)	-.0794 (-.250)	-.2783 (-.607)	.1244 (.386)	.0341 (.101)	.8803	5.349
3819	86	-.0438 (-.496)	.7057 (4.656)	.2339 (2.833)	.2117 (2.761)	-.1524 (-.383)	.0303 (1.895)	.0260 (.376)	.0070 (.094)	.0058 (.039)	-.0089 (-.216)	.8588	13.567
3822	30	.0197 (.153)	.3572 (2.215)	.5764 (4.798)	.1800 (2.002)	-.0211 (-.038)	.0782 (2.467)	.0307 (.327)	.0193 (.072)	.0204 (.166)	-.0202 (-.215)	.8929	3.138
3824	19	-.1429 (-.782)	.0569 (.235)	1.1619 (2.894)	-.0668 (-.256)	.1693 (.252)	.2367 (2.981)	-.1289 (-.405)	-.1927 (-.418)	-.3874 (-.873)	.3237 (.949)	.8677	1.495
3829	89	-.1209 (-1.374)	.2540 (1.777)	.5760 (5.256)	.1858 (2.178)	-.0485 (-.282)	.0668 (2.999)	-.0329 (-.407)	.0132 (.235)	-.0121 (-.132)	.0059 (.259)	.9006	18.840
3839	19	.0799 (.349)	-.1985 (-.544)	.7805 (1.612)	.2709 (1.198)	.6094 (.746)	.6439 (1.008)	-.0230 (-.144)	-.8114 (-1.056)	-.1075 (-.524)	.1080 (.463)	.0950	2.049
3841	19	.2533 (-1.334)	.5058 (1.324)	.4955 (1.279)	.0232 (.191)	.3142 (.433)	.7743 (2.340)	.6745 (5.962)	-.4132 (-.935)	.2226 (1.319)	-.6364 (-3.752)	.9920	.310
3843	73	-.3994 (-3.514)	.4041 (2.069)	.4784 (2.704)	.3894 (2.735)	-.8777 (-1.928)	-.1405 (-.897)	.1105 (.660)	.4210 (1.491)	.0411 (.273)	-.0061 (-.069)	.8536	20.364

Table 5.2   **Cobb-Douglas with CRTS**

$\ln y = \alpha_0 + \alpha_1 \ln LM + \alpha_2 \ln LS + \alpha_3 \ln K$: subject to $\alpha_1 + \alpha_2 + \alpha_3 = 1.0$

ISIC Code	Number of Observations	α_0	α_1	α_2	α_3	R^2	SSR	F
3111	100	−.168 (−2.126)	.396 (5.577)	.357 (5.666)	.247 (4.333)	.758	42.766	1.491
3112	46	−.163 (−1.347)	.506 (4.865)	.118 (2.000)	.377 (3.307)	.828	21.733	2.040
3113	32	.072 (.507)	.429 (3.516)	.237 (4.740)	.334 (3.408)	.820	8.886	.295
3114	37	.335 (2.681)	.648 (8.307)	.094 (2.350)	.258 (3.440)	.808	8.550	2.598
3115	34	.033 (.251)	.556 (4.672)	.316 (1.745)	.128 (.969)	.670	13.624	4.111
3119	26	.015 (.151)	.213 (2.505)	.372 (4.428)	.416 (6.933)	.958	3.082	1.490
3121	39	−.912 (−6.561)	.389 (3.087)	.261 (3.222)	.351 (3.375)	.817	15.490	2.178
3131	25	.003 (.018)	.263 (1.574)	.463 (2.967)	.274 (1.764)	.705	11.496	4.740
3132	70	−.111 (−1.219)	.692 (6.989)	.018 (.666)	.289 (3.010)	.591	31.249	.307
3211	232	.096 (2.181)	.584 (16.680)	.208 (8.320)	.207 (6.088)	.874	53.764	8.102*
3212	22	.045 (.542)	.438 (4.132)	.163 (1.273)	.399 (3.764)	.847	2.384	2.583

3213	145	-.177 (-3.933)	.578 (11.115)	.172 (5.058)	.250 (5.681)	.890	25.509	.503
3231	57	-.127 (-1.628)	.527 (5.377)	.365 (3.842)	.109 (1.379)	.835	13.799	.716
3233	30	.076 (.783)	.329 (2.350)	.450 (4.639)	.221 (2.511)	.797	4.976	1.240
3240	138	-.122 (-2.541)	.397 (8.446)	.338 (8.243)	.264 (6.285)	.908	24.680	3.646
3311	252	.116 (2.829)	.646 (18.450)	.088 (5.866)	.266 (7.600)	.751	80.192	15.267*
3312	27	.172 (1.653)	.710 (8.160)	.083 (3.458)	.208 (2.337)	.638	4.922	3.855
3320	132	-.111 (-2.055)	.672 (14.933)	.073 (3.041)	.255 (5.666)	.800	29.685	3.640
3411	19	.105 (1.019)	.406 (3.123)	.333 (1.947)	.262 (4.158)	.979	1.629	.712
3420	149	.073 (1.520)	.411 (10.024)	.233 (9.708)	.357 (9.394)	.870	32.850	19.710*
3511	32	.083 (.439)	.352 (2.378)	.547 (3.022)	.101 (.782)	.574	18.059	3.131
3521	25	-.148 (-1.510)	.221 (.884)	.291 (1.841)	.487 (2.459)	.851	4.757	1.268
3522	45	.044 (.666)	.210 (2.121)	.369 (3.690)	.421 (5.134)	.905	6.645	2.841
3523	52	.011 (.098)	.146 (1.315)	.562 (4.973)	.292 (3.792)	.883	14.498	.407

Table 5.2 (continued)

ISIC Code	Number of Observations	α_0	α_1	α_2	α_3	R^2	SSR	F
3529	37	.123 (1.230)	.386 (3.446)	.322 (2.576)	.292 (2.862)	.815	10.538	.875
3559	24	.022 (.266)	.554 (3.668)	.481 (4.219)	−.035 (−.284)	.919	3.322	.572
3560	77	−.083 (−1.238)	.417 (5.712)	.289 (5.160)	.295 (4.538)	.827	20.101	3.905
3620	32	.048 (.475)	.506 (4.147)	.231 (1.560)	.262 (2.977)	.914	6.355	2.311
3710	42	.062 (.738)	.219 (2.281)	.464 (4.000)	.317 (4.594)	.892	9.787	.174
3811	26	−.123 (−1.149)	.608 (5.477)	.264 (1.639)	.128 (1.040)	.873	5.064	.966
3812	47	−.190 (−2.043)	.498 (6.225)	.390 (5.416)	.112 (1.349)	.849	11.050	6.851[*]
3813	76	−.137 (−1.851)	.489 (8.890)	.200 (4.444)	.311 (5.759)	.833	20.837	2.790

3814	56	.086 (1.303)	.418 (8.360)	.140 (3.888)	.441 (8.480)	.898	10.292	3.563
3815	31	−.063 (−.583)	.434 (3.312)	.194 (1.437)	.372 (2.676)	.843	7.016	.825
3819	86	−.098 (−1.606)	.657 (14.600)	.109 (4.360)	.235 (5.875)	.842	15.140	1.689
3822	30	.023 (.244)	.561 (7.480)	.230 (5.111)	.209 (3.370)	.821	5.235	4.842
3824	19	.011 (.082)	.544 (4.000)	.036 (.642)	.419 (3.103)	.560	4.972	8.027*
3829	89	−.139 (−2.074)	.574 (10.830)	.131 (4.517)	.296 (5.285)	.874	23.965	5.909*
3839	19	.102 (.980)	.072 (.452)	.612 (3.517)	.316 (4.051)	.856	2.803	.820
3841	19	.007 (.058)	.446 (3.185)	.375 (2.884)	.179 (2.486)	.956	1.707	4.493
3843	73	−.455 (−5.617)	.292 (2.891)	.507 (5.761)	.202 (2.589)	.819	25.237	.775

NOTE: An asterisk denotes that the hypothesis that the Cobb-Douglas specification is correct can be rejected (see text).

For linear restrictions, the existence of a linear logarithmic index for L and K was rejected in all six cases. We cannot reject the existence of a linear logarithmic aggregator for L and S in industries 3311, 3812, 3824, and 3829. For S and K, the existence of a linear logarithmic aggregator is rejected for all sectors except 3824.[12]

Finally, for the three sectors for which the CRTS hypothesis was rejected, we tested for complete global separability. In all three cases we found that a linear logarithmic aggregator can be built for labor (L) and skill (S), but for only one out of these three sectors is a linear aggregator of S and K possible.

It thus appears that, for most cases, there is some slight evidence in support of building an aggregator of labor and skill rather than of skill and capital. Furthermore, in most cases the proper aggregator is a geometric one (linear in the logs) rather than an arithmetic one with equal weights as used in most of the testing of trade theories. If these results can be extended to other countries, we might find that, with a proper aggregation of L and S, a two-factor model with labor (in efficiency units) and capital can be used to study the pattern of trade.

The next task is to evaluate technological differences across tradable sectors. To do this we estimate the elasticities of output with respect to each factor. Table 5.3 provides three rankings of the factor elasticities (labor, skill, and capital) ordered from higher to lower values for the forty-four manufacturing sectors. Of these forty-four sectors, five are manufacturing industries producing exportable goods: canning and pre-serving of fruits and vegetables (3113);[13] canning, preserving, and pro-cessing of fish, crustaceans, and similar foods (3114); wine industries (3132); sawmills, planing, and other wood mills (3311); and manufacture of pulp, paper, and paperboard (3411). Two of the forty-four sectors are industries classified as noncompeting import industries; these are cutlery, hand tools, and general hardware (3811) and special industrial machinery and equipment except metal and woodworking machinery (3824). The remaining thirty-seven manufacturing sectors are classified as import-competing industries.[14]

As we have stated above, it is not possible to reject a CRTS Cobb-Douglas production function as a representation of the technology for most of the industries used in this study; as a consequence, no significant difference has been found between export and import-competing manu-facturing in relation to the degree of complementarity or substitution between their productive factors (labor, skill, and physical capital). In fact, in only one case out of five export industries, and in seven cases out of thirty-seven import-competing industries, a CRTS Cobb-Douglas pro-duction function was rejected.

To observe the existence of some other technological differences be-tween export and import-competing industries, we have computed the value-added productive factor elasticities. These factor elasticities could be used, specially in the case of a three-input production function, as a sort of measurement of the relative factor intensity of an industry; this is what is done below.

Looking at factor elasticity rankings, we have found the following (see table 5.3): (1) Export-producing sectors are generally clustered above the median value of the labor elasticity. (2) Export-producing sectors are clustered, in general, below the median value of the skill elasticity. (3) Export-producing sectors are clustered around the median value of the capital elasticity. (4) No clear pattern arises for the two sectors classified as noncompeting import industries.

An important dynamic implication of these findings should be stressed. An equal output expansion of tradables will have, in general, a higher employment creation for exportables than for importables; for skill, requirements will be exactly the opposite. For capital, the results are unclear and require the consideration of the specified output mix.

5.4 Conclusions

Perhaps the most striking feature of our findings is the high proportion of cases where estimation of a translog production function indicated that the Cobb-Douglas production form was a satisfactory representation of the technology; if this is valid for most situations, then, it would not be worthwhile the effort to estimate translog production functions (however, this is only known expost). Even more striking, perhaps, is that, in all but three of the forty-four industries for which estimates could be made, the constant returns to scale hypothesis could not be rejected. The remaining three sectors, all import-competing, provided evidence of increasing returns to scale. As a consequence of this type of results, no significant difference has been found between export and import-competing manufacturing industries with respect to the degree of complementarity or substitution between factors of production.

Using the results to investigate some other differences between exportable and import-competing manufacturing industries, the most striking finding is that the output elasticities of exportable industries with respect to labor were generally higher than the median, while those with respect to skills were generally below the median. For capital, no such pattern emerged. It may thus be that differences in the skill composition of the labor force are more important in affecting comparative advantage than are differences in capital/labor endowments.

Finally, for those industries for which the Cobb-Douglas specification could not be rejected, it obviously makes no difference whether skills and unskilled labor are aggregated or whether skills and capital are aggregated. For the industries that were not Cobb-Douglas but had constant

Table 5.3 **Ranking of Manufacturing Sectors by Value-Added Elasticities**

Numerical Ranking	Labor	Skill	Capital
1	.851 (3117)[a]	.612 (3839)	.487 (3521)
2	.850 (3220)	.562 (3523)	.441 (3814)
3	.846 (3693)	.547 (3511)	.421 (3522)
4	.710 (3312)	.507 (3843)	.419 (3824)
5	.692 (3132)	.464 (3710)	.416 (3119)
6	.672 (3320)	.463 (3131)	.399 (3212)
7	.657 (3819)	.450 (3233)	.377 (3112)
8	.648 (3114)	.390 (3812)	.372 (3815)
9	.646 (3311)	.375 (3941)	.357 (3420)
10	.608 (3811)	.372 (3119)	.351 (3121)
11	.584 (3211)	.369 (3522)	.334 (3113)
12	.578 (3213)	.365 (3231)	.317 (3710)
13	.574 (3829)	.357 (3111)	.316 (3839)
14	.561 (3822)	.338 (3240)	.311 (3813)
15	.556 (3115)	.333 (3411)	.296 (3829)
16	.544 (3824)	.322 (3529)	.295 (3560)
17	.527 (3231)	.316 (3115)	.292 (3529)
18	.506 (3112)	.302 (3559)	.292 (3523)
19	.506 (3620)	.291 (3521)	.289 (3132)
20	.498 (3812)	.289 (3560)	.274 (3131)
21	.489 (3813)	.264 (3811)	.268 (3559)
22	.446 (3941)	.261 (3121)	.266 (3311)
23	.438 (3212)	.237 (3113)	.264 (3240)
24	.430 (3559)	.233 (3420)	.262 (3411)
25	.430 (3815)	.231 (3620)	.262 (3620)
26	.429 (3113)	.230 (3822)	.258 (3114)
27	.418 (3814)	.208 (3211)	.255 (3320)
28	.417 (3560)	.200 (3813)	.250 (3213)
29	.411 (3420)	.194 (3815)	.247 (3111)
30	.406 (3411)	.172 (3213)	.235 (3819)
31	.397 (3240)	.163 (3212)	.232 (3693)
32	.396 (3111)	.140 (3814)	.229 (3117)
33	.389 (3121)	.140 (3220)	.221 (3233)
34	.386 (3529)	.131 (3829)	.209 (3822)
35	.352 (3511)	.124 (3693)	.208 (3312)
36	.329 (3233)	.118 (3112)	.207 (3211)
37	.292 (3843)	.109 (3819)	.202 (3843)
38	.263 (3131)	.094 (3114)	.194 (3220)
39	.221 (3521)	.088 (3311)	.179 (3941)
40	.219 (3710)	.083 (3312)	.128 (3115)
41	.213 (3119)	.073 (3320)	.128 (3811)
42	.210 (3522)	.055 (3117)	.112 (3812)
43	.146 (3523)	.036 (3824)	.109 (3231)
44	.072 (3839)	.018 (3132)	.101 (3511)

NOTE: For sectors 3211, 3311, 3420, 3812, 3824, and 3829, values obtained in table 5.2 have been used as a local approximation. For sectors 3117, 3220, and 3693, values used correspond to a nonconstant returns to scale Cobb-Douglas function; see Corbo and Meller (1979*b*).

[a]Figures in parentheses correspond to the four-digit ISIC code.

returns to scale, a linear logarithmic aggregator was valid in all cases, but in only one case could a skilled-capital aggregator be defended. These results provide some slight evidence in support of aggregating skilled and unskilled labor into efficiency units.

Notes

1. To our knowledge, Stern (1976) is the only author in the literature who attempted this approach, but data limitations did not allow him to study this question fully.

2. The procedure by which we obtain the number of labor-efficient units to aggregate blue- and white-collar workers is an example of consistent aggregation. The index of consistent quantity Q is $Q = X_1 + (P_2/P_1) X_2$. Using $P = P_1$ as an aggregate price index, the product PQ gives the total wage bill (for blue- and white-collar workers).

3. For details see Berndt and Christensen (1973a, p. 102).

4. There is a link between pairwise and global separability; if two sets of weak separability conditions are satisfied, then global separability conditions are automatically satisfied. The hypothesis of constant returns to scale (CRTS) can be tested directly from (1). Constant returns to scale also implies a set of restrictions on the parameters of the function. In the special case of CRTS, the fulfillment of the conditions for global separability implies that the translog function becomes a Cobb-Douglas function. See Berndt and Christensen (1973a, p. 84).

5. Preliminary statistical tests and regressions were performed using the number of annual man-hours worked by production workers; however, this variable turned out to be highly unreliable. Therefore the only available variable measurement of a flow was the number of days worked by an establishment during the year of the census of manufactures. The use of this variable implies that in all establishments of the same industry: workers work the same number of hours; absenteeism and part-time workers are equally distributed (part-time workers are negligible in Chilean manufacturing); and the number of shifts worked is the same (most Chilean manufacturing establishments work only one shift).

6. The implicit assumption here is that each worker is composed of two parts: body and skills; see Griliches (1967).

7. The wage rate of entrepreneurs is assumed to be twice the average wage rate of white-collar workers within a given firm. The minimum wage rate of the whole industrial sector is computed as the simple average of the ten lowest wage rates of blue-collar workers observed in the census.

8. The use of book values to measure the capital services factor (besides the traditional limitations of ignoring differences in capacity utilization, accounting procedures, and depreciation rates) in a persistently inflationary economy like Chile's leads to an underestimation of the capital factor of the older establishments, exaggerating their technical efficiency. One of the authors (Meller 1975) earlier used a measure of capital services instead of the value of the stock. The capital service variable was defined as $K = .10 K_M + .03 K_B + .20 K_V + .10 (K_M + K_B + K_V + K_I)$, where K_M, K_B, K_V, and K_I are the book values of machinery, buildings, vehicles, and inventory goods. Geometric depreciation rates of .10, .03, and .20 were used for machinery, buildings, and vehicles, and a 10 percent real interest rate was used as the cost of capital. The simple correlation between the capital service measure and the book value of machinery measure was above .95 in sixteen out of the twenty-one industrial sectors considered in that study, with the smallest correlation coefficient being .823. Similar high correlation coefficients were obtained with standard alternative capital measures like electricity consumed by the establishment measured in kilowatt hours and installed capacity of the production machinery measured in horsepower.

9. Even at the four-digit industry level the product homogeneity objection is valid; establishments could be producing goods that are far from being substitutes for each other. Moreover, they produce a great variety of goods and very different proportions of each type, and they also differ considerably in the proportion of value added to the final product. Dividing the four-digit industries according to establishment size should increase the product homogeneity within each industrial group; see Meller (1975). Therefore, at the four-digit ISIC level, the resulting elasticity of substitution would be a sort of measure of the substitution possibilities between productive techniques and the substitution possibilities between different commodities within the same four-digit ISIC industry.

10. For example, we find in the literature statements like: "Industry in Chile is typically monopolistic or oligopolistic" (Harberger 1963, p. 245); "about 17% of all enterprises control 78.2% of total assets in the corporate sector" (Garretón and Cisternas 1970, p. 8); "The level of industrial concentration is rather high—the 52 largest firms of the country (they represent less than 1% of all firms) generate 38% of the value added in the industrial sector" (Lagos 1966, p. 104).

11. This was done by performing a Chow test; for details of the econometric results see Corbo and Meller (1979b). Using the CRTS translog for all industries for which the null hypothesis of CRTS was not rejected and a non-CRTS for the other three sectors, we verify whether the estimated functions are well behaved. A table showing the percentage of observations satisfying the monotonicity and quasi-concavity conditions for each one of the forty-four four-digit ISIC industries is available from the authors on request.

12. For details of the test using nonlinear pairwise separability restrictions, see Corbo and Meller (1979b).

13. Figures in parentheses correspond to the four-digit ISIC (International Standard Industrial Classification) code.

14. For the trade classification criteria see Corbo and Meller (1981).

References

Baldwin, R. E. 1971. Determinants of the commodity structure of U.S. trade. *American Economic Review* 61 (March): 126–46.

Berndt, E. R., and Christensen, L. R. 1973a. The internal structure of functional relationships: Separability, substitution and aggregation. *Review of Economic Studies* 40 (July): 403–10.

———. 1973b. The translog function and the substitution of equipment, structures and labor in U.S. manufacturing 1929–68. *Journal of Econometrics* 1 (March): 81–113.

———. 1974. Testing for the existence of a consistent aggregate index of labor inputs. *American Economic Review* 64 (June): 391–404.

Corbo, V., and Meller, P. 1979a. The translog production function: Some evidence from establishment data. *Journal of Econometrics* 10 (June): 193–99.

———. 1979b. La substitución de trabajo, capital humano y capital físico en la industria manufacturera chilena. *Estudios de Economia*, no. 14 (second semester), pp. 15–43.

———. 1981. Alternative trade strategies and employment implications: Chile. In *Trade and employment in developing countries*, vol. 1, *Indi-*

vidual studies, ed. A. O. Krueger, H. B. Lary, T. Monson, and N. Akrasanee. Chicago: University of Chicago Press for National Bureau of Economic Research.

Garretón, O. G., and Cisternas, J. 1970. Algúnas características del proceso de toma de decisiónes en la gran empresa: La dinámica de concentración. Servicio de Cooperación Técnica. Mimeographed.

Green, H. A. J. 1964. *Aggregation in economic analysis*. Princeton: Princeton University Press.

Griliches, Z. 1967. Production functions in manufacturing: Some preliminary results. In *The theory and empirical analysis of production*, ed. M. Brown. New York: Columbia University Press for National Bureau of Economic Research.

Griliches, Z., and Ringstad. V. 1971. *Economies of scale and the form of the production function*. Amsterdam: North-Holland.

Harberger, A. C. 1963. The dynamics of inflation in Chile. In *Measurements in economics*, ed. C. Christ. Palo Alto: Stanford University Press.

Hildebrand, G. H., and Liu, T. C. 1965. *Manufacturing production functions in the United States, 1957*. Ithaca: Cornell University.

Humphrey, D. B., and Moroney, J. R. 1975. Substitution among capital, labor and natural resource products in American manufacturing. *Journal of Political Economy* 83 (1): 57–82.

Keesing, D. 1966. Labor skills and comparative advantage. *American Economic Review* 61 (May): 249–58.

Kenen, P. B. 1965. Nature, capital and trade. *Journal of Political Economy* 73 (October): 437–60.

Lagos, R. 1966. *La industria en Chile: Antecedentes estructurales*. Santiago: Universidad de Chile, Instituto de Economia.

Leontief, W. 1956. Factor proportions and the structure of American trade: Further theoretical and empirical analysis. *Review of Economics and Statistics* 3 (November): 386–407.

Meller, P. 1975. Production function for industrial establishments of different sizes: The Chilean case. *Annals of Economic and Social Measurement* 4 (fall): 595–634.

Stern, R. M. 1976. Capital-skill complementarity and U.S. trade in manufactures. In *Quantitative studies of international economic relations*, ed. H. Glejser. Amsterdam: North-Holland.

6   Do Multinational Firms Adapt Factor Proportions to Relative Factor Prices?

Robert E. Lipsey, Irving B. Kravis, and Romualdo A. Roldan

6.1   Introduction

A major issue in the discussion of the effects of multinational firms' operations on host country employment has been whether these firms use "inappropriately" capital-intensive methods of production and are therefore responsible in some degree for underutilization of the presumably abundant labor, or unskilled labor, resources of less developed countries. There are many aspects to this issue; here we consider one: whether multinational firms respond to differences in labor costs by using more labor-intensive methods of production where labor costs are low. In contrast to the case studies that have examined this question in individual countries or industries, our work investigates the pattern that emerges from an analysis of the main manufacturing industries across many countries. We make particular use of data on multinational firms collected by the Bureau of Economic Analysis (BEA) of the United States Department of Commerce for 1966 and 1970 and similar data for Swedish-based multinational firms collected by the Industriens Utredningsinstitut of Stockholm for 1970 and 1974.

Robert E. Lipsey is associated with NBER and with Queens College, City University of New York; Irving B. Kravis is associated with NBER and with the University of Pennsylvania; and Romualdo A. Roldan is associated with Chase Econometrics.

We are indebted to Dennis Bushe and Linda O'Connor, helped in the late stages by Stanley Lewis, for statistical calculations and programming, and to Arnold Gilbert and Michael Liliestedt for programming and advice on United States Department of Commerce data. Anne O. Krueger, Hal B. Lary, and several referees read the paper carefully and made valuable comments on it. The Industriens Utredningsinstitut provided hospitality in Stockholm and information and calculations on Swedish multinational firms from its surveys, and Birgitta Swedenborg guided us in using the Swedish data and supervised the Swedish calculations. We are grateful also to the City University of New York for a grant of computer time.

The question of degree of adaptation to factor costs has received considerable attention. Unfortunately there are many possible definitions of adaptation, and a good deal of effort has been spent, often unprofitably, we believe, in attempting to distinguish one from another.

A question frequently raised is whether any observed differences between production methods in developed countries and those in LDCs are the result of factor substitution within a single technology (along a single production function), as in figure 6.1, or the result of the use of a more labor-intensive technology in LDCs: one that would be more labor-intensive under any set of factor price ratios, as in figure 6.2. Observed differences in factor input ratios could be a combination of substitution between and within technologies, as in figure 6.3. Courtney and Leipziger (1975), for example, assume two technologies in each industry—one for developed country affiliates of each firm and one for affiliates in LDCs. They fit production functions accordingly and attempt to divide the observed differences between DC and LDC factor use ratios (k_1 and k_3 in fig. 6.3) into the unobserved differences between k_1 and k_2 (ex ante substitution in their terms) and the unobserved differences between k_2 and k_3 (ex post substitution). "By ex ante factor substitution we refer to choices of plant design and by ex post factor substitution, we refer to the way in which the plant is run" (Courtney and Leipziger 1975, p. 297).

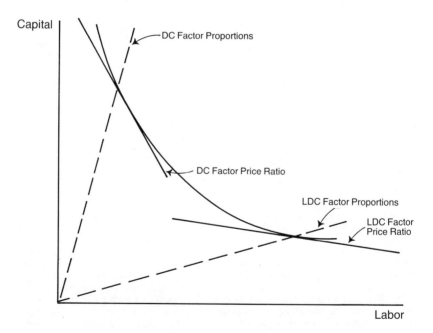

Fig. 6.1   Substitution of capital for labor within a single technology.

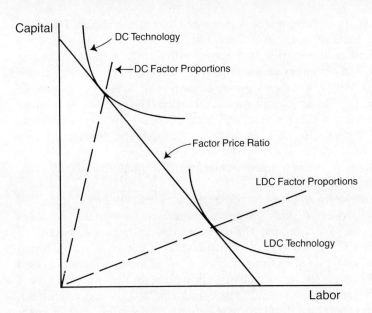

Fig. 6.2   Substitution of labor-intensive technology for capital-intensive technology.

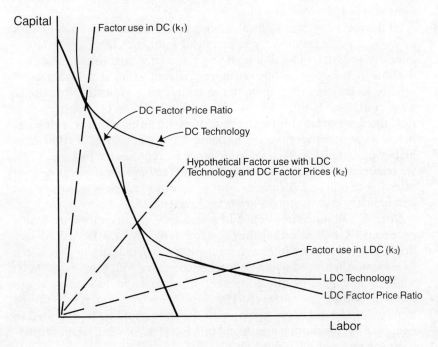

Fig. 6.3   Substitution of labor for capital between and within technologies.

In our study we have not only compared parent companies, DC affiliates, and LDC affiliates as groups, but also compared affiliates in an industry across all countries, treating individual affiliates or the aggregate of affiliates in a country as the units of observation. The parent firm is viewed as having a technology set consisting of a variety of ways of producing that differ in their capital intensity. The question is whether the parent firm's choices from this technology set for use in different countries reflect differences in factor costs. Of course this picture of a single technology set is a simplification, more appropriate for a single product than for the heterogeneous industries distinguished in any available collection of data.

We concentrate on the observed differences in factor proportions (the difference between k_1 and k_3 in fig. 6.3) and relate them to differences in factor prices. We examine the relationships taking as our units of observation for a country, in turn, manufacturing as a whole, broad industries, and individual firms. We ask what adaptation there is to host country factor prices, how much of it takes place through the selection of industries (labor-intensive industries producing in low-wage countries), how much takes place through the selection of firms within each industry (labor-intensive firms in each industry producing in low-wage countries), and, finally, how much takes place through the choice of factor proportions within industries or firms.

At the most aggregative level, among broad industries such as textiles or chemicals, adaptation by selection of industries means that labor-intensive industries based in high-wage countries establish affiliate production in low-wage countries more frequently, or at a higher level relative to home output, than do capital-intensive industries from high-wage countries. In other words, if there is adaptation by industry selection, the share of labor-intensive industries will be higher among affiliates in low-wage countries than among home-country industries or affiliates in high-wage countries. Such selection could be represented by figure 6.2 if we relabeled DC and LDC technology and factor proportions as instead referring to industry A (noninvestor or investor in high-wage countries) and industry B (investor in low-wage countries).

Virtually all industries defined by statistical classifications are heterogeneous in the sense that they include more and less labor-intensive firms. The more labor-intensive firms within each industry might choose to relocate their production to foreign countries with low wage levels, while more capital-intensive firms did not invest abroad at all or chose locations with high wage levels. That would be adaptation by selection of firms within an industry. Again, such selection could be represented in figure 6.2 by substituting firm A and firm B technology and factor proportions for those of DCs and LDCs.

In the cases of selection of investing industries and investing firms there are, of course, influences other than the price of labor on the extent and location of foreign operations. It has been suggested, in fact, that the typical advantage of United States firms, which enables them to compete effectively in foreign markets with host country firms and other foreign firms, is technological skill. If high technology is associated with high capital intensity there will be a tendency for capital-intensive firms and industries to locate abroad. For firms in a home country with high labor costs, such a tendency will operate in the opposite direction from the influence of labor costs on the selection of industries and firms to operate abroad. Also operating against the influence of labor costs would be high capital intensity in industries based on natural resource availability if the natural resources were concentrated in countries with low labor costs.

Even within the firm there could be differences in the type of output produced in different countries. Since the typical firm produces more than one final or intermediate output and can supply one market by production from another market, it will have an incentive to produce the labor-intensive product in LDCs and the capital-intensive product in developed countries or at home. This phenomenon would appear in the statistical data as substitution of labor for capital in LDCs even if each product were produced in exactly the same way at home and abroad. Since most large firms' home country operations extend over several industries, the selection of products within the firm may be a selection not only among the products of a single industry but also among the industries of the parent. Once again we could represent the selection using figure 6.2, with products A and B, produced in high-wage and low-wage countries respectively, substituted for DC and LDC technology and factor proportions.

Thus there are three types of adaptation to low wages in LDCs that involve selection rather than the adaptation of production processes. One is the greater tendency of labor-intensive industries, compared with capital-intensive industries, to move production to low-wage countries. The second is the same tendency for labor-intensive firms within any industry. The third is, for a given firm, the same tendency to select among products or production processes. Of course the division between adaptation by selection among industries and adaptation by selection within industries depends on the fineness of the industry classification. The broader the industry groups, the more apparent adaptation within industries; the narrower the industries, the more important industry selection appears.

Also embedded in factor proportions comparisons among countries may be differences in capital intensity due to differences in scale of production, if the production function is not homothetic. This possibility

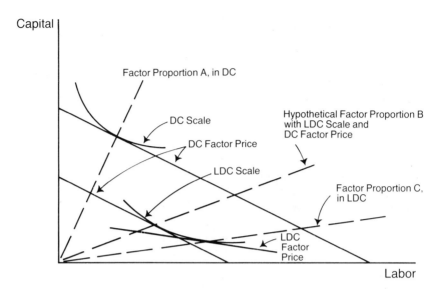

Fig. 6.4   Effect of scale of production on factor proportions: one tech-
                     nology, two production levels, two factor prices.

would be obscured if a single production function were fitted to all
countries, assuming homotheticity. Differences in factor proportions that
were really related to scale of production would then be attributed to
factor prices, since these are, among countries, generally related to scale
of production, the least developed countries having both low labor costs
and small plants. In figure 6.4, for example, the existence of some
indivisibilities in plant or capital equipment means that capital-intensive
methods of production (DC scale) would be used only in developed
countries, resulting in factor proportion A. Labor-intensive methods
would be used in LDCs, resulting in factor proportion C. If the production function were assumed to be homothetic, the entire difference
between A and C would be attributed to factor price differences, even
though at LDC scale DC factor prices would bring about a capital
intensity only as high as B.

   In our direct comparisons of capital intensities between developed
countries and LDCs we are, in effect, treating low capital intensities that
result from small-scale operations in LDCs as one more form of adaptation to low labor costs. Although the differences in capital intensities
between LDC affiliates and parents or DC affiliates in such a case do not
represent substitution along an isoquant, they may still be a consequence
of differences in factor costs. Low labor costs in LDCs may make eco-
nomical the operation of small labor-intensive plants that would be
hopelessly uneconomical at high labor costs.

A more fundamental difficulty plagues attempts to measure scale effects from production functions fitted to data across countries. Typically no physical output data are available, and output is measured by value added. This practice biases the result toward obscuring economies of scale, if they exist. Presumably, plants of uneconomically small size, perhaps in markets too small to sustain plants of optimal size, can survive only if they are afforded high protection or subsidies. The level of protection must be high enough to provide standard levels of wages for the workers and profits sufficient to attract and retain capital. Each worker enters the production function on the right-hand side, and his wage enters on the left, in value added. Each unit of capital is also entered on both sides of the function because the investment (on the right-hand side) will not be made unless the level of protection or subsidy is sufficient to provide a standard return, which enters the equation on the left-hand side.

Within a single economy the presumption is that all producers must sell at the same price, since they are in competition with each other. Any inefficiently small plant with too many workers per unit of output would have the high wage bill included in its value added; but, since it is selling in competition with, and at the same price as, efficient plants, the inefficiency will be reflected in a low or even negative return on capital, and a low or negative value added, which will truly reflect net output. The same would happen in the case of a plant with too much capital per unit of output. What is different in a comparison across countries is that prices need not be the same if there are trade barriers and plants in one country that do not compete freely with those in another. The value added by inefficient plants is inflated in segregated, protected markets. The results in studies across countries are thus biased toward proportionality between inputs and outputs: that is, constant returns to scale.[1] This analysis assumes, of course, that the degree of protection is that needed for survival by inefficient plants rather than that achieved by politically powerful firms or industries seeking high profits.

6.2 Data

The basic data for our analysis came from two sources: surveys of the foreign operations of United States firms by the Bureau of Economic Analysis (BEA), formerly the Office of Business Economics (OBE) of the United States Department of Commerce, and surveys of foreign operations of Swedish firms by the Industriens Utredningsinstitut of Stockholm. The United States surveys took place in 1966 (a complete census) and 1970, and the Swedish surveys, believed to have virtually complete coverage, took place in 1970 and 1974. The United States data are described in United States Department of Commerce (1972, 1975), and the 1970 Swedish data in Swedenborg (1973, 1979). The Swedish data for 1974 had not yet been published at the time these calculations were done and are therefore referred to below as unpublished data.

Although the United States and Swedish survey questionnaires are very similar, there are differences that are reflected in the way they are used below. The United States data give more detailed balance-sheet information, including net and gross book values for property, plant, and equipment. The Swedish data provide a breakdown of products and industries for both parents and overseas subsidiaries and also, in addition to book value, the value of property, plant, and equipment based on fire insurance values, an approximation to current gross market value. Although the fire insurance valuation presumably does not include revaluations of land, we are inclined to the view that it is better than book value as an estimate of the amount of capital in market values. The United States data, on the other hand, characterize each parent and each affiliate only by its single most important industry affiliation and provide only book values of assets.

6.3 Factor Proportions of Domestic Industry, Parent Companies, and Foreign Affiliates: Aggregate Data

The basic facts about capital intensity for all manufacturing in multinationals' home countries, home country operations of parent companies, and foreign affiliates are set out in table 6.1. In every case for which we have data to make a comparison, capital intensity in home country domestic manufacturing as a whole and in parent companies' domestic operations was higher than in foreign affiliates, even those in other developed countries. And capital intensities of affiliate operations in other developed countries were consistently higher than those of operations in less developed countries. The comparisons clearly indicate that some form of adaptation to differences in wage levels does take place and that the adaptation, or the sum of all the different types of adaptation, was large. Capital intensities of affiliates in less developed countries were typically 40 percent or more below those of parents or home countries.

As we mentioned earlier, there are many possible reasons for such differences. One is that we are observing only industry selection. The more labor-intensive industries might choose to go abroad to benefit from lower wage levels, particularly in less developed countries, but might produce abroad exactly as at home. A test for this possibility is to make comparisons of capital intensity within industries, as in tables 6.2 and 6.3. If all the differences in table 6.1 were accounted for by industry selection there would be no differences within industries. If industry selection were unimportant, the differences in tables 6.2 and 6.3 would be as large as those in table 6.1.

Table 6.1   **Capital Intensity (Capital per Employee) in Manufacturing, United States and Swedish Domestic Industry, Parents, and Foreign Affiliates**

| | | | | Foreign Affiliates | |
Capital Stock Measure		Domestic Industry	Parents	Developed Countries	Less Developed Countries
		Thousands of Dollars			
United States					
Total assets	1966	n.a.	22.1[a]	17.0	14.8
	1970	n.a.	29.3	20.8	16.2
Net property, plant, and	1966	11.7[b]	8.6[a]	6.7	5.7
equipment, book value	1970	14.6[c]	12.0	8.0	6.0
		Thousands of Kronor			
Sweden					
Total assets	1960	n.a.	n.a.	37.9[d]	27.7
	1965	n.a.	n.a.	57.8[d]	38.7
	1970	117.6	n.a.	91.9[d]	59.0
	1974	176.0	n.a.		
Net property, plant, and	1970	31.9	n.a.	25.7	19.4
equipment, book value	1974	40.2	n.a.	35.1	22.6
Gross property, plant and	1970	108.0	n.a.	50.8	29.2
equipment, fire insurance	1974	177.5	206.8	73.2	43.9
value					

SOURCES: United States Department of Commerce (1972), Sweden, Statistiska Centralbyrån (1972*a*, *b*, 1976*a*, *b*), Swedenborg (1973), and unpublished data of the Industriens Utredningsinstitut.
[a]Includes only those parents reporting in 1970.
[b]Gross property plant and equipment for 1967; 1966 not available.
[c]Gross property, plant, and equipment.
[e]Includes Europe, North America, Australia, New Zealand, and South Africa. No Japanese manufacturing subsidiaries are reported.

It is clear that, even within broad industry groups, home production is most capital-intensive, production in developed country affiliates next, and production in LDC affiliates least capital-intensive. In the case of the United States (table 6.2), twenty-two out of twenty-four possible comparisons between parents and developed country affiliates show parent production more capital-intensive. All sixteen possible comparisons between developed country affiliates and those in LDCs show that the former are more capital-intensive, and all sixteen possible comparisons show parent production more capital-intensive than affiliate production in LDCs. Adaptation, in other words, is visible within industries, at least within industry groups as broad as these. That impression is strengthened by the averages. The averages of the industry relatives of affiliate to parent capital intensity show at least as much relation to the type of host country as do the aggregates, and possibly more in the case of LDCs.

The adaptation in capital intensity shown by manufacturing industry as a whole in table 6.1, put in index form in the "all manufacturing" rows of table 6.2, can be divided into two parts. One is the adaptation within industries, and the other is adaptation by selection among broad indus-

Table 6.2   **Capital Intensity (Capital per Employee) in Manufacturing Industry Groups, United States Parents and Foreign Affiliates (Unit: Thousand Dollars per Employee)**

Manufacturing Industry Group	1970			1966[a]		
		Affiliates in			Affiliates in	
	Parents	Developed Countries	LDCs	Parents	Developed Countries	LDCs
Total Assets per Employee						
Food products	28.27	20.17	14.44	21.62	17.42	13.26
Chemicals and allied products	35.95	37.77	20.46	29.94	28.27	17.27
Primary and fabricated metals	33.71	21.31	—	26.11	21.33	—
Machinery	24.25	18.02	12.08	16.28	13.54	12.26
Transport equipment	30.01	19.07	—	22.04	17.30	—
Other	29.69	21.26	16.31	23.75	15.99	13.94
Total Assets per Employee (Parent Ratio = 100)						
All manufacturing	100.0	70.9	55.2	100.0	76.6	66.8
Average of industry relatives[b]	100.0	74.8	53.0	100.0	80.4	63.6
Net Property, Plant, and Equipment per Employee						
Food products	11.17	7.72	4.18	8.33	6.55	4.68
Chemicals and allied products	17.67	17.37	8.28	14.78	13.24	7.33
Primary and fabricated metals	18.28	7.52	—	13.04	7.79	—
Machinery	9.86	5.84	3.60	6.38	4.52	3.51
Transport equipment	8.09	7.78	—	5.75	6.97	—
Other	13.12	8.05	7.24	9.62	6.55	6.15
Net Property, Plant, and Equipment per Employee (Parent Ratio = 100)						
All manufacturing	100.0	67.2	50.3	100.0	78.6	66.3
Average of industry relatives[b]	100.0	72.3	44.1	100.0	81.9	60.5

SOURCE: United States Department of Commerce (1972).

[a]Includes only those parents reporting in 1970.

[b]Weighted by parent employment in each industry.

tries, discussed earlier. Adaptation within industries is shown in the individual industry rows of table 6.2 and summarized in the "average of industry relatives" rows. It is calculated by putting each industry row into relative form (parent capital intensity = 100) and averaging across industries with parent employment as weights. If within-industry adaptation were the only type that took place, the "all manufacturing" entries and the "average of industry relatives" entries would be identical. If there were, in addition, some selection by choice of industries, in the sense that labor-intensive industries had a larger share of overseas activity than of home country activity, it would tend to make the "all manufacturing" relatives lower than the "average of industry relatives." Such selection does appear to have taken place in the case of affiliates in developed countries. Labor-intensive industries are more important than in the home countries. However, the opposite seems to be true for less developed countries. The industry selection seems to lean toward capital-intensive industries there and offsets, to a small degree, the effect of adaptation within industries. Thus, not only does selection of industries play a small role in the total extent of adaptation for manufacturing as a whole, but it even plays a role apparently opposite to that of labor cost in LDCs, for reasons suggested earlier. The major adaptation to labor costs takes place within these broad industries.

The Swedish data in table 6.3 point to roughly the same conclusions. In the overwhelming majority of cases the capital intensities in Swedish industries were higher than those in developed country affiliates (fifteen out of seventeen) and those in LDC affiliates (nine out of eleven). The capital intensities in Swedish parent companies were higher than those in developed country affiliates in fifteen out of eighteen cases and higher than those of LDC affiliates in all twelve comparisons we could make. By far the largest part of the difference in capital intensity between companies in Sweden and foreign affiliates in developed countries and between affiliates in developed countries and those in LDCs is accounted for by differences within broad industries. Comparing the aggregate ratios with the averages of industry ratios for fire insurance values, we find for LDCs that the aggregate is a bit lower, indicating some selection of labor-intensive industries for production in LDCs. However, the effects of that selection were again, as in the United States, minor compared with the use in LDCs of relatively labor-intensive production methods within industries.

We conclude from these aggregate data that the large differences in capital intensity, especially between LDCs and the DC affiliates of United States and Swedish companies and between DC affiliate and parent or home country capital intensity, are not primarily expressions of industry mix, at least among the broadly defined manufacturing industries we consider, but reflect differences within industries.

Table 6.3   Capital Intensity (Capital per Employee) in Manufacturing Industry Groups, Swedish Domestic Industry, Parent Companies, and Foreign Affiliates (Unit: Thousand Kronor per Employee)

	1970				1974			
			Affiliates in				Affiliates in	
Manufacturing Industry Group	Swedish Industry	Parent Companies	Developed Countries	LDCs	Swedish Industry	Parent Companies	Developed Countries	LDCs
Fire Insurance Value of Gross Property, Plant, and Equipment per Employee								
Food, drink, and tobacco	108.6	142.4	76.6	—	186.6d	252.6	120.4	—
Textiles and apparel	57.8c	62.7	12.2	—	91.7d	114.8	16.5	—
Pulp, paper, and printing	182.2	n.a.	108.1	71.0	338.1	325.4	193.7	110.6
Pulp and paper	341.6d	234.2	156.7	—	589.4d	365.0	233.1	—
Paper products and printing	73.2d	118.0	66.0	71.0	109.3d	125.8	137.7	110.6
Chemicals and plastics	164.0e	92.6	94.0	31.9	258.4d	165.3	170.7	95.1
Metal products a	65.7d	117.1	67.1	35.2	113.6d	172.1	88.3	36.7
Machinery	100.3	106.7	48.3	27.4	118.3	128.5	57.7	35.9
Nonelectrical	82.7d	78.0	54.7	28.6	122.2d	125.2	71.6	17.7
Electrical	77.6d	108.6	29.8	24.1	100.1d	130.9	40.0	32.4
Transport equipment f	107.9d		43.7	22.5	139.8d	128.8	126.8	51.6
Fire Insurance Value of Gross Property, Plant, and Equipment per Employee (Swedish ratio = 100)								
All manufacturing	100.0	100.0	53.6	26.2	100.0	100.0	47.5	24.7
Average of industry relatives b	100.0	100.0	55.6	32.6	100.0	100.0	52.6	31.9

SOURCES: For industries, Sweden, Statistiska Centralbyrån (1972a, b, 1976a, b), except as indicated. For companies, directly from Industriens Utredningsinstitut.

a Published industry figures include primary metals, excluded from company data. This is a very capital-intensive industry and tends to distort the comparisons. We have therefore used the figure for metal products alone, from the Industriens Utredningsinstitut.

b Weighted by industry employment.

c Including rubber products.

d Estimates from Industriens Utredningsinstitut.

e Excluding rubber products.

f Excluding shipping industry.

6.4   Measures of the Price of Labor and Capital Intensity

The theoretical determinant of capital-intensity decisions, if scale of production is not a factor, is the relative prices of labor and capital. In examining factor choices within the firm we have assumed that the prices of capital are identical for the firm in all locations, and that ratios of the price of labor to the price of capital are therefore proportional to the price of labor (wage rates) alone. The price of capital may be considered to consist of two elements, one the opportunity cost to the firm of tying up assets in a particular form, and the other the price of a physical capital good. If there were no restrictions on transferring profits or repatriating capital, and if risks and tax rates were the same among countries, capital costs in the first sense could be taken to be the same for a given firm all over the world. That might not be a bad assumption for comparisons among developed countries. In at least some developing countries it would be far from accurate, and in extreme cases restrictions on repatriation might make capital for reinvestment almost free to an affiliate. Such circumstances would tend to produce high capital intensities in low-income countries and limit or obscure adaptation to factor prices.

With respect to physical capital, the assumption of equal prices in all countries is clearly not valid. This is particularly true for construction costs, which are strongly affected by wage or real income levels. It is not quite such a bad assumption for equipment, which tends to have more of a world market. Price indexes for construction costs in 1970, relative to those in the United States, ranged from 37 and 26 percent in the poorest and next-poorest group of countries to 62 percent in the highest-income countries, while those for producer durables ranged from 91 percent in the middle group of countries up to 106 percent in the poorest group (Kravis, Heston, and Summers 1978a, p. 120). Thus the price relationships for the two groups have somewhat offsetting effects.

The high level of producer durable prices in low-income countries reflects, to some extent, the degree of protection to domestic production of these products. The effective protection rates vary widely, but quite a few are over 100 percent.[2]

It would be desirable to take account of these differences in capital costs if the price comparisons were available. Since construction costs and wage rates are positively correlated, we exaggerate the differences between countries in relative factor prices and underestimate elasticities of substitution by using wage rates alone to measure factor price ratios.

The price of labor we would like to measure is that for completely unskilled labor or for labor of a given quality. Lacking any such price measure, we have used several approximations, or proxies. These include real GDP per capita, the average wage paid by all United States manufacturing affiliates in a country, the average wage paid by a particular affiliate, and the latter two deflated by an index of the average quality of labor.

Real GDP per capita is of course not a measure of the price of labor. It was used as a proxy under the assumption that the higher the real GDP per capita, the higher the standard of living and the higher the cost of unskilled labor. The estimates, which are from Kravis, Heston, and Summers (1978b), are based on data from the United Nations International Comparison Project and are not subject to the usual problems of comparisons via exchange rates (see Kravis, Kenessey, Heston, and Summers 1975; Kravis, Heston, and Summers 1978a).

Average wages, converted into dollars at current exchange rates, come closer to measures of the price of labor, but they obviously reflect differences in quality as well as differences in price. To remove the effect of quality differences, we have devised a rough index of labor quality for about fifty countries from various measures calculated by others, including Denison (1967), Harbison and Myers (1964), and Krueger (1968). In using the quality index to deflate money wages for a specific industry, for example, we in effect assume that each company within a country hires workers of average quality and that any deviation of a company's wage or an industry's wage from the average wage represents a higher cost rather than higher quality. Where we use average country wages without distinguishing companies or industries, however, we are making a very different assumption—namely, that all companies and industries in a country face the same price of labor and that any variation in average wages among companies or industries represents differences in quality.

Measures of capital intensity raise at least as many problems. We have experimented with assets per worker, book and replacement values of property, plant, and equipment per worker, value added, and nonwage value added per worker. Assets per worker have the advantage of being comprehensive. If one thinks of inventories, bank accounts, and loans as being production inputs, that comprehensiveness seems desirable. However, there is no assurance that the financial assets of a subsidiary are held entirely to assist production in that subsidiary's host country. It is quite conceivable that a parent company might arrange to have the subsidiary hold assets for the use of the parent or of other affiliates, and it would then be improper to treat those financial assets as necessarily contributing to host country output. Similarly, the parent might hold financial assets for the use of all its affiliates, in which case we might be understating the amount of capital involved in a given affiliate's production.

We have, for these reasons, leaned toward fixed assets, or property, plant, and equipment per worker. Most of the data are for net property, plant, and equipment, with all the associated problems of depreciation rates, valuation of assets purchased in the past, and so on. However, for Swedish affiliates and their parents and for Swedish domestic firms in each industry we also have data on the valuation of gross property, plant, and equipment for fire insurance, which should come closer to current replacement cost.

It would be desirable to have a measure of the flow of capital services instead of the stock of capital, since that would be the appropriate measure of the contribution of capital to production. We do not have adequate measures, however, and the proxies that have been suggested, such as value added or nonwage value added per worker (see, for example, Lary 1968), do not seem satisfactory, especially for comparisons within firms. The problem centers on the ability of the firm to manipulate the location of profits, presumably to minimize taxes or to evade other host country or home country regulations. The result is that there are large numbers of affiliates with negative or zero value added and others in which value added has been inflated for similar reasons. To the extent that companies kept subsidiary books in local currencies and translated into dollars or kronor via current exchange rates in answering questionnaires, there may be a bias from under- or overvaluation of currencies that enters the value of capital (part of the dependent variable) and the wage rate (one of the independent variables) in the same direction. As a check on such bias we have run equations using real GDP per capita as a wage-cost proxy, since that measure, while it may be subject to error as a wage proxy, is free of currency translation bias because it does not depend on exchange rate conversions.

We should have liked to investigate differences in skill mix and prices of skilled labor, but the data are poor for this purpose. The United States survey forms included questions on the breakdown of the labor force and payrolls by type of worker, but the answers were considered unsatisfactory by BEA and were not used. We could not treat differences among countries in average wages as representing skill differences, as one might within a country. The average wage of each country, deflated by average labor quality, is our measure of the price of standard labor, though it can incorporate skill differences as well. To the extent that it does, the relationship between the price of labor and capital intensity is blurred.[3]

The Swedish affiliate data did include a usable distinction between production workers and others. We have made some use of the proportion of nonproduction workers as a measure of skill intensity. It is a crude measure, but the fact that nonproduction workers have higher earnings per worker than the production workers suggests that they are of higher average skill.

6.5 Labor Costs and Factor Proportions
in Individual Countries and Industries

We begin our analysis of the effect of labor costs on capital intensity with a series of regressions across countries, using data on the characteristics of United States and Swedish multinationals' affiliates in different countries.

In the first set of regressions, summarized in table 6.4, each observation is for the sum of all United States–owned manufacturing affiliates in a country. The equations, which are in double-log form, show that capital intensity responds significantly to country differences in the price of labor. Equations 5 and 6, which make use of what we consider our best measures of the price of labor (the average affiliate wage divided by our measure of average labor quality in each country, described earlier), show strongly significant coefficients for the price of labor of about 0.7 (with property, plant, and equipment as the capital measure) and 0.8 (for all capital). If we assume that the production functions are CES and that capital costs do not differ among countries, these coefficients are measures of the elasticity of substitution between capital and labor. Comparing equations 1 and 2 with equations 3 and 4 indicates that adding more countries to the thirty-eight covered by our labor quality index would tend to raise the coefficients, their significance, and the $\bar{r}^2$ but would not change the main findings.

Real GDP per capita, which we expected to be a good proxy for the price of labor, performed poorly, explaining very little of the variation in capital intensity. To check whether the greater explanatory power of the wage rates might be spurious, stemming from a common price level effect on both wage rates and the capital intensity measure, we ran equations 7 and 8 with price level as the explanatory variable. Price level had no apparent explanatory power, and the coefficients were not statistically significant. However, the fact that the coefficients were positive and fairly large does raise the possibility that the elasticity of substitution we calculate may be somewhat exaggerated by spurious price effects.

The Swedish data of table 6.5, like the United States data, show strong effects of wage levels on capital intensity. The coefficients for average wage and for quality-adjusted average wage range from 0.75 to 0.87, somewhat above those in the United States equations. What is different about the Swedish results is that both price level and real GDP are related to capital intensity. The high price level coefficient hints at some exaggeration of the calculated substitution elasticities, but the considerable explanatory power of real GDP, the labor price proxy most clearly cleansed of price effects, shows that the price of labor is an influential factor.

The results summarized in tables 6.4 and 6.5 indicate that factor proportions do respond in a significant way to differences in wage levels.

We ask next whether the response involves only the choice of industries for investment (labor-intensive industries in low-wage countries) or includes choices among companies or production methods within industries. We can get some notion of the answer to this question from tables

Table 6.4   **Relation of Capital Intensity of Production
to the Price of Labor, United States–Owned Affiliates,
by Country (All Manufacturing Combined, 1966)**

$$\ln\left(\frac{K}{L}\right) = a + b \ln w$$

Equation Number[a]	Number of Observations (Countries)[b]	Capital Intensity Measure	Labor Price Measure	Coefficients		
				Labor Price[c]	Constant Term	$\bar{r}^2$
1[d]	66	PPE	Average affiliate wage	0.72 (4.73)	2.97 (2.55)	.25
2[d]	66	Assets	Average affiliate wage	0.68 (5.55)	4.28 (4.53)	.31
3	38	PPE	Average affiliate wage	0.60 (2.80)	3.96 (2.38)	.16
4	38	Assets	Average affiliate wage	0.62 (3.26)	4.76 (3.21)	.21
5	38	PPE	$\dfrac{\text{Average affiliate wage}}{\text{Average quality}}$	0.73 (3.10)	6.29 (8.31)	.19
6	38	Assets	$\dfrac{\text{Average affiliate wage}}{\text{Average quality}}$	0.79 (3.84)	7.07 (10.73)	.27
7	38	PPE	Price level	.26 (.76)	7.57 (5.49)	.00
8	38	Assets	Price level	.31 (1.01)	8.32 (6.62)	.00

NOTE:
PPE = Gross property, plant, and equipment per worker, in $ thousand.
Assets = Total assets per worker, in $ thousand.
Average affiliate wage = Average wage in United States manufacturing affiliates.
Average quality = Index of average quality of the labor force.
Price level = Money GDP, translated into dollars by exchange rate, divided by real GDP.
[a]Each equation is in double-log form, with capital intensity as the dependent variable and the price of labor as the independent variable.
[b]Each observation is for all affiliates of United States manufacturing companies in a foreign country.
[c]Assuming the production function is CES and that capital costs do not differ across countries for an individual firm, this coefficient is a measure of the elasticity of substitution.
[d]Equations 1 and 2 are based on all observations for which average affiliate wage is available. The other equations are confined to countries for which the labor quality measure could be constructed.

Table 6.5   **Relation of Capital Intensity of Production**[a]
                   to the Price of Labor, Swedish–Owned Affiliates,
                   by Country (All Manufacturing Combined, 1970 and 1974)

$$\ln \left(\frac{K}{L}\right) = a + b \ln w$$

Equation Number[b]	Number of Observations (Countries)[c]	Year	Labor Price Measure or Proxy	Labor Price	Constant Term	$\bar{r}^2$
1	27	1970	Average affiliate wage[d]	0.75 (3.29)	1.16 (1.41)	.27
2	25	1974	Average affiliate wage[d]	0.80 (2.53)	1.31 (1.12)	.18
3	27	1970	$\dfrac{\text{Average wage}^d}{\text{Average quality}}$	0.84 (3.22)	4.69 (6.71)	.27
4	25	1974	$\dfrac{\text{Average wage}^d}{\text{Average quality}}$	0.87 (2.30)	5.05 (13.82)	.15
5	28	1970	Real GDP	0.46 (3.71)	2.23 (4.98)	.32
6	26	1974	Real GDP	0.49 (3.07)	2.40 (3.94)	.25
7	28	1970	Price level	0.89 (2.92)	0.18 (0.14)	.22
8	26	1974	Price level	0.98 (2.87)	0.14 (0.10)	.22

NOTE: For definitions of labor price measure see table 6.4.
[a]Fire insurance value of property, plant, and equipment per worker.
[b]Each equation is in double-log form, with capital intensity as the dependent variable and the price of labor as the independent variable.
[c]Each observation is for all affiliates of Swedish manufacturing companies in a country other than Sweden.
[d]Average wages in United States affiliates.

6.6 and 6.7, which show the same relationships within broad industry groups for both United States and Swedish affiliates.

The United States equations for aggregate manufacturing (table 6.4) and for pooled individual industries (table 6.6) are very similar, except that the latter imply lower elasticities of substitution, 0.50–0.55 instead of 0.6–0.7. In other words, the substitution between labor and capital in the manufacturing aggregates of table 6.4 owes a little to the choice of industries but mostly takes place within the broad industry groupings found in the table. There is some tendency for labor-intensive industries to be more heavily represented in lower-income countries, in contrast to our earlier results from treating all LDCs as a group, but it accounts for only a small part of the apparent substitution of labor for capital there.

The equations for individual United States industries almost all show significant labor price coefficients, implying substitution of labor for capital in low-wage countries. The exception was transport equipment, for which the number of observations was very small. The largest coefficient, suggesting an elasticity of substitution above one, was for the chemicals industry.

In every industry, whether property, plant, and equipment or total assets was used as the capital measure, the response to differences in wages adjusted for labor quality was somewhat stronger than that to the unadjusted wage differences. The same was true in the pooled industry data, as can be seen in the comparison between equation 2 and equation 3. The higher coefficients for quality-adjusted wage levels are apparently not simply a characteristic of the smaller group of countries for which we have the labor quality data; these countries and the whole set produce almost identical equations, as can be seen by comparing equations 1 and 2.

A similar analysis of Swedish affiliates is made in table 6.7. Since we had no wage data by country for Swedish affiliates, the elasticities were estimated using average wages paid in each country by United States affiliates: the same wage variable as in tables 6.4 and 6.5. Both 1970 and 1974 equations indicated strong response to labor prices, as measured by average wages or by quality-deflated average wages, and the degree of response was virtually the same as in the corresponding country aggregates of table 6.5. Industry mix, in other words, contributed very little, if anything, to the appearance of response to wage differences. Both real GDP and price level were also related to capital intensity and, in fact, explained it better than did the presumably more appropriate wage variable.

Although there were not enough observations to calculate an equation for each industry among Swedish affiliates, there did seem to be some industry differences large enough to affect the elasticity measure. When we distinguished two industries, which seemed to be outliers, paper products and printing and metal products, from the others, we found them to have somewhat higher capital intensities, and the explanatory power of the equation increased greatly.

On the whole, the Swedish affiliates appeared to respond to prices of labor as the United States affiliates did, and perhaps to a greater degree, with elasticities of substitution mainly over 0.7. Little of this apparent response in either country is attributable to selection of industries. Almost all the response took place within industries.

Table 6.6   Relation of Capital Intensity of Production to the Price of Labor, United States Affiliates Aggregated by Industry Group within Each Country (Five Industry Groups, Separately and Pooled, 1966)

$$\ln\left(\frac{K}{L}\right) = a + b \ln w$$

Equation Number[a]	Industry Group	Number of Observations[b]	Capital Intensity Measure	Labor Price Measure[c]	Coefficients Labor Price	Coefficients Constant Term	$\bar{r}^2$
1	All manufacturing industry groups, pooled	179	PPE[d]	Average wage	0.50 (4.97)	−5.28 (6.82)	.12
2		128[e]	PPE[d]	Average wage	0.51 (4.30)	−5.32 (5.76)	.12
3		128	PPE[d]	Average wage / Average quality	0.55 (4.18)	−3.12 (7.36)	.11
4	Food manufacturing	45	PPE	Average wage	0.40 (3.66)	5.33 (6.48)	.22
5		31	PPE	Average wage / Average quality	0.56 (4.35)	6.68 (16.70)	.37
6		45	Assets	Average wage	0.53 (5.17)	5.21 (6.70)	.37
7		31	Assets	Average wage / Average quality	0.61 (5.57)	7.45 (21.78)	.50
8	Chemicals	52	PPE	Average wage	1.07 (4.70)	0.26 (0.14)	.29
9		33	PPE	Average wage / Average quality	1.20 (3.60)	4.80 (4.31)	.27

10		52	Assets	Average wage	0.73 (5.02)	4.06 (3.56)	.32
11		33	Assets	Average wage / Average quality	0.78 (3.25)	7.24 (9.01)	.23
12	Metals	29	PPE	Average wage	0.54 (1.91)	4.45 (1.99)	.09
13		23	PPE	Average wage / Average quality	0.81 (1.96)	5.97 (4.34)	.11
14		29	Assets	Average wage	0.55 (2.73)	5.40 (3.43)	.19
15		23	Assets	Average wage / Average quality	0.66 (2.20)	7.49 (7.50)	.15
16	Machinery	38	PPE	Average wage	0.49 (3.80)	4.22 (4.27)	.27
17		28	PPE	Average wage / Average quality	0.51 (2.82)	6.42 (11.18)	.20
18		38	Assets	Average wage	0.56 (5.65)	5.02 (6.64)	.46
19		28	Assets	Average wage / Average quality	0.62 (4.42)	7.40 (16.71)	.41
20	Transport equipment	15	PPE	Average wage	0.44 (1.12)	4.71 (1.51)	.02
21		13	PPE	Average wage / Average quality	0.64 (1.33)	6.12 (3.82)	.06

Table 6.6 (continued)

| Equation Number[a] | Industry Group | Number of Observations[b] | Capital Intensity Measure | Labor Price Measure[c] | Coefficients | | $\bar{r}^2$ |
					Labor Price	Constant Term	
22		15	Assets	Average wage	0.30 (1.20)	7.10 (3.57)	.03
23		13	Assets	$\dfrac{\text{Average wage}}{\text{Average quality}}$	0.40 (1.32)	8.15 (7.91)	.06

[a]Each equation is in double-log form with capital intensity as the dependent variable and the price of labor as the independent variable.

[b]Each observation is the sum of all United States affiliates in an industry group in a country.

[c]Average wage paid by all United States-owned affiliates in an industry in a country.

[d]In pooled equations the capital intensity (gross property, plant, and equipment per worker) of United States affiliates is taken as a percentage of the capital intensity in the corresponding United States industry.

[e]Equation 2 is the same as equation 1 but is run only over those countries for which labor quality data are available. Thus equation 2 is comparable in country coverage to equation 3.

6.6   Labor Costs and Factor Proportions within United States Firms

The next question we address is whether the degree of adaptation we have found to exist within industries might be a matter of selection, either among subindustries or among companies within each industry, with each company producing in the same way at home and abroad and in each foreign location. We cannot work with much finer industry classifications than those of table 6.6, for lack of data or of sufficient numbers of observations, but we can, for both the United States and Sweden, use information for individual companies and their affiliates to look for adaptation within companies. The within-company adaptation might be within a given technology (fig. 6.1), between technologies (fig.6.2), some combination of these (fig.6.3), or some selection of processes for LDC production. In addition, the capital/labor ratio may reflect the effects of scale economies or diseconomies within the firm (fig.6.4).

Table 6.7   **Relation of Capital Intensity of Production[a]
to the Price of Labor, Swedish Affiliates Aggregated by Country
within Industry (Manufacturing Industries, Pooled, 1970 and 1974)**

$$\ln \left(\frac{K}{L}\right) = a + b\,D + c \ln w$$

Equation Number	Year	Labor Price Measure	Coefficients			Number of Observations	$\bar{R}^2$
			Labor Price or Proxy	Constant Term	Dummy Variable for two Industries[b]		
1	1970	Average wage[c]	.68 (3.83)	−3.44 (5.25)	.61 (4.19)	106	.25
2	1974	Average wage	.77 (3.79)	−3.75 (4.92)	.58 (3.95)	96	.22
3	1970	Average wage[c]/ quality	.74 (3.54)	−1.95 (6.67)	.62 (4.25)	106	.24
4	1974	Average wage[c]/ quality	.79 (3.25)	−2.02 (5.58)	.58 (3.91)	96	.19
5	1970	Real GDP	.45 (4.69)	−2.64 (7.18)	.62 (4.45)	108	.30
6	1974	Real GDP	.53 (4.95)	−2.95 (6.94)	.56 (4.15)	100	.28
7	1970	Price level	.91 (4.34)	−4.77 (5.40)	.62 (4.36)	108	.28
8	1974	Price level	1.00 (4.64)	−5.13 (5.58)	.54 (3.92)	100	.27

[a]Fire-insurance value of property, plant, and equipment per worker relative to that of the same industry in Sweden.
[b]Paper products and metal products.
[c]Average wage in manufacturing affiliates of United States companies.

A sampling of United States results for all industries in 1966 and 1970 is given in table 6.8. Since we are using individual affiliates as the units of observation here, we can include, in addition to the price of labor in the host country, the scale of operations for the affiliate itself as an explanatory variable.

The data for 1966 have some advantages and some drawbacks compared with those from the 1970 survey. The main advantage is that they are from a complete census of foreign direct investment, and the number of observations is therefore much greater. Second, the 1966 questionnaire was much more detailed than the later one, a fact that permits us to measure more and different variables. On the other hand, the 1966 census did not include as much parent data as in 1970. Therefore the capital-intensity variables for 1966 could not be calculated relative to those of parents because we lack parent data. The result is that some selection of parents may be mixed in with the adaptation by individual companies.

The wage level coefficients in equations 2 and 3 are close to, but a little smaller than, those of table 6.6 where we used country aggregates of affiliates. We can therefore say that most of the response to wage level within industries takes place within individual companies, but there is also a tendency for firms with low capital intensity to operate in low-wage countries, reinforcing the effects of intrafirm adaptation.

The scale variable proves to be highly significant and in the expected direction for capital intensity as measured by physical plant and equipment. That is, larger scale is associated with more capital-intensive methods of production. But this was not true where capital intensity was measured by total assets per worker (equations 7, 8, and 9). By that measure, larger size had no relation, or even a negative relation, to capital intensity.

The measure of the price of labor used here (except in equations 3, 6, and 9) is different for each affiliate. It is the affiliate's average wage per worker or average wage deflated by the average labor quality of the country in which the affiliate is located. Use of the individual firm average wage as a measure of the price of labor implies that, within a country, higher wages represent a higher price for standard labor rather than higher labor quality. If this is not the case (if internal labor markets are competitive, for example) the price of labor might be better measured by the average manufacturing affiliate wage for the country as a whole. Equations 3, 6, and 9 of table 6.8 use this wage level measure, but the results are not consistently higher or lower labor price coefficients than those of the equations using the affiliate wage levels.

The pooling of observations from all industries implies that labor price and scale effects are identical among them, an assumption in which we have no great confidence. Coefficients from equations for the individual manufacturing industries are given in table 6.9 and 6.10, the former showing those for the price of labor and the latter those for scale of production, for both 1966 and 1970. The equations for 1966 differ from those for 1970 in several respects. As mentioned earlier, affiliate capital intensity is not calculated relative to that of the parent for 1966, and we have omitted the equations for net property, plant, and equipment per worker because they are similar to those for gross PPE but show slightly lower elasticities and $\bar{R}^2$s.

Within industries, physical capital intensity is clearly responsive to differences in the price of labor (table 6.9). The variable is significant in eleven out of fourteen equations for 1970 and twelve out of fourteen for 1966, not counting groups such as chemicals for which we also have subgroup equations. The mean and median of the statistically significant wage level coefficients is 0.45 for 1970, when each affiliate is compared with its parent, and 0.50 for 1966, both a little lower than the coefficient of 0.55 from the country aggregates for the same year in table 6.6. Apparently, most all of the response to wage level differences we have observed takes place within, rather than between, individual firms.

Somewhat surprisingly, in view of the doubts we expressed earlier about assets as a capital measure for individual affiliates, we are able to explain variation in total capital per worker better than variation in physical capital per worker. The levels of the $\bar{R}^2$ and the average labor price coefficients are substantially above those for physical capital. The coefficients are higher than those in the equations of table 6.8 using pooled industry data. Apparently industries with affiliates having high total assets per worker tend to locate in low-wage countries. Such a selection of industries would run counter to what we would expect from adaptation to wage levels through selection of industries, and it therefore implies that industry selection is not the reason for the labor price response we observe.

Scale is significant in only three of the fourteen individual industry equations, excluding duplicated groups, for 1970, when capital intensity was measured by net PPE assets. However, the coefficient is positive, as expected, where it is significant (table 6.10). For 1966, with many more observations, a gross PPE measure, but no comparison with parents, scale was significant in eight of the industries. The absence of scale effects in many industries, particularly for 1970 when capital intensity was measured relative to parents, suggests that in the pooled data of table 6.8 we might have been observing an interindustry effect rather than a true effect of scale on capital intensity within industries. That is, industries with small-scale operations tended to have affiliates that were labor-intensive relative to their parents, but within most industries there was little relation between scale and capital intensity of individual affiliates. That possibility of industry effects is also suggested by the fact that two of

Table 6.8 Relation of Capital Intensity of Production to the Price of Labor: Individual United States Affiliates (All Manufacturing Industries, Pooled, 1966 and 1970)

$$\ln\left(\frac{K}{L}\right) = a + b \ln w + c \ln NS$$

Equation Number[a]	Year	Number of Observations (Affiliates)	Capital Intensity Measure[b]	Labor Price Measure	Coefficients Labor Price	Scale[c]	Constant	$\bar{R}^2$
1	1966	4,502	Gross PPE[d]	Average affiliate wage	0.44 (14.29)	0.13 (11.54)	8.88 (98.51)	.08
2	1966	4,336[f]	Gross PPE	Average affiliate wage / Average quality	0.47 (13.18)	0.14 (12.27)	−9.73 (101.40)	.08
3	1966	4,336	Gross PPE	Average country wage / Average quality	0.34 (7.96)	0.15 (13.06)	−9.62 (96.18)	.06
4	1970	2,305	Net PPE[e]	Average affiliate wage	0.45 (9.89)	0.08 (4.53)	−2.18 (14.30)	.06

	Year		Capital intensity	Independent variable				R^2
5	1970	2,256	Net PPE	Average affiliate wage / Average quality	0.45 (8.98)	0.09 (4.86)	−2.23 (14.20)	.06
6	1970	2,213	Net PPE	Average country wage / Average quality	0.62 (9.20)	0.09 (5.12)	−2.55 (15.15)	.06
7	1970	2,315	Assets[c]	Average affiliate wage / Average quality	0.60 (20.05)	−0.02 (1.95)	−1.11 (11.28)	.15
8	1970	2,266	Assets	Average affiliate wage / Average quality	0.60 (18.38)	−0.02 (1.39)	−1.17 (11.47)	.13
9	1970	2,223	Assets	Average country wage / Average quality	0.59 (13.08)	0.00 (0.27)	−1.37 (12.12)	.07

[a]Each equation is in double-log form with capital intensity as the dependent variable and labor price as the independent variable.

[b]Gross PPE = Gross property, plant, and equipment per worker.
Net PPE = Net property, plant and equipment per worker.
Assets   = Assets per worker.

[c]Scale (SC) = Net sales of affiliate (total sales less imports from the United States).

[d]Affiliate relative to United States industry.

[e]Affiliate relative to parent.

[f]Equation 2 is the same as equation 1 but is run only over those countries for which labor quality data are available. Thus equation 2 is comparable in country coverage to equation 3.

Table 6.9   Coefficients for Labor Price in Equations
                   Relating Physical and Total Capital Intensity
                   to the Price of Labor[a] and Scale of Production[b]
                   (Individual United States Affiliates, by Industry, 1966 and 1970)

$$\ln \left(\frac{K}{L}\right) = a + b \ln w + c \ln NS$$

| | Coefficients in Equations for | | | |
| | Physical Capital Intensity[c] | | Total Capital Intensity[d] | |
Industry	1970	1966	1970	1966
Food processing	0.45	0.53	0.91	0.85
Paper and allied products	0.44	0.70	0.40	0.71
Chemicals	0.55	0.67	0.64	0.78
Drugs	0.41	0.29	0.37	0.58
Other chemicals	0.58	0.75	0.76	0.82
Rubber and plastics	0.19[e]	0.50	0.27	0.68
Primary and fabricated metals	0.44	0.45	0.59	0.62
Non-electrical machinery	0.52	0.39	0.60	0.69
Computers and office machinery	1.04	0.70	0.78	0.78
Other nonelectrical machinery	0.32	0.25	0.56	0.63
Electrical machinery	0.54	0.57	0.82	0.85
Radio, television, and electronics	0.47	0.70	0.90	0.92
Household appliances	1.28	0.41	1.00	0.65
Other electrical machinery	0.33[e]	0.47	0.58	0.83
Transport equipment	0.54	0.28	0.29	0.67
Motor vehicles	0.59	0.22[e]	0.30[e]	0.60
Other transport equipment	−0.43[e]	0.65[e]	−0.19[e]	1.04
Other manufacturing	0.38	0.47	0.49	0.81

[a]Average wage per worker in each affiliate, deflated by average labor quality in the country in which the affiliate is located.
[b]Net sales of an affiliate (total sales less imports from the United States).
[c]For 1970, affiliate net property, plant, and equipment per worker relative to the same measure for the parent company; for 1966, affiliate gross property, plant, and equipment per worker.
[d]For 1970, affiliate total assets per worker relative to the same measure for the parent company; for 1966, affiliate total assets per worker.
[e]Not significant at the 5 percent level.

the three significant scale effects on physical capital intensity in 1970 are for combinations of industries: other chemicals, and other nonelectrical machinery.

When we did measure capital intensity by total, rather than physical, assets per worker, the coefficient for scale, while it is statistically significant in only a minority of cases, is negative in all of these. That is, the larger the affiliate, the lower the total assets per worker even though some of the same industries' equations showed that the larger the affiliate, the higher the gross property, plant, and equipment per worker.

These negative scale coefficients are a surprise. There is virtually no relationship between size of affiliate and assets per worker in simple regressions within industries, and the few significant coefficients are split between positive and negative ones. However, there is a strong relationship between affiliate size and gross property, plant, and equipment per worker, and all the statistically significant coefficients are positive. These results suggest that indivisibilities in machinery and equipment are responsible for the relationship with physical capital intensity and that the effect of these is offset in other types of assets.

6.7   Labor Costs and Factor Proportions within Swedish Firms

The data for Swedish firms and their foreign affiliates differ from the United States data in several respects. One of the chief advantages of the Swedish data is that they give production, by industry, for each parent and affiliate. We can thus distinguish industry-mix choices even within the firm from choices of factor proportions within an industry in a way that is impossible with the United States data, in which each parent and each affiliate is characterized as being in a single industry. We calculate, for each Swedish parent and affiliate, capital intensities at Swedish industry coefficients. Any difference between the capital intensities of parents and affiliates at Swedish industry coefficients then represents a choice of industry mix, while the differences between the actual capital intensity of an affiliate and its calculated capital intensity at Swedish industry coefficients represents a choice of production methods or product mix within industries. Thus we can calculate the affiliate's capital input at Swedish coefficients as

$$AK^{sw} = \sum_{i=1}^{m} Aq_i \frac{K_i^{sw}}{q_i^{sw}}$$

and its labor input at Swedish coefficients as

$$AL^{sw} = \sum_{i=1}^{m} Aq_i \frac{L_i^{sw}}{q_i^{sw}},$$

where AK_i^{sw} and AL_i^{sw} are affiliate capital and labor inputs at Swedish industry coefficients, Aq_i is the affiliate's production in industry i, and K_i^{sw}, L_i^{sw}, and q_i^{sw} are capital input, labor input, and output in the domestic Swedish industry i. We can similarly calculate parent capital and labor inputs at Swedish industry ratios, PK^{sw} and PL^{sw}, and we can compare all of these with actual affiliate and parent inputs, AK, AL, PK, and PL.

Table 6.10   **Coefficients for Scale Variable in Equations Relating Physical and Total Capital Intensity to the Price of Labor[a] and Scale of Production[b] (Individual United States Affiliates, by Industry, 1966 and 1970)**

$$\ln\left(\frac{K}{L}\right) = a + b \ln w + c \ln NS$$

| | Coefficients in Equations for | | | |
| | Physical Capital Intensity[c] | | Total Capital Intensity[d] | |
Industry	1970	1966	1970	1966
Food processing	0.10**	0.06**	−0.10**	−0.06**
Paper and allied products	0.09*	0.06*	0.02	−0.06*
Chemicals	0.15**	0.21**	0.02	0.01
Drugs	0.10*	0.26**	0.08*	0.03*
Other chemicals	0.15**	0.19**	−0.00	0.00
Rubber and plastics	0.03	0.13**	−0.01	−0.04*
Primary and fabricated metals	−0.06	0.09**	−0.07*	−0.04**
Non-electrical machinery	0.12**	0.11**	0.01	−0.02*
Computers and office machinery	0.02	0.32**	−0.07**	0.05*
Other nonelectrical machinery	0.12**	0.07**	0.04*	−0.02*
Electrical machinery	−0.05	0.02	−0.11**	−0.09**
Radio, television, and electronics	−0.03	0.02	−0.17**	−0.06**
Household appliances	−0.11	0.04	−0.08*	−0.17**
Other electrical machinery	−0.06	0.03	−0.08*	−0.10**
Transport equipment	−0.01	0.05*	0.02	−0.04*
Motor vehicles	−0.01	0.06**	0.02	−0.02
Other transport equipment	0.04	−0.08	0.01	−0.02*
Other manufacturing	0.08*	0.03*	−0.02	−0.09**

[a]Average wage per worker in each affiliate, deflated by average labor quality in the country in which the affiliate is located.
[b]Net sales of an affiliate (total sales less imports from the United States).
[c]For 1970, affiliate net property, plant, and equipment per worker relative to the same measure for the parent company; for 1966, affiliate gross property, plant, and equipment per worker.
[d]For 1970, affiliate total assets per worker relative to the same measure for the parent company; for 1966, affiliate total assets per worker.
** $= t \geqslant 1.96$.
* $= 1.00 \leqslant t < 1.96$.

Another advantage of these data is that both numbers and payroll are given separately for wage and salaried workers, enabling us to calculate average earnings for each. The wage per wage worker, while not standardized for quality, may be a little less subject to wide differences in mix than the average wage in the United States figures, which lump wage and salaried workers together.

One way to use the Swedish affiliate data is to compare affiliates in the aggregate with their parents and with Swedish industry, taking advantage of the information on industry composition instead of relying on the single-industry designations as in the earlier comparisons of aggregates in tables 6.1 and 6.3. For example, we can calculate the average ratios of affiliate industry/parent industry capital intensities and skill intensities at Swedish industry coefficients in 1974

$$\frac{AK^{sw}}{AL^{sw}} \bigg/ \frac{PK^{sw}}{PL^{sw}} = 1.06$$

$$\frac{ALS^{sw}}{AL^{sw}} \bigg/ \frac{PLS^{sw}}{PL^{sw}} = 1.01,$$

where AK^{sw} is the amount of capital, AL^{sw} the number of workers, and ALS^{sw} the number of salaried workers an affiliate would have if it used the Swedish industry ratio of capital, all workers, and salaried workers to output and the figures for parents are analogous.

The actual capital intensities of the affiliates and parents can be compared with Swedish and parent levels for the same industries as follows:

$$\text{Average} \frac{AK}{AL} \bigg/ \frac{AK^{sw}}{AL^{sw}} = .81$$

$$\text{Average} \frac{\dfrac{AK}{AL} \bigg/ \dfrac{AK^{sw}}{AL^{sw}}}{\dfrac{PK}{PL} \bigg/ \dfrac{PK^{sw}}{PL^{sw}}} = .79 \, .$$

We can interpret these ratios in the light of the fact that Swedish wages were high in comparison with those in affiliates' host countries. Adjusted for labor quality or not, Swedish wage levels in 1966 and 1970 were higher, by all our measures of the price of labor, than those of every country except the United States and Canada.

If we take Swedish capital intensities in parent company industries (PK^{sw}/PL^{sw}) as 100, the capital intensities for aggregates of parents and affiliates were:

Affiliate industry mix relative to parents

$$\left(\frac{AK^{sw}}{AL^{sw}} \bigg/ \frac{PK^{sw}}{PL^{sw}} \right)$$
                                                                    106

Parent capital intensity relative to all
Swedish firms in same industries

$$\left(\frac{PK}{PL} \bigg/ \frac{PK^{sw}}{PL^{sw}} \right)$$
                                                                    102

Affiliate capital intensity relative to
Swedish industry in parent industries

$$\left(\frac{AK}{AL} \Big/ \frac{PK^{sw}}{PL^{sw}}\right)$$

86

Affiliate capital intensity was 14 percent below that of Swedish companies in the industries of parents. We can divide that difference into two elements. The actual capital intensity of affiliate production was almost 20 percent below what would have been expected (difference between 106 and 86), given the industry composition of affiliate activities and Swedish capital intensity. The 20 percent could reflect the degree of adaptation by affiliates, within industries, to lower prices of labor outside Sweden. That lower capital intensity within industries was partly offset by the fact that the affiliates were in industries that were 6 percent more capital-intensive than those of the affiliates' parent companies. Thus there was no adaptation to wage level differences in the selection of affiliate industry mix as compared with parent company industry mix. Furthermore, parent companies tended to be slightly more capital-intensive than the corresponding Swedish industries, and there was thus no indication of adaptation through selection of labor-intensive parents within industries.

With respect to our indicator of skill intensity, the only calculation we made shows that affiliates are in industries with substantially the same skill requirements (as measured by the importance of salaried workers) as those of their parents' industries.

Using the data for individual affiliates and individual countries, we test first for adaptation by choice of industry mix. Do affiliates in labor-intensive industries tend to be in low-wage countries? For this purpose we related the capital intensity of each affiliate's parent and of each affiliate itself, at Swedish factor coefficients (AK^{sw}/AL^{sw} and PK^{sw}/PL^{sw}), to measures of wage levels, as in equations (1) through (3).

(1) $\ln\dfrac{AK^{sw}}{AL^{sw}} = 4.83 + .09 \ln w_c$ $\bar{R}^2 = .00$
        Number of observations = 428

(2) $\ln\dfrac{PK^{sw}}{PL^{sw}} = 5.08 + .16^* \ln w_c$ $\bar{R}^2 = .01$
        Number of observations = 424

(2) $\ln\dfrac{PK^{sw}}{PL^{sw}} = 5.09 + .15 \ln w_a$ $\bar{R}^2 = .02$
        Number of observations = 402

*Statistically significant at the 5 percent level. The calculations performed for us on the Swedish data did not include t-statistics for the coefficients.

w_c is the average wage in all Swedish affiliates in a country, and w_a is the average wage in a particular affiliate, both divided by the average quality of labor, estimated from data on the educational level of the population, as described earlier. There is only a very faint tendency for affiliates with parents in labor-intensive industries to be in countries where wage levels are low.

Our measure of adaptation to factor costs within industries by individual firms is the ratio of affiliate factor proportions to what they would have been if there had been no adaptation. The factor proportions that represent no adaptation within an industry are those of Swedish parents or of a Swedish industry in the aggregate in each industry. Thus the factor input ratios AK^{sw}/AL^{sw} and AK^p/AL^p represent no adaptation to factor prices outside Sweden, and we compare the actual factor ratio of each affiliate, AK/AL, with that at Swedish or parent coefficients, in table 6.11. When we use affiliate wage, either adjusted for average labor quality in each country as in equations 3 and 4, or unadjusted, but compared with Swedish or parent wages (assuming an industry or company hires the same quality of labor abroad as in Sweden), as in equations 5 and 6, the labor cost coefficients are statistically significant and range between 0.47 and 0.55. However, only a small part of the variation in capital intensities is explained. If we substitute average wages in Swedish affiliates in a country for the individual affiliate wages, as in equations 1 and 2, the wage level coefficient rises substantially, to about 0.75. We might guess from this change that the apparent variation in the price of labor among affiliates within a country may be spurious, representing mainly quality differences rather than price differences.

If we aggregate not only wage levels but also capital intensities within host countries, as in table 6.12, the sensitivity to wage level differences is much greater. The wage level coefficients are 0.90 or above, and the equations explain much more of the variation in capital intensities, up to 40 percent. The variation in capital intensities is adjusted for differences in industry mix and is the closest we can come to within-industry substitution between capital and labor. If we accept the results from these country aggregates, we would conclude that Swedish firms respond even more strongly to wage level differences than do United States firms.

Since the Swedish data contain information on aggregate wages, aggregate salaries, and numbers of wage and salary workers, we can calculate the average wage and average salary for each parent, affiliate, and Swedish industry. If each group of workers is assumed to be homogeneous—clearly a risky assumption—we can calculate prices for wages and salary and also amounts of input (employment) of each group. We have calculated a relative price of skilled labor for each affiliate as the ratio of the average salary to the average wage divided by the ratio of average Swedish or parent salary to average Swedish or parent wage,

Table 6.11   **Relation of Physical Capital Intensity to the Price of Labor (Individual Swedish Affiliates, 1974)**

$$\ln\left(\frac{K}{L}\right) = a + \ln w$$

Equation Number	Dependent (Capital Intensity) Variable	Labor Cost Variables	Coefficients Labor Price	Coefficients Constant Term	Number of Observations	$\bar{R}^2$
1	$\dfrac{AK}{AL} \Big/ \dfrac{AK^{sw}}{AL^{sw}}$	$\dfrac{w_c}{Q_c}$	.74*	.30	334	.09
2	$\dfrac{AK}{AL} \Big/ \dfrac{AK^p}{AL^p}$	$\dfrac{w_c}{Q_c}$	.79*	.31	334	.10
3	$\dfrac{AK}{AL} \Big/ \dfrac{AK^{sw}}{AL^{sw}}$	$\dfrac{w_a}{Q_c}$	.48*	−.02	326	.06
4	$\dfrac{AK}{AL} \Big/ \dfrac{AK^p}{AL^p}$	$\dfrac{w_a}{Q_c}$	.47*	−.08	326	.06
5	$\dfrac{AK}{AL} \Big/ \dfrac{AK^{sw}}{AL^{sw}}$	$\dfrac{w_a}{w_s}$	.55*	−.55	353	.09
6	$\dfrac{AK}{AL} \Big/ \dfrac{AK^p}{AL^p}$	$\dfrac{w_a}{w_p}$	.48*	−.50	349	.08

NOTE:

AK = Fire insurance value of affiliate plant and equipment.
AL = Number of workers in affiliate.
AK^{sw} = Fire insurance value of affiliate plant and equipment if affiliate had the same ratio of plant and equipment to sales in each industry as Swedish industry.
AL^{sw} = Number of workers in affiliate if affiliate had the same ratio of employment to sales in each industry as Swedish industry.
AK^p = Fire insurance value of affiliate plant and equipment if affiliate had the same ratio of plant and equipment to sales as among Swedish parents in each industry.
AL^p = Number of workers in affiliate if affiliate had the same ratio of workers to sales as among Swedish parents in each industry.
w_c = Average wage in Swedish manufacturing affiliates in a country.
w_a = Average wage in a Swedish affiliate.
w_s = Average wage in Sweden in affiliate industries.
w_p = Average wage in parent firm.
Q_c = Average quality of labor in a country as estimated from data on education.
*   = Statistically significant at the 5 percent level.

weighted by the affiliate's mix of industries. We thus measure the relative price of skill adjusted for industry mix, and the same ratio is aggregated over Swedish affiliates to produce country measures of the relative price of skilled, as compared with unskilled, labor.

The skill input measure is the ratio of salaried to wage workers, again adjusted for the industry composition of the affiliate's output. The skill input measure can be related to the relative price of skill across affiliates and across countries.

Table 6.12   **Relation of Physical Capital Intensity to the Price of Labor (Swedish Affiliates Aggregated by Country, 1974)**

$$\ln\left(\frac{K}{L}\right) = a + \ln w$$

Equation Number	Dependent (Capital Intensity) Variable	Labor Cost Variable	Coefficients		Number of Observations	$\bar{R}^2$
			Labor Price	Constant Term		
1	$\dfrac{AK}{AL}\Big/\dfrac{AK^{sw}}{AL^{sw}}$	$\dfrac{w_c}{Q_c}$	.94*	.65	30	.41
2	$\dfrac{AK}{AL}\Big/\dfrac{AK^{p}}{AL^{p}}$	$\dfrac{w_c}{Q_c}$	.95*	.55	30	.41
3	$\dfrac{AK}{AL}\Big/\dfrac{AK^{sw}}{AL^{sw}}$	$\dfrac{w_c}{w_s}$	1.04*	−.37	35	.40
4	$\dfrac{AK}{AL}\Big/\dfrac{AK^{sw}}{AL^{sw}}$	$\dfrac{w_c}{w_p}$	.95*	−.20	35	.30
5	$\dfrac{AK}{AL}\Big/\dfrac{AK^{p}}{AL^{p}}$	$\dfrac{w_c}{w_s}$	.98*	−.48	35	.36
6	$\dfrac{AK}{AL}\Big/\dfrac{AK^{p}}{AL^{p}}$	$\dfrac{w_c}{w_p}$	.89*	−.32	35	.27

NOTE: For definitions of terms see notes to table 6.11.

* = Statistically significant at the 5 percent level.

An attempt is made in the equations of table 6.13 to test for response to relative prices of skilled (salaried) and unskilled (wage) labor. Although little of the variation in skill ratios was explained by the relative price variable, there was a statistically significant response in the expected direction. In affiliates where the price of skilled labor was high, the proportion of skilled workers, adjusted for the industry mix of the affiliate's production, tended to be low (equations 1 and 2). The relationship was stronger among countries (equations 3 and 4). In countries where the price of skilled labor was relatively high, the proportion used was low. Whatever this crude "skill" ratio measures, whether it is truly skill or education, or perhaps the distinction between white-collar and blue-collar workers, Swedish firms did appear to respond to differences in relative prices among countries by adjusting the proportions of the two types of labor.

6.8 Results of Other Studies

The study most similar to ours was that of Courtney and Leipziger (1975), who used the same data on United States affiliates abroad. As

Table 6.13   **Relation of Skill Intensity to Price of Skilled Labor (Individual Swedish Affiliates and Affiliates Aggregated by Country, 1974)**

$$\ln\left(\frac{L_{sal}}{L_{wage}}\right) = a + \ln\frac{w_{sal}}{w_{wage}}$$

Equation Number	Skill Intensity (Dependent) Variable	Skilled Labor Price Variable	Coefficients		Number of Observations	$\bar{R}^2$
			Skilled Labor Price	Constant Term		
1	$\frac{L_{sal}}{L_{wage}}\left|\frac{L_{sal}^{sw}}{L_{wage}^{sw}}\right.$	$\frac{w_{sal}}{w_{wage}}\left|\frac{w_{sal}^{sw}}{w_{wage}^{sw}}\right.$	$-.27^*$	.15	427	.04
2	$\frac{L_{sal}}{L_{wage}}\left|\frac{L_{sal}^{P}}{L_{wage}^{P}}\right.$	$\frac{w_{sal}}{w_{wage}}\left|\frac{w_{sal}^{P}}{w_{wage}^{P}}\right.$	$-.32^*$	$-.01$	423	.07
3	$\left(\frac{L_{sal}}{L_{wage}}\left|\frac{L_{sal}^{sw}}{L_{wage}^{sw}}\right.\right)_c$	$\left(\frac{w_{sal}}{w_{wage}}\left|\frac{w_{sal}^{sw}}{w_{wage}^{sw}}\right.\right)_c$	$-.42^*$	.19	31	.08
4	$\left(\frac{L_{sal}}{L_{wage}}\left|\frac{L_{sal}^{P}}{L_{wage}^{P}}\right.\right)_c$	$\left(\frac{w_{sal}}{w_{wage}}\left|\frac{w_{sal}^{P}}{w_{wage}^{P}}\right.\right)_c$	$-.46^*$	.03	31	.12

NOTE:

L_{sal} and L_{wage} = Number of salaried and wage workers.

L_{sal}^{sw} and L_{wage}^{sw} = Number of salaried and wage workers that would be employed by an affiliate at Swedish industry ratios of salaried and wage workers to output.

L_{sal}^{P} and L_{wage}^{P} = Number of salaried and wage workers that would be employed by an affiliate at parent ratios of salaried and wage workers to output.

w_{sal} and w_{wage} = Average salary per salaried worker and wage per wage worker.

w_{sal}^{sw} and w_{wage}^{sw} = Average salary per salaried worker and average wage per wage worker that affiliate would have given at affiliate industry. mix and Swedish salary levels.

w_{sal}^{P} and w_{wage}^{P} = Average salary per salaried worker and average wage per wage worker in parent companies.

c = Country aggregates.

* = Statistically significant at the 5 percent level.

already noted, their study concentrated on separating observed differences in capital intensity between affiliates in developed countries and those in LDCs (k_1 and k_3 in figure 6.3) into the unobserved differences in the choice of technology (k_1 and k_2), or "ex ante substitution" in their terms, and the unobserved substitution within the chosen technology (k_2 and k_3), or "ex post substitution." Courtney and Leipziger assumed two technologies in each industry, one for developed country affiliates and one for affiliates in LDCs.

Their results contained some puzzling findings. They found significant differences in technology between affiliates in developed countries and those in LDCs in six out of eleven industries, and in three of these it was the affiliates in LDCs that were using the more capital-intensive technology: that is, they were using, by the authors' interpretation, more capital-intensive plant designs. However, the response to wage levels being lower in LDCs than in developed countries was so large that even industries using more capital-intensive technologies in LDCs ended up with comparatively labor-intensive production there. Since the most capital-intensive technologies in LDCs, relative to developed countries, were associated with the highest elasticities of substitution, there is a question whether the authors were really successful in separating the choice of technology or plant design from the response to factor prices.

Other studies of factor use in multinational firms' operations in LDCs have been mainly case studies of particular industries or groups of plants. On the whole, the results have been inconclusive, with some reporting extensive adaptation and others reporting virtually none. Since adaptation is not always clearly defined, or the definitions differ among studies, and since most studies refer to narrow segments of industry, it is not certain whether they contradict each other or simply observe actual differences in behavior among industries or countries.

A study by Morley and Smith (1974) examined the choice of technology by multinational firms in Brazil, largely on the basis of interviews and the authors' views rather than any substantial statistical evidence on the operation of plants. Their main conclusion was that there were very large differences in technology between the United States firms at home and their affiliates in Brazil. However, they explained the difference as an adaptation to differences in the scale of production rather than in relative factor prices. They argued that the production function is not homothetic and that at any factor prices small-scale production would be relatively labor-intensive and large-scale production capital-intensive.

It is worth mentioning again in this connection that a major role for scale in determining factor proportions does not preclude a role for factor costs in adaptation even if there is no response to factor prices at a given level of production. It may be only the cheapness of labor in LDCs that permits the existence of small, labor-intensive plants that could not survive in the high labor cost environment of the developed countries. The amount of protection required to sustain small-scale, labor-intensive production may be much less in LDC, with low wages, than in a developed country with its high wage levels. The adaptation by multinational firms may thus be attributable to both the smallness of LDC markets and the low labor costs.

Examples of adaptation in the sense of both selection of stages of production and selection of production techniques were found in a study by Finan (1975) of United States direct investment and technology transfer in the semiconductor industry. American firms tended to place the labor-intensive assembly stage of production in low-wage foreign countries while confining the more capital-intensive and technology-intensive wafer fabrication stage to the United States and to affiliates in developed countries. However, within the assembly stage, production was more capital-intensive in the United States than abroad. A substantial number of automated assembly lines were in operation in the United States, but there were none in foreign operations.

Cohen (1975), in a study of foreign-owned and locally owned plants in Taiwan, South Korea, and Singapore, not identified by industry, mentions that National Semiconductor and Texas Instruments were producing integrated circuits using highly automated techniques in these countries, a fact he interprets as lack of adaptation, though he presents no comparison with home country methods of production.

6.9 Conclusions

The purpose of our investigation was to learn whether multinational firms responded to differences among countries in the price of labor by using more labor-intensive methods of production in low-wage countries, either by selecting labor-intensive subindustries, selecting labor-intensive processes within industries, selecting small-scale operations for which only labor-intensive methods were available, or operating in a labor-intensive way whatever technologies were selected. We found that, for both Swedish and United States multinational firms, parent company or home country capital intensities of production, as measured by total assets per worker or by fixed assets alone, were higher than those of affiliates in developed countries, and that these in turn were higher than those of affiliates in less developed countries. These differences were not primarily the result of industry selection, at least among the broad industry groups used here: in fact, in some cases it was capital-intensive industries that tended to invest abroad, particularly in less developed countries.

Among countries in which affiliates were located, a higher price of labor was associated with higher capital intensities of affiliates in the aggregate for all manufacturing and within manufacturing industries. Some of the relation for manufacturing as a group represented a tendency for affiliates in labor-intensive industries to settle in low-wage countries, but the main element was the relation of capital intensity to wage levels within industries.

Within individual companies there is again a strong effect of wage levels on capital intensity. Some of the intraindustry effect noted above could have been the result of selection among companies, more labor-intensive companies being more attracted to low-wage countries. However, the main intraindustry effect was the result of adaptation within companies, whether by selection among products or processes or by adaptation of particular production processes. We also found, in the data for individual companies, a strong effect of scale of operations on capital intensity when that was defined as property, plant, and equipment per worker. Scale had very little effect, and sometimes a negative effect, on capital intensity measured by total assets per worker.

While the United States data, even for individual firms in an industry, could contain some industry-mix effects, because some firms and even affiliates produce in several industries and could vary the industry mix from country to country, we could reduce that effect in the Swedish data, for which we know the industry mix of each affiliate's production. The results there seem to show even stronger indications that firms respond to low wage rates by producing in a labor-intensive way.

Notes

1. We can see this relationship most clearly in a very simple example, abstracting from transport costs, differences in factor costs and factor prices, and the possible existence of intermediate products. If there are decreasing costs up to some level of output, j, perhaps the level at which some indivisible unit of capital is fully utilized, and constant costs above j, we have the type of unit cost function shown in the accompanying diagram.

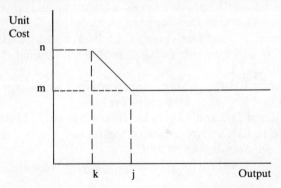

A producer in a small country, operating at output k, could not compete in his own market with large producers unless he had a protective tariff of 50 percent. Such a tariff would inflate both the value of his output and his value added. If output is then measured by value added in a production function fitted across countries, the inefficiency of the small producer is concealed, different scales of production appear to be equally efficient, and the estimated production function implies constant returns to scale.

2. Among the seven countries included in the two poorest groups above, four were studied in NBER's project on foreign trade regimes and economic development. The effective rates of protection for years closest to 1970, as calculated in the NBER studies or taken from other publications, were as follows:

	Nonelectrical Machinery	Electrical Machinery
Colombia (1970)	33	57
India (1968–69)	88	120
Philippines (1965)	112[a]	
	103[b]	
South Korea (1968)	44[a]	
	30[b]	

[a]Balassa measure.
[b]Corden measure.

Data are from Bhagwati and Srinivasan (1975), p. 179, Balassa (1971), p. 279, Díaz-Alejandro (1976), p. 60), and Frank, Kim, and Westphal (1975, pp. 198–99).

3. A possibility that might be worth exploring is to measure the price of labor by average wage for the country as a whole deflated by the average labor quality index and to measure skill intensity for a given affiliate or group of affiliates by the ratio of average wage paid to the average national wage.

References

Balassa, Bela, and Associates. 1971. *The structure of protection in developing countries*. Baltimore and London: Johns Hopkins University Press for the International Bank for Reconstruction and Development and the Inter-American Development Bank.

Bhagwati, Jagdish N., and Srinivasan, T. N. 1975. *Foreign trade regimes and economic development: India*. New York: National Bureau of Economic Research.

Cohen, Benjamin I. 1975. *Multinational firms and Asian exports*. New Haven and London: Yale University Press.

Courtney, William H., and Leipziger, Danny M. 1975. Multinational corporations in LDCs: The choice of technology. *Oxford Bulletin of Economics and Statistics* 57:297–303.

Denison, Edward. 1967. *Why growth rates differ*. Washington, D.C.: Brookings Institution.

Díaz-Alejandro, Carlos F. 1976. *Foreign trade regimes and economic development: Colombia*. New York: National Bureau of Economic Research.

Finan, William. 1975. The international transfer of semiconductor technology through U.S.-based firms. NBER Working Paper no. 118. Xeroxed.

Frank, Charles R., Jr.; Kim, Kwang Suk; and Westphal, Larry E. 1975. *Foreign trade regimes and economic development: South Korea*. New York: National Bureau of Economic Research.

Harbison, Frederick, and Myers, Charles A. 1964. *Education, manpower, and economic growth*. New York: Macmillan.

Kravis, Irving B.; Heston, Alan W.; and Summers, Robert. 1978a. *United Nations international comparison project: Phase II; International comparisons of real product and purchasing power*. Baltimore and London: Johns Hopkins University Press.

———. 1978b. Real GDP per capita for more than one hundred countries. *Economic Journal* 88:215–42.

Kravis, Irving B.; Kenessey, Zoltan; Heston, Alan; and Summers, Robert. 1975. *A system of international comparisons of gross product and purchasing power*. Baltimore and London: Johns Hopkins University Press.

Krueger, Anne O. 1968. Factor endowments and per capita income differences among countries. *Economic Journal* 78:641–59.

Lary, Hal B. 1968. *Imports of manufactures from less developed countries*. New York: National Bureau of Economic Research.

Leipziger, Danny M. 1976. Production characteristics in foreign enclave and domestic manufacturing: The case of India. *World Development* 4:321–25.

Morley, Samuel A., and Smith, Gordon W. 1974. The choice of technology: Multinational firms in Brazil. Paper no. 58 (fall), Rice University Program of Development Studies.

Sweden, Statistiska Centralbyrån. 1972a. Företagen 1970. Ekonomisk redovisning.

———. 1972b. Industri 1970. Del. 1. Data fördelade enligt standard för svensk näringsgrensindelning (SNI).

———. 1976a. Företagen 1974. Ekonomisk redovisning.

———. 1976b. Industri 1974. Del. 1. Data fördelade enligt standard för svensk näringsgrensindelning (SNI).

Swedenborg, Birgitta, 1973. *Den svenska industrins investeringar i utlandet*. Stockholm: Industriens Utredningsinstitut.

———. 1979. *The multinational operations of Swedish firms*. Stockholm: Industriens Utredningsinstitut.

United States Department of Commerce. 1972. *Special survey of U.S. multinational companies, 1970*. Washington, D.C.: Bureau of Economic Analysis.

———. 1975. *U.S. direct investment abroad, 1966: Final data*. Washington, D.C.: Bureau of Economic Analysis.

Contributors

Jere R. Behrman
Department of Economics
University of Pennsylvania
Philadelphia, Pennsylvania 19174

José L. Carvalho
Fundação Getúlio Vargas—EPGE
Caixa Postal 9052 ZC-02
Rio de Janeiro 20000 R.J.
Republic of Brazil

Vittorio Corbo
Instituto de Economía
Pontificia Universidad Católica
Casilla 114-D
Santiago, Chile

Cláudio L. S. Haddad
Fundação Getúlio Vargas—EPGE
Caixa Postal 9052 ZC-02
Rio de Janiero 20000 R.J.
Republic of Brazil

James M. Henderson
Department of Economics
University of Minnesota
Minneapolis, Minnesota 55455

Irving B. Kravis
Department of Economics
University of Pennsylvania
Philadelphia, Pennsylvania 19174

Anne O. Krueger
Department of Economics
University of Minnesota
Minneapolis, Minnesota 55455

Robert Lipsey
National Bureau of Economic
  Research
269 Mercer Street, 8th Floor
New York, New York 10003

Patricio Meller
CIEPLAN
Departamento de Economía
Universidad de Chile
Casilla 3861
Santiago, Chile

Romualdo A. Roldan
Chase Econometrics
150 Monument Road
Bala Cynwyd, Pennsylvania 19004

T. Paul Schultz
Economic Growth Center
Yale University
52 Hillhouse Avenue
New Haven, Connecticut 06520

257

Author Index

Subject Index

ACMS model of capital/labor substitution, 160, 161–66; variants of, 171–87

Aggregation, in capital–labor substitution, xiii, 160, 187, 193, 194, 195–97, 208, 209–11

Agriculture: in Belgium, 26; capital services in, 43–44; in Chile, 26; in Colombia, 88, 89, 94, 95, 97, 103, 105, 106, 107, 109, 144 n.11; in France, 26, 30; in Germany, 26, 30; income in, 96–97; in Italy, 26; in Ivory Coast, 22, 26, 29; in Kenya, 22, 26; labor in, 17, 20–21, 22–26, 40, 43–44; protected, 86, 94, 106, 109; in South Korea, 22, 29, 30; in Taiwan, 29; in Tunisia, 22, 30, 32; in Turkey, 26, 29; in Uruguay, 29, 31

Alcohol, 18

Balance of payments, 88; constraints on, 32

Belgium: agriculture in, 26; manufacturing in, 26, 31; optimal trade model in, 16, 26

Brazil: coffee in, 149, 151, 154; export promotion in, xii, 149–57; gross domestic product in, 154, 156, 157; influence on world prices of, 151; manufacturing in, 154, 156; multinationals in, 251; real exchange rate in, 152–53, 154, 156; technology in, 251

Capital: cost of, 12, 37, 144 n.7, 187, 227–29; human, xiii, 90, 91, 193, 194; physical, xiii, 17, 193, 194, 227, 239–43; as production input, 4, 7–8, 12, 15, 20, 21, 86–87, 162, 215, 221, 228; rate of return on, 86–

87, 162, 171, 221; services, 34–38, 43, 48, 80; shifts, 34, 38; stock/flow measures of, 8, 21, 229; and skill, 208, 209. *See also* Capital intensity; Capital/labor substitution

Capital intensity, xii, 86, 145 n.18, 218, 219, 220, 222–29; in Colombia, 88; and cost of capital, 227–29; in developing countries, 37–38, 216–21; and labor costs, 227–53; measures of, 197–98, 211 n.8, 222, 228–29, 233, 239–43, 253; in manufacturing, 222–26; of multinationals, xiii, 215, 222–26; and protection, 98, 108, 110; studies of, 249–52; in Sweden, 225, 230–33, 243–49, 252–53; and technology, 249–52; in United States, 223, 230–33, 237–43, 252–53

Capital/labor ratios, 34–38, 80, 81, 237–43

Capital/labor substitution, xi, xii, 2, 41, 159–211; ACMS model of, 160, 161–66, 171–87; aggregation in, xiii, 160, 187, 193, 194, 195–97, 208, 209–11; in Chile, xiii, 37, 38–40; cross-country estimates of, 159, 160–61, 164, 165, 166–71, 180–86; in developing countries, 34–38, 81; effects of, 159–60; exchange rates in, 182; GDP per capita in, 178, 179, 180; GNP per capita in, 185–86; and income, 159, 182–83; inflation and, 182; life expectancy and, 167, 180–81; model for, 161–87; by multinationals, 216–18, 219, 230, 232–33, 251; quality of labor in, 171, 176, 180, 181; returns to scale in, 175–76, 177; technology in, 176, 178, 179, 186, 187, 208–9;